Governance for Peace

Governance for Peace presents a comprehensive analysis of the dimensions of governance that are most likely to prevent armed conflict and foster sustainable peace. It is an accessible study written for the general reader that brings together the best empirical evidence across numerous disciplines showing how effective governance and inclusive, participatory and accountable institutions help to reduce violence by addressing social needs and providing mechanisms for resolving disputes. This balanced and incisive book gives meaning to the term 'good governance' and identifies the specific features of political and economic institutions that are most likely to promote peace within and between states. Concepts and topics examined in the book include political legitimacy, human security, 'political goods,' governance and power, inclusion, accountability, social cohesion, gender equality, countering corruption, the role of civil society, democratic participation, development as freedom, capitalism and economic growth, the governance of markets, China and the 'East Asian peace,' the European Union, and global institutions.

David Cortright is the Director of Policy Studies at Notre Dame's Kroc Institute for International Peace Studies. He is the author or editor of 20 books, including *Civil Society, Peace, and Power* and *Peace: A History of Movements and Ideas*.

Conor Seyle is the Director of Research at One Earth Future Foundation, an operating foundation focused on developing good governance systems for sustainable peace. His most recent book, co-edited with John Forrer, is *The Role of Business in the Responsibility to Protect*.

Kristen Wall edits scholarship on peace evaluation at George Mason University's School for Conflict Analysis and Resolution. She has written on global civil society's engagement in the New Deal and co-edited *Drones and the Future of Armed Conflict: Ethical, Legal, and Strategic Implications*.

Governance for Peace

*How Inclusive, Participatory and
Accountable Institutions Promote
Peace and Prosperity*

DAVID CORTRIGHT

Notre Dame

CONOR SEYLE

One Earth Future Foundation

KRISTEN WALL

Notre Dame

CAMBRIDGE
UNIVERSITY PRESS

CAMBRIDGE
UNIVERSITY PRESS

University Printing House, Cambridge CB2 8BS, United Kingdom

One Liberty Plaza, 20th Floor, New York, NY 10006, USA

477 Williamstown Road, Port Melbourne, VIC 3207, Australia

4843/24, 2nd Floor, Ansari Road, Daryaganj, Delhi – 110002, India

79 Anson Road, #06-04/06, Singapore 079906

Cambridge University Press is part of the University of Cambridge.

It furthers the University's mission by disseminating knowledge in the pursuit of education, learning, and research at the highest international levels of excellence.

www.cambridge.org
Information on this title: www.cambridge.org/9781108415934
DOI: 10.1017/9781108235471

First published 2017

Printed in the United States of America by Sheridan Books, Inc.

A catalogue record for this publication is available from the British Library.

ISBN 978-1-108-41593-4 Hardback
ISBN 978-1-108-40251-4 Paperback

Contents

Preface

This book argues that peace and prosperity are advanced through accountable systems of governance and effective institutions of mature democracy. Ours is an optimistic analysis, drawing from a large body of empirical evidence to show that myriad indicators associated with good governance, international development, and peace and security are moving in positive directions. This research shows, we believe, that consolidated forms of democratic governance that deliver public goods equitably are capable of preventing war and maintaining stability. We recognize that governance can be weak, corrupt and abusive, and that violence is prevalent in these conditions, but the dominant pattern in much of the world in recent decades has been toward stronger institutions, more democracy and less war.

In the last few years, however, trends have moved in the opposite direction. In much of the world, progress toward greater political freedom and democracy has stalled, and authoritarian regimes have consolidated. Even in Europe and the United States, democracy is facing significant challenges. Far-right populist parties, such as France's National Front and the Dutch Party for Freedom, have risen from obscurity to transform the politics of virtually every Western European country.[1] Demagogic leaders in Hungary, the United States and other countries have used xenophobic messages to gain and consolidate political power. Populist leaders are questioning the value of international institutions and norms that have

---

[1] Roberto Stefan Foa and Yascha Mounk, "The Danger of Deconsolidation: The Democratic Disconnect," *Journal of Democracy* 27, no. 3 (July 2016): 5–17.

increased global prosperity and, as we show in this book, have contributed to a more peaceful world.[2]

Many people in the West are losing faith in democratic institutions. The 2015 Eurobarometer survey revealed that 62 percent of Europeans distrusted their national governments.[3] In the United States, a 2014 Gallup Mood of the Nation poll showed that 65 percent of Americans were dissatisfied with their system of government, continuing a pattern of increased discontent over the past decade.[4] Job approval ratings of the US Congress have been abysmal in recent years, averaging just 17 percent in 2016.[5] The declining health of democracy is evident in low levels of voter participation, distrust of political leaders, the corrupting influence of money in elections, and increasing polarization and gridlock. Out of this discontent leaders like Viktor Orban in Hungary and Donald Trump in the United States have been elected to power.[6]

The elements of this 'illiberal' democracy are common across different countries. The use of distortion, innuendo and even charges of criminality against political adversaries. Attempts to suppress the vote of opposing constituencies. Disregard for existing political conventions and norms. Pressures against independent media. These and related practices are a threat to the core institutions of democracy.

Some analysts see disturbing parallels between the right-wing populism of today and the rise of extremism during the 1930s. They draw lessons from the breakdown of democracies in Europe and Latin America in the 1930s, and from episodes of political intolerance in US history, citing classic studies by Juan Linz, Seymour Martin Lipset and others.[7]

---

[2] Joseph S. Nye, "Will the Liberal Order Survive?" *Foreign Affairs* 96, no. 1 (January/February 2017): 15.

[3] European Commission, *Standard Eurobarometer 83*, Spring 2015, http://ec.europa.eu/public_opinion/archives/eb/eb83/eb83_first_en.pdf.

[4] Justin McCarthy, "In U.S., 65% Dissatisfied With How Gov't System Works," *Gallup Politics*, January 22, 2014, www.gallup.com/poll/166985/dissatisfied-gov-system-works.aspx.

[5] Art Swift, "U.S. Congressional Approval Averages Weak 17% for 2016," *Gallup Politics*, December 15, 2016, www.gallup.com/poll/199445/congressional-approval-averages-weak-2016.aspx?g_source=Politics&g_medium=newsfeed&g_campaign=tiles.

[6] John Shattuck, "Resisting Trumpism in Europe and the United States," *American Prospect* Longform, December 2, 2016, http://prospect.org/article/resisting-trumpism-europe-and-united-states.

[7] Juan J. Linz and Alfred Stepan, eds., *The Breakdown of Democratic Regimes* (Baltimore: Johns Hopkins University Press, 1979); Seymour Martin Lipset and Earl Rabb, *The Politics of Unreason: Right-Wing Extremism in America, 1790–1970* (New York: Harper & Row, 1970).

Democracy is at risk when leaders encourage, tolerate or justify actions that go beyond the limits of acceptable politics. Critics contend that Trump exhibited these tendencies in his 2016 campaign by denigrating women and religious and ethnic minorities, pledging to jail his opponent, and suggesting he might not accept the electoral results.[8] Larry Diamond described the failure to challenge such behavior as a form of "democratic disloyalty."[9]

Other writers question the analogy with the past. Today's populists may be anti-liberal, but they are not fascists, Sheri Berman writes.[10] To describe Orban or other leaders as 'fascist' obscures more than it clarifies. The extremists of the 1930s shared a virulent opposition to democracy and a deep suspicion of capitalism. Today's leaders claim they want to improve democracy. They criticize the system but propose no alternative to it, offering vague promises to make government better and more responsive. They are not threatening to close legislatures or cancel elections, at least not yet. Joseph Nye argues that there are sufficient institutional buffers against turbulence now at both the domestic and international level that a descent into the economic and geopolitical chaos of earlier decades "is not in the cards."[11] The institutions of democracy in the United States and Europe have deep roots. Robust civil societies provide citizens with myriad ways of voicing their concerns and influencing political outcomes.

Berman and Nye do not discount the seriousness of the current challenges, however, and they emphasize the need for political leaders and citizens to address the underlying causes of public discontent. The problems of democracy are deeply rooted and go beyond the practices of particular leaders. As Berman notes, the way to ensure that right-wing populism does not threaten the peace is "to make democratic institutions, parties, and politicians more responsive to the needs of all citizens."[12] This means addressing the problems of rising economic and social inequality, ending

---

[8] Steven Levitsky and Daniel Ziblatt, "Is Donald Trump a Threat to Democracy," *New York Times*, December 16, 2016, www.nytimes.com/2016/12/16/opinion/sunday/is-donald-trump-a-threat-to-democracy.html?&moduleDetail=section-news-o&action=click&contentCollection=Opinion&region=Footer&module=MoreInSection&version=WhatsNext&contentID=WhatsNext&pgtype=article.

[9] Larry Diamond, "It Could Happen Here," *The Atlantic*, October 19, 2016, www.theatlantic.com/international/archive/2016/10/trump-democracy-election-2016/504617/.

[10] Sheri Berman, "Populism is not Fascism," *Foreign Affairs* 95, no. 6 (November/December 2016): 39–44.

[11] Nye, "Will the Liberal Order Survive?"

[12] Sheri Berman, "Populism is not Fascism."

political gridlock through more inclusive citizen participation, and reducing the corrosive influence of corruption. In short, strengthening the institutions of democratic governance.

These are the challenges we address in the chapters that follow. We argue that the capacity and quality of governance both domestically and internationally are key factors in determining the prospects for peace and the well-being of society. This is true in Western democracies as much as it is in fragile states and conflict-affected regions. Stability and peace are most assured in settings of consolidated democracy, where governing institutions enforce the rule of law and provide effective services for all, and where people are able to participate actively and hold government institutions accountable. An informed and engaged citizenry is an essential bulwark against authoritarianism and an important force for peace.

Acknowledgments

This book is a collective effort not only of the co-authors but of many colleagues, reviewers and friends who contributed to the research and reviewed and critiqued the evolving manuscript. We benefited enormously from the support and guidance of our respective institutions, the University of Notre Dame's Kroc Institute for International Peace Studies and the One Earth Future Foundation. We are grateful to the many who encouraged this work and helped to make it a better book, although we alone take responsibility for any errors of fact or interpretation contained here.

Many people commented upon all or portions of the manuscript or attended workshops to evaluate our arguments and analyses. We received detailed critical feedback and suggestions for revision in the manuscript from Håvard Hegre and Margit Bussmann. The critical contributions of Hegre and Bussmann led to significant revisions and improvements in the volume. We owe a special debt of gratitude to the anonymous reviewers at Cambridge University Press who provided extensive and sometimes sharp critical commentary on the initial version of the manuscript. The Cambridge reviews prompted a major process of revision and resubmission that greatly improved the substantive content and quality of the book.

We are grateful to Bruce Russett for co-hosting a workshop at Yale University on the early research for this volume. Participants in that workshop included Russett, Nicholas Sambanis, Bethany Lacina, Madhav Joshi and Virginia Haufler. We received written comments from Joshua Goldstein and Erica De Bruin. The comments and critiques provided by the participants at Yale were foundational in shaping the direction of our research and writing.

We also received valuable feedback and insights from Steven Pinker during a meeting at MIT and from Barbara Walter and Erik Gartzke during a visit to the University of California San Diego.

We gained many useful insights from a workshop at Notre Dame's Kroc Institute that included critical presentations from Caroline Hartzell and Peter Wallensteen and commentary and feedback on the manuscript from John Paul Lederach, Robert Johansen, Lindsay Heger, Patrick Regan, Erik Melander, Madhav Joshi and other workshop participants. We received research, editorial and logistical support from a number of Kroc Institute colleagues over the years, including Eliot Fackler, Rachel Fairhurst, Lucy Dunderdale and Laurel Stone.

We are most grateful for the support of Scott Appleby, former Director of the Kroc Institute and now Dean of Notre Dame's Keough School of Global Affairs. Appleby provided institutional support and intellectual encouragement throughout the project. We are also grateful for the assistance of Hal Culbertson, the Institute's Executive Director and now Associate Dean of Operations at the Keough School, and to Ruth Abbey, who as Interim Director of the Kroc Institute provided sustained support for the latter stages of this effort. Without the institutional backing of Notre Dame and the Kroc Institute this project would not have been possible.

The project originated with and received significant institutional support from the One Earth Future Foundation in Colorado. Former OEF project manager Meadow Didier contributed early research for the book, managed the early writing process, and helped to coordinate workshops and planning sessions. Scholars and experts who participated in the initial workshop on the book in Colorado included Virginia Haufler, Colleen Scanlon Lyons, Stan Deetz, Heidi and Guy Burgess, and Chet Tchozewski. Also participating from OEF were Eamon Aloyo, former research associate at OEF and now at the Hague Institute for Global Justice. This discussion was critical for setting our initial thinking about the content of the book. Later in the writing process invaluable feedback and assistance were provided by Lindsay Heger, Tracie Ware and the staff of the OEF Research program.

Our greatest debt of gratitude is to Marcel Arsenault, founder and chair of OEF, and Cynda Collins Arsenault, adviser and member of the OEF board. Marcel Arsenault founded OEF as a 'think and do tank,' a center for generating research on the linkages between governance and peace and for creating practical projects and activities to develop that linkage in practice. The idea for this book emerged from discussions at OEF with Marcel Arsenault and Cynda Collins Arsenault, who encouraged us to synthesize the voluminous research on governance into a single volume that would illuminate the ways in which governance promotes prosperity and peace. OEF provided sustained institutional support for this project through the several years that were required to conduct the research and complete the manuscript. This volume owes its existence to the inspiration, guidance and support of Marcel Arsenault and the One Earth Future Foundation.

We express deep personal thanks to our family members and loved ones who sustained us through this work: David to Karen Jacob for her love and encouragement through the long process of bringing this book to fruition; Conor to Amanda Seyle Jones for her support and patience with the work; Kristen to Steve, Betsy and Rebecca Wall for their interest and support for this endeavor.

Introduction

Governance and Conflict Prevention

In the American west disputes over land and power contributed to an often bloody history featuring the iconic image of a cowboy with a Winchester rifle and a six-shooter by his side. In the nineteenth and early twentieth centuries, the flood of farmers and ranchers pouring into the frontier territories generated ongoing disputes over grazing rights, ownership of stock, access to water and the control of land. These 'Range Wars' often spilled over into armed violence. In the case of one such feud, the Sutton-Taylor range war in southern Texas, a dispute between two ranching families grew into a tit-for-tat killing spree that eventually left more than 35 people dead and required the intervention of the State Police and the fabled Texas Rangers (as well as the notorious outlaw John Wesley Hardin, eventual subject of the Johnny Cash song "Hardin Wouldn't Run").

These disputes did not end with the dawn of the twentieth century, or even the twenty-first. In large tracts of the American west, sharp differences continue over how public and private rangelands should be developed. Competing constituencies of environmentalists, Native American communities, weekend hikers, ranchers, logging companies and the federal government regularly engage in intense arguments over regulations regarding access and development. In these modern disputes, however, the disagreements are not contested with revolvers and Bowie knives, but rather through lawsuits, op-eds, political advocacy, digital media campaigns and neighborhood organizing. While the emotions attached to these disputes may be as strong as in the past, they are settled today through political and legal agreements, not by the Texas Rangers.

In some parts of the world the conditions of the 'Wild West' still prevail, and many people are trapped in cycles of violent conflict. Legitimate institutions for resolving disputes are weak, non-existent, or have been shattered. Corrupt and oppressive forms of governance are prevalent. The local forces engaged in fighting are not ranchers but insurgents and militias. Terrorist networks pose a global threat, and brutal civil wars rage in Syria, Iraq and other countries.

In much of the world, however, the trend has been toward less violence. As societies have become more economically developed and interdependent, they have acquired structures of effective governance and are able to settle disputes without armed conflict. Rival communities and groups that once used weapons today rely on governmental institutions and legal systems to resolve conflicts. A zone of relative peace and prosperity has emerged, stretching across North America, Europe, East Asia and beyond. This zone is characterized by mature systems of governance that provide the full range of public goods and enable individuals and communities to make decisions and resolve disputes without bloodshed. The European Union has been at the core of this development, although its future is more uncertain after Brexit and other recent shocks. East Asia has also become less warlike and prosperous. More stable and less violent political conditions have emerged in much of Latin America and parts of Africa. Although the prospects for peace are being threatened on many fronts – strains within the EU, authoritarianism in Russia and other countries, weak and oppressive states across the Middle East, deep inequalities in many countries and an increase in the number of armed conflicts over the last five years – the general trend has been toward less war.

Steven Pinker highlights this in his influential book, *The Better Angels of Our Nature*. Pinker documents a long-term trend in human affairs toward a reduction in armed violence, which he calls perhaps "the most important thing that has ever happened in human history."[1] His analysis has been hotly contested,[2] but the available evidence indicates a "real and remarkably large" historical decline of human violence.[3] Pinker

[1] Steven Pinker, *The Better Angels of Our Nature: Why Violence Has Declined* (New York: Viking, 2011), xxi.
[2] See, for example, Elizabeth Kolbert, "Peace in Our Time: Steven Pinker's History of Violence," *New Yorker*, October 3, 2011; and the critical essays by Bradley Thayer, Jack Levy and William Thompson in "The Forum: The Decline of War 2013," *International Studies Review* 15, no. 3 (2013): 393–419.
[3] *The Human Security Report 2013: The Decline in Global Violence: Evidence, Explanation, and Contestation* (Vancouver, BC: Human Security Research Group, Simon

attributes this development to improved governance and the emergence of the nation state, economic growth, the empowerment of women, and greater social mobility and literacy. Peace becomes more likely, he argues, in societies that are governed well – in mature and prosperous democracies with greater gender equality that are economically and politically interdependent. These trends – consolidated state governance, commerce, feminization, cosmopolitanism and what he calls "the escalator of reason" – are enduring forces that over the centuries have made armed violence less prevalent.[4]

Noticing this long-term trend is not equivalent to claiming that the world is peaceful. Armed violence remains a persistent reality. Contending groups often resort to violence as they vie for power and control over resources, causing massive civilian suffering and instability. Since the end of World War II tens of millions of people have lost their lives in violent conflict. Forty active armed conflicts were recorded in the world in 2015, according to data provided by the Uppsala Conflict Data Program in Sweden. This was a nearly 20 percent increase over the previous year. Nearly all of the reported armed conflicts were within states rather than between them. Eleven of the conflicts were characterized as wars, with more than a thousand deaths annually.[5] The bloodiest was in Syria, followed by Iraq, Afghanistan, Nigeria, Pakistan, Ukraine, Israel, South Sudan and Somalia. The recent increase is worrisome, but since the end of the Cold War levels of armed conflict have declined and even with the increase are lower now than during much of the twentieth century.

Fraser University, 2014), 10, www.hsrgroup.org/human-security-reports/2013/overview.aspx.

[4] Others have emphasized the trend toward reduced armed conflict. See John Mueller, *Retreat from Doomsday: The Obsolescence of Major War* (New York: Basic Books, 1989); Randall Forsberg, "The End of War," *Boston Review*, October/November 1997; Azar Gat, *War in Human Civilization* (Oxford University Press, 2006); Joshua S. Goldstein, *Winning the War on War: The Decline of Armed Conflict Worldwide* (New York: Dutton, 2011); John Horgan, *The End of War* (San Francisco: McSweeney's Books, 2012); and the Human Security Research Group's Human Security Reports for the years 2005, 2009/2010, 2012 and 2014, at www.hsrgroup.org/human-security-reports/human-security-report.aspx.

[5] See Thérése Pettersson and Peter Wallensteen, "Armed Conflicts, 1947–2014," *Journal of Peace Research* 52, no. 4 (July 2015): 536–550. Throughout this volume we use the UDCP definitions. Armed conflicts are defined as contested incompatibilities concerning government and/or territory involving the use of armed force in which at least one of the parties is a state that has between 25 and 999 battle-related deaths per year. Wars are such conflicts that have more than 1,000 battle-related deaths per year, at www.pcr.uu.se/research/ucdp/definitions/definition_of_armed_conflict/.

Social science has identified some of the key pathways toward peace. New knowledge is accumulating to illuminate more precisely the conditions associated with preventing war and maintaining peace. Increasingly rigorous quantitative methods are available to document and offer explanations for the presence or absence of war, generating significant findings on the drivers of conflict and the conditions conducive to peace. While many uncertainties and lacunae remain in the emerging body of research, sufficient evidence now exists to say with confidence that the reduction of armed conflict is possible. Trends are moving generally in that direction, despite recent headlines suggesting otherwise. Greater understanding of the lessons to be drawn from this research can help in shaping policies and structures for conflict prevention.

In this book, we review diverse findings from a wide body of literature to examine the role of governance in determining the prospects for peace. We argue that systems of 'good' governance are essential conditions for reducing the risk of armed violence. Many studies on peace and development emphasize the importance of good governance, but few define precisely what this means. We attempt to unpack the term and give it definition through a focus on the conditions that are most likely to enhance the prospects for peace. Ours is an evidence-based analysis that identifies the elements of governance that foster prosperity and peace. We synthesize the most significant empirical studies to show that armed conflict is less prevalent in states that deliver public goods effectively and equitably, and in societies that are fully democratic, with high levels of per capita income, where women are empowered, and which are extensively integrated with transnational trade networks and global governance institutions.

Within these findings are deeper patterns of congruence. Governance that promotes peace tends to be inclusive, participatory and accountable. It provides public goods to all stakeholders, guarantees economic freedom and the rule of law, protects human rights, and offers inclusive and participatory forms of equitable representation for major constituencies. Inclusive, participatory and accountable institutions and policies enhance public legitimacy and help to reduce the risk of armed conflict. Governance enhances peace when people trust the political system and turn to it to resolve their differences. As the capacity and quality of governing institutions improve, the numbers of disagreements that might lead to armed conflict diminish and the means for resolving disputes increase. Conflicts and differences among individuals and communities remain, but they are less likely to lead to violence.

We define peace as the absence of armed conflict. Our focus is on the negative peace of avoiding war rather than the broader concept of positive peace which encompasses human rights and social justice. We adopt this approach not for lack of sympathy with the concerns of justice but to prioritize the prevention of violent conflict. We agree with Joshua Goldstein that ending war is important in itself, not as a derivative of a broader agenda for social justice.[6] In this book we focus on what can be measured empirically. We present social science evidence on the predictors of armed conflict and the conditions of peace.

As we examine this evidence, we find that the conditions associated with the absence of armed conflict, negative peace, are strongly correlated with factors that are commonly identified with the social justice dimensions of positive peace. Equitable access to social opportunity, institutions of inclusion rather than exclusion, the opportunity to voice grievances and hold leaders accountable, guarantees of political and economic freedom, the empowerment of women – all are directly related to peace. They are also associated with conditions usually subsumed under the heading of social justice. The conditions of positive peace lead to the avoidance of armed conflict. Negative peace and positive peace are thus interdependent and mutually reinforcing. The indicators that measure one define the other.

The concept of quality peace helps to bridge the two approaches. As developed by Peter Wallensteen it refers to the conditions for preventing the recurrence of armed conflict. The essential ingredients for assuring peace are safety, dignity and predictability in people's lives. "Quality peace means the creation of conditions that make the inhabitants of a society ... secure in life and dignity now and for the foreseeable future."[7] Peace is not simply the absence of war but the maintenance of conditions that reduce the risk of armed conflict. Chief among these is good governance, which is a lens broad enough to encompass the dynamic interrelatedness of many complex factors. It encompasses not only protection against armed violence but human rights and the rule of law, freedom from discrimination and repression, and equitable access to education, health care, and other public goods and services. Quality peace emerges when governance systems establish durable conditions of safety, economic well-being and human dignity.

---

[6] Goldstein, *Winning the War on War*, 204.
[7] Peter Wallensteen, *Quality Peace: Peacebuilding, Victory, and World Order* (Oxford University Press, 2015), 6.

GOVERNANCE CAPACITY AND QUALITY

Governance is the means of making and implementing collective decisions. It is a general term that encompasses the functions of government, but it goes beyond the role of the state to include civil society and the private sector. Our focus is primarily on governance within states, the locus of most armed conflicts, but we also address inter-state, regional and global dimensions. When we speak of governance we refer not only to the institutions of state but to the organizations and networks of society, and the ways in which social cohesion and public perceptions of legitimacy influence state behavior and contribute to peace. Governance is exercised through formal and informal institutions, networks, and widely shared values and norms that guide behavior. It applies to political, economic and social realms at local, national and transnational levels.

Governance is about power. It is about how decisions are made, by whom, for what purpose and for whose benefit. Struggles about political and military power and control over resources and territory are at the heart of almost all armed conflicts. Power can be exercised through coercive means and the threat of punishment, through economic exchange and patronage, or through shared identity and public trust. Governance is more efficient and less costly when it achieves cooperation through trust rather than coercion. We develop these ideas in Chapter 1 and throughout the book.

Governance is not always peaceful or good, nor is it intended to be. In many countries governance is not established to serve the common good but is a system for preserving and increasing the power and wealth of corrupt elites. It is an instrument of domination and exploitation rather than social betterment. Nor is civil society always a force for good. Non-state actors sometimes promote hatred and intolerance. Violent extremists use the Internet to build support for terrorism. The world is often a nasty and brutish place, as Hobbes wrote, not only in the competition for power between states but in abusive systems of governance within states and in society. The possibilities for good governance are nonetheless real, and it is important to understand the factors that generate cooperation and peace so that their benefits can spread further.

With Pippa Norris we emphasize both the capacity and the quality of governance as essential conditions for assuring development and peace.[8]

---

[8] Pippa Norris, *Making Democratic Governance Work: How Regimes Shape Prosperity, Welfare, and Peace* (Cambridge University Press, 2012).

Governance capacity includes the ability to provide security and deliver social goods. Preserving public safety is an essential function of governance and is obviously necessary for peace, but research shows that security is also enhanced through the provision of social goods. The extent of education and literacy, the availability and quality of health care, the reliability of public infrastructure – all are elements of social capacity and are correlated with greater prospects for peace and stability. Social capacity empowers people to play an active role in shaping the political and economic decisions that affect their lives. High levels of human capital and the presence of strong social safety nets facilitate economic growth and development, which are fundamental to the creation of more peaceful societies. The political, economic and social empowerment of women is a measure of both social capacity and quality and also helps to reduce the likelihood of armed conflict.

Effective governance fosters peace in two fundamental ways, by ameliorating the conditions and grievances that cause people to fight, and by offering mechanisms for resolving and transforming disputes without violence. Decision-making structures that provide inclusive channels for hearing grievances and settling disputes reduce the risk of armed violence. The evidence shows that institutionally mature democracies are more peaceful than other forms of governance. This is the liberal peace theory. Fully developed democratic states almost never wage war on one another and are less likely than partial democracies or autocracies to experience civil conflict. Regime type matters greatly in reducing the risk of war.

As we explore below, however, the relationship between democracy and peace is subject to qualification. Well established and highly institutionalized democracies are indeed less likely to experience internal armed conflict and also tend to have higher levels of prosperity and economic growth. When states are transitioning from authoritarianism to democracy, however, they face a greater risk of civil conflict and tend to be unstable and poorly governed. This is especially true for states with low per capita income.

China poses a different kind of challenge to the liberal theory. It is an authoritarian regime with strong institutions that has achieved high levels of economic growth and in recent decades has not experienced internal armed conflict or war with its neighbors, although its military and economic assertiveness is growing. The experience of China seems to show that institutional capacity and high levels of economic growth can bring peace and stability even in the absence of formal democracy. This does not mean that democracy is unimportant, but it indicates that other aspects of governance, especially the ability to deliver public goods and achieve economic growth, may be equally important. When democracy is fully mature it is an essential element of good governance for peace, but institutional capacity and economic development are also critically necessary.

The empirical evidence reviewed in this volume suggests that governance systems are more likely to advance the prospects for peace when they are:

1. inclusive in their scope, with guarantees of civil and human rights and systems of fair representation for sharing power and gaining access to resources;
2. participatory in their form, with opportunities available for all individuals and significant social groups to voice their concerns in political and social systems and play an active role in economic and public life; and
3. accountable in their operations, based on the rule of law and accessible mechanisms of judicial and political redress, with transparency and the right of citizens to organize and express opinions.

As societies develop more inclusive institutions, they tend to become more peaceful. Studies show that conflict risk is reduced when significant ethnic groups are included in decision making and have equitable access to resources. Inclusive systems increase the willingness of participants to accept institutional decisions. As political, economic and social equality becomes institutionalized the risks of armed violence diminish. Ethnic exclusion and marginalization, by contrast, make conflict more likely. Governance systems that successfully include diverse social groups are more likely to avoid violence.

Inclusion and participation are closely related, the former referring to universal rights, the latter defining how those rights are exercised through active political, economic and social engagement. Inclusion means that governance programs incorporate and apply equally to all communities, while participation means that those communities play an active role in creating and shaping the programs that affect their lives. Participation incorporates democratic forms of political decision making but also includes access to economic opportunity and membership in associations that bridge ethnic and social divides. Participatory political regimes in which all significant constituencies can participate and voice their concerns are less likely to experience internal armed conflict and rarely wage war on each other. Economic growth and development are greatest in open and fair market systems that provide opportunities for all to engage in commerce. Studies of social capital show that interethnic associational linkages are associated with a lower risk of armed conflict. Participatory systems are more likely to create peaceful outcomes.

Accountability enhances peace by bolstering the effectiveness, legitimacy and capacity of governance institutions to provide necessary public goods. Accountability is the means of ensuring that public decisions are implemented according to agreed rules and procedures in a manner that is perceived as fair and legitimate. When governance systems are unable or unwilling to guarantee the rule of law or provide basic services to all groups, the risk of armed conflict increases. Accountability is reflected in political mechanisms for constraining executive authority, controlling corruption and subordinating security forces to civilian control. Accountability also depends upon transparency, access to information and a vibrant civil society.

Inclusivity, participation and accountability define the essential qualities of governance that enhance the prospects for peace. These qualities apply to economic as well as political decision making and implementation. Economic systems promote peace when property rights and opportunities for market access are available to all, and when market freedoms are balanced by social protections against exploitation, corruption and oligopoly. Political systems reduce the risk of conflict when they are highly representative and participatory and provide equitable opportunities for people to voice their concerns. Empirical evidence consistently confirms the importance of these qualities of inclusion, participation and accountability. They go together and reinforce one another in advancing peace.

AN EMERGING CONSENSUS

The importance of governance for peace and development is widely recognized in international policy. This is reflected in the 2030 Agenda for Sustainable Development, adopted by the UN General Assembly in September 2015. Many of the 17 Sustainable Development Goals in that Agenda refer to governance and peace. Goal 16 makes the connection explicit, calling upon nations to: "Promote peaceful and inclusive societies for sustainable development, provide access to justice for all and build effective, accountable and inclusive institutions at all levels." The targets approved by the UN for achieving Goal 16 include reducing corruption; developing effective, accountable and transparent institutions;

ensuring responsive, inclusive, participatory and representative decision making; and strengthening national institutions, including through international cooperation, for building capacity at all levels.[9] This linkage of development with peace, governance and the rule of law is unprecedented and was forged through extensive consultation and debate among many governments, international institutions and civil society groups leading up to the 2015 General Assembly.[10]

A milestone in this process was the 2013 High-level Panel report, *A New Global Partnership*, which called for "a fundamental shift – to recognize peace and good governance as core elements of well-being." The report described freedom from fear, conflict and violence as "the most fundamental human right" and the essential foundation for building more peaceful and prosperous societies. People everywhere expect and deserve their governments to be "honest, accountable, and responsive to their needs," the report observed. It called for building "sound institutions" and urged a "transparency revolution" so that people can see how taxes, aid and revenues from extractive industries are spent.[11] Advancing good governance, the Panel concluded, is essential for creating conditions of peace and prosperity. To achieve economic development and reduce the risk of armed conflict requires "building effective and accountable institutions" of governance.[12]

One of the most influential reports in building this awareness was the World Bank's 2011 World Development Report (WDR). Success in overcoming poverty, the report argued, depends upon preventing armed conflict and building more legitimate and capable systems of governance. The risk of armed conflict in any society is determined by "the *combination* of the exposure to *internal and external stresses* and the strength of that society's 'immune system'" [emphasis in original].[13] Preventing

---

[9] United Nations Development Program, *Sustainable Development Goals, Goal 16: Promote Just, Peaceful, and Inclusive Societies*, www.un.org/sustainabledevelopment/peace-justice/.

[10] See Erin McCandless, "Civil Society and the 2030 Agenda: Forging a Path to Universal Sustainable Peace through Policy Formulation," in *Civil Society, Peace and Power*, edited by David Cortright, Melanie Greenberg and Laurel Stone (Lanham: Rowman & Littlefield, 2016).

[11] United Nations, *A New Global Partnership: Eradicate Poverty and Transform Economies through Sustainable Development*, The Report of the High-level Panel of Eminent Persons on the Post-2015 Development Agenda (United Nations, 2013), 9.

[12] Ibid., 27.

[13] World Bank, *World Development Report 2011: Conflict, Security, and Development* (Washington, DC: World Bank, 2011), 7.

armed violence depends upon responsive and capable institutions that enable societies to cope with shocks and potential flashpoints for violence. "Legitimate institutions and governments that give everyone a stake in national prosperity are the immune system that protects from different types of violence," states the WDR.[14]

Within the US military as well, interest in governance has increased. A 2010 Joint Forces Command handbook notes an emerging "interagency consensus about the critical role of governance in transforming conflict, promoting national unity, and addressing extremism. Building government, electoral, and media institutions are essential objectives of any post-conflict reconstruction and stabilization mission."[15] When he took command in Afghanistan in 2009 General Stanley McChrystal promised 'government in a box' and instructed American forces to work with local partners in attempting to create "a country at peace, the foundations of good governance, and economic development."[16] A major retrospective on the Iraq War observed the "central importance of governance and economics" in US strategy, but noted tensions and uncertainty over the balance of civilian and military responsibilities in these areas.[17]

The problem of armed conflict and terrorism can be viewed from an epidemiological perspective, as a disease that needs to be prevented and cured.[18] The first task is to contain the 'illness' and prevent its spread, which requires security capacity and effective law enforcement that respects human rights and the rule of law. Next is finding the cause and applying proper remedies. For conflict and militancy this means addressing unresolved grievances, overcoming political and economic exclusion, and providing economic and social opportunity. States and societies improve their 'health' through development and more inclusive and accountable systems of governance.

---

[14] Ibid., 18.

[15] United States Joint Forces Command, *Handbook for Military Support to Governance, Elections and Media*, United Action Handbook Series, Book Three, February 11, 2010, www.dtic.mil/doctrine/doctrine/jwfc/gem_hbk.pdf.

[16] NATO, International Security Assistance Force, *Tactical Directive*, Kabul, Afghanistan, July 6, 2009, cited in Rosa Brooks, *How Everything Became War and the Military Became Everything: Tales from the Pentagon* (New York: Simon & Schuster, 2016), 94.

[17] Catherine Dale, Congressional Research Service, *Operation Iraqi Freedom: Strategies, Approaches, Results, and Issues for Congress*, April 2, 2009, 7-5700, RI 34387, 127.

[18] Paul Stares and Monica Yacoubian, "Terrorism as a Virus," *Washington Post*, August 23, 2005.

No single factor can explain the outbreak of armed conflict, but the increasing body of literature looking at predictors of conflict suggests that many of the influences that reduce or increase the likelihood of war are linked to the capacity and quality of national and international governance structures. States without adequate governing systems are more likely to experience internal armed conflict and war. It is no coincidence that regions without effective governance – Afghanistan, Somalia, South Sudan and eastern Congo – have high rates of armed violence. Or that states where previous government systems have been shattered – Iraq, Syria and Libya – face civil war and persistent armed conflict. In states without legitimate public authority and effective institutional capacity violence is more likely.

Failures of governance can set in motion a series of negative cascades and a downward spiral that undermines both development and security. The WDR emphasizes the link between governance deficits and the likelihood of armed conflict:

> Where states, markets, and social institutions fail to provide basic security, justice, and economic opportunities for citizens, conflict can escalate ... Countries and subnational areas with the weakest institutional legitimacy and governance are the most vulnerable to violence and instability and the least able to respond to internal and external stresses.[19]

A 2012 UNDP report traces armed violence to fragility, which it defines as contexts in which "public authorities no longer have the monopoly on legitimate violence, the ability to deliver services, or the capacity to collect public revenues." These "overlapping deficits" reflect a collapse in governance mechanisms for providing public goods or mediating social disputes and may prompt aggrieved constituencies to pick up arms.[20]

INSTITUTIONS AND RESILIENCE

Many studies emphasize the importance for preventing conflict of effective, stable and legitimate institutions of governance that provide security, economic opportunity and the delivery of public goods in inclusive, accountable ways. To measure institutional capacity researchers often use proxy indicators for corruption, rule of law and bureaucratic efficiency.

---

[19] World Bank, *World Development Report 2011*, 7.
[20] United Nations Development Programme, *Governance for Peace: Securing the Social Contract* (New York: United Nations Development Programme and Bureau for Crisis Prevention and Recovery, 2012), 17.

These indicators are an order of magnitude more important than other tested variables in predicting the risk of armed violence.[21] High values for these indicators show a strong relationship with peace.[22] States with the best institutional performance are the most likely to avoid the onset of armed conflict.[23]

In their respective background papers for the WDR, James Fearon and Barbara Walter build upon their previous work on these subjects to provide new evidence on the linkages between weak governance and the risk of armed violence. Fearon uses per capita income as a proxy for state capacity and models the impact of elements of governance quality. To address the methodological risk of selection bias he observes governance ratings of countries at the same level of per capita income. This allows him to identify what he calls "surprisingly good governance," which exists in a country that has high-quality governance ratings in comparison to other countries at the same level of per capita income. Correlating this governance rating with subsequent conflict onset, he finds "very large substantive effects" of high governance quality ratings on reduced likelihood of armed conflict.[24] His study shows that a country with "surprisingly good governance" has a lower risk of armed conflict in the subsequent 5–10 years than countries with similar per capita income but lower governance ratings.[25]

Walter also finds a direct correlation between favorable ratings of institutional quality and the likelihood of peace. Countries that score high on the World Bank's Country Policy and Institutional Assessment (CPIA) index "are significantly less likely to experience armed conflict" than those with lower governance ratings.[26] She finds that the presence of a democratic constitution substantially reduces the odds of conflict renewal. "Political institutions are the key to explaining why some countries can escape the conflict trap while others do not," she writes. Armed

---

[21] World Bank, *World Development Report 2011*, 84.

[22] Institute for Economics and Peace, *Pillars of Peace: Understanding the Key Attitudes and Institutions Underpinning Peaceful Societies* (2013), 10–11, available at http://economicsandpeace.org/wp-content/uploads/2011/10/Pillars-of-Peace-Report-IEP.pdf.

[23] Zeynep Taydas, Dursun Peksen and Patrick James, "Why Do Civil Wars Occur? Understanding the Importance of Institutional Quality," *Civil Wars* 12, no. 3 (September 2010): 206.

[24] James D. Fearon, "Governance and Civil War Onset," World Development Report 2011 Background Paper (World Bank, 2010), 45, 49.

[25] World Bank, *World Development Report 2011*, 85.

[26] Barbara F. Walter, "Conflict Relapse and the Sustainability of Post-conflict Peace," World Development Report 2011 Background Paper (World Bank, September 2010), 19.

conflict is a sign that government is weak, unresponsive and unreliable.[27]
A greater focus on building viable and credible political institutions may
be the most effective way to manage conflicts and prevent the outbreak
of armed violence.

The linkage between governance systems and the prospects for peace
is confirmed in the work of the Political Instability Task Force (PITF).
Through analyses of a wide range of governance variables, the PITF team
has been able to identify weak institutional structures and poor provision
of public goods as factors that increase the risk of civil war and mass
violence. Their research also points the way toward overcoming these
factors and underscores the critical role of high-quality institutions for
achieving security and peace.

Four significant variables stand out as predictors of political instability
and armed conflict: regime type, infant mortality, conflict in the region,
and state-led discrimination. Regime type measures the degree of democracy, based on indicators of political openness, competitiveness and participation. Infant mortality is a proxy for the level of economic and social
development. Regional spillover effects reflect poor or weak governance
systems that fail to control borders or address the grievances of contiguous ethnic groups. State discrimination reflects government policies that
repress or marginalize significant ethnic groups and minority populations. High ratings in these indicators increase the likelihood of political
instability and armed conflict. Using these variables Jack Goldstone et al.
report 80 percent accuracy in predicting all forms of political instability
within two years of measurement.[28] A related analysis by Ted Gurr et al.
using the same variables also found significant correlations with political
instability and armed violence.[29]

Overcoming the problems of instability and state fragility depends
upon institutional resilience. Every society has conflicts, and all governments face periodic crises and shocks. The challenge for peace is managing these risks in a way that avoids violence. The systemic approach
developed by Goldstone et al. offers a framework for meeting this
challenge:

---

[27] Ibid., 7.
[28] Jack A. Goldstone, Robert H. Bates, David L. Epstein, Ted Robert Gurr, Michael
      B. Lustik, Monty G. Marshall, Jay Ulfedler and Mark Woodward, "A Global Model for
      Forecasting Instability," *American Journal of Political Science* 54, no. 1 (2010): 195.
[29] Ted Robert Gurr, Mark Woodward and Monty G. Marshall, "Forecasting Instability: Are
      Ethnic Wars and Muslim Countries Different?" Presented at the Annual Meeting of the
      American Political Science Association, September 2005.

If the factors that appear associated with stability ... are in place – high income, low discrimination, few conflicts in the neighborhood, and most important, a non-contested or unified political regime – the model suggests that the polity will remain stable. This result suggests that we may need to think more about the factors that ... provide resilience in a troubled world, rather than about the diverse and often idiosyncratic causes of varied types of conflicts.[30]

A policy approach that focuses on quality governance and capable institutions offers the best prescription for enhancing resilience and reducing the risk of armed violence. Good governance systems are like healthy organisms that are capable of fending off threats and infection. They provide the institutional capacity and qualities of inclusion and accountability that are needed to protect against violence.

The studies reviewed here and examined throughout this volume show that governance systems increase the prospects for peace when they are inclusive, participatory and accountable and have sufficient capacity to ensure security and provide the full range of public goods. Fully democratic regimes with high levels of economic development are more stable politically and are less prone to armed conflict. The indicators of good governance are mutually reinforcing. Representative government and human rights, inclusive and accountable institutions, public welfare provision, effective security capacity, support for economic and social development – all are conditions for peace. No single dimension of governance by itself is sufficient to explain the irenic effects. Good governance is a complementary package of capacities and qualities that enhance the ability of human communities to make and implement decisions in ways that reduce the risk of armed conflict.

We offer this theory of good governance knowing full well that the reality in many places is far from the idealized model we posit. Governance is often a mechanism of exploitation, oppression and abuse. It is an instrument of control or a faceless form of neglect, with vital services and promised benefits falling short of public need or never arriving. Collective action is organized not for public benefit but to enrich and empower corrupt elites, to divert wealth and power for the privileged while excluding and marginalizing others. People who experience such abuse may be skeptical of the very idea of good governance. For the Afghan villager alienated from the kleptocracy of Kabul, the refugee from Syria seeking safety for her family, or the impoverished worker of the Niger delta seeing the region's oil wealth squandered by distant leaders, the concept

---

[30] Goldstone et al., "A Global Model for Forecasting Instability," 205.

of governance as a mechanism to serve the public good may seem like a
cruel joke. Yet many people struggle against these harsh realities, and we
strive in this volume to identify the dimensions of governance that can
serve as the foundation for better alternatives.

THE CHAPTERS OF THE BOOK

In the chapters that follow we develop these points and explore in greater
depth the many connections between governance and peace. We begin in
the first chapter with an examination of the various definitions and dimensions of governance. This is followed by three parts. The first focuses on
governance capacity, examining both security and social capacity and
the importance of both for assuring sustainable peace. The second part
looks at various qualities of governance, focusing on inclusion, participation and accountability as they are reflected in systems for managing disputes, enhancing gender equality and containing corruption. In the third
part we examine the political and economic dimensions of governance
that are most determinative of peace, including regime type, economic
development and the role of markets. This is followed by two concluding
chapters that look at global governance systems and implications of our
perspective for international policy.

Our discussion of the meaning of governance in Chapter 1 focuses on
the challenge of collective action, convincing people to forego near-term
advantage for the sake of longer-term community benefit. Individuals
and groups are more likely to cooperate for the common good if they
have trust in public authority and consider governance systems legitimate. These beliefs depend upon governance performance (the capacity to
meet public needs) and procedures (when they are perceived as fair and
accessible). We use Robert Rotberg's framework to evaluate governance
systems according to their ability to deliver essential political goods.[31]
Governments that guarantee security, the rule of law, social services,
economic opportunity and human rights are more accountable to their
citizens and less likely to experience instability and armed conflict. We
examine the 'faces of power' that are reflected in different approaches to
governance and consider how more decentralized and horizontal forms
of 'new governance' create additional possibilities for participation and
accountability. New social actors and means of discourse are entering the

---

[31] Robert I. Rotberg, ed., *On Governance: What It Is, What It Measures and Its Policy Uses*
(Waterloo: Centre for International Governance Innovation, 2015).

public arena, for good or ill, transforming the nature of public authority and governance.

Part I addresses governance capacity, beginning with the bedrock requirement for security. Providing for the safety of citizens and protecting against aggression and armed violence are first-order priorities of government, as we explore in Chapter 2. Security is an essential foundation of good governance, but the relationship between security capacity and peace is complex. A basic level of security is needed, but an excessive emphasis on military solutions is problematic. Research shows that countries maintaining large armed forces in the wake of armed conflict are more likely to experience renewed armed conflict.[32] Structural issues related to the accountability of security forces are critically important, especially the principle of subordination to civilian political authority.[33] Military forces that are structured along patronage lines can be dangerous and increase the risk of military coups and armed conflict.[34] According to von Clausewitz, as affirmed by Rupert Smith, the utility of force is judged not by its destructive capacity but by its ability to achieve intended political purposes.[35] A similar political principle applies to the evaluation of security capacity. Security systems contribute to good governance when they are under civilian political control and are more representative of the communities they are intended to serve. New conceptions of human security broaden the framework of protection beyond the state to individuals and communities and emphasize bottom-up approaches and better accountability to society as requirements for assuring public safety.

The other side of governance capacity is the ability to provide social services, to meet public needs and increase human capital. Social capacity is as important as security capacity for creating well governed and more peaceful societies. The evidence examined in Chapter 3 shows that measures for welfare spending, health care availability and other forms of social capacity correlate significantly with the prospects for peace.[36]

---

[32] Paul Collier, *The Bottom Billion: Why the Poorest Countries are Failing and What Can Be Done About It* (Oxford University Press, 2007), 132.

[33] Todd Sechser, "Are Soldiers Less War-Prone Than Statesmen?" *Journal of Conflict Resolution* 48, no. 5 (2004): 763–764, 771.

[34] Kristen A. Harkness, "The Ethnic Army and the State: Explaining Coup Traps and the Difficulties of Democratization in Africa," *Journal of Conflict Resolution* 60, no. 4 (2016): 587–616.

[35] Rupert Smith, *The Utility of Force: The Art of War in the Modern World* (London: Penguin Books, 2006).

[36] Zeynep Taydas and Dursun Peksen, "Can States Buy Peace? Social Welfare Spending and Civil Conflicts," *Journal of Peace Research* 49, no. 2 (2012); Clayton Thyne, "ABC's,

Especially important is the role of education. More than a dozen recent studies show a direct relationship between lower conflict risk and higher levels of literacy and educational attainment.[37] Investments in public education raise the value and productivity of labor and stimulate economic growth. They create opportunities for young people who might otherwise be tempted to join armed rebel groups. The beneficial impacts of education are contextual, however, and depend on the content of what is taught and whether educational opportunities are equitably available to all social groups. Inclusive and participatory access to education is an essential element of social capacity for peace.

The second part of the book looks at the qualities of governance, exploring the ways in which elements of inclusion, participation and accountability influence the performance of governing institutions. In Chapter 4 we assess the relevance of governance quality for understanding and mitigating the most prevalent forms of war – ethnically based struggles over the control of power, resources and territory. We show how the degree of inclusion in a governance system helps to determine whether such disputes turn violent. Countries in which oil exports are a major source of revenue account for one-third of all armed conflicts in the world. It is not the presence of oil that causes conflict, however, but the lack of capable, accountable and inclusive institutions for managing natural resource development. States with strong institutions and representative systems of governance have lower levels of armed conflict and are able to escape the so-called resource curse. Competing claims over the control of territory are also frequent causes of armed conflict. In these settings boundaries are in dispute and aggrieved communities and social groups seek to realign or break away from existing states. Territorial disputes often grow out of conditions of horizontal inequality and political, economic and social exclusion, in which governing regimes systematically favor one social or ethnic community over another. Inclusive and participatory governance systems avoid these causes of conflict and are better able to manage territorial and political disputes.[38]

123's, and the Golden Rule: The Pacifying Effect of Education on Civil War, 1980–1999," *International Studies Quarterly* 50, no. 4 (2006).

[37] Gudrun Østby and Henrik Urdal, "Education and Civil Conflict: A Review of the Quantitative, Empirical Literature," Background paper prepared for the Education for All Global Monitoring Report 2011, *The Hidden Crisis: Armed Conflict and Education*, 2011/ED/EFA/MRT/PI/29 (2010).

[38] Joan Esteban and Debraj Ray, "Polarization, Fractionalization and Conflict," *Journal of Peace Research* 45, no. 2 (2008): 165, 180.

In Chapter 5 we examine the empowerment of women as an essential element of governance quality, perhaps the most important manifestation of inclusion and participation. Empirical studies confirm that gender equality is strongly associated with reduced rates of armed conflict. Peace is more likely in societies with high levels of female educational achievement, professional employment and participation in government decision making, as well as lower fertility rates.[39] The ability of women to exercise agency in matters of family and social life is directly related to higher levels of socioeconomic status. The empowerment of women is also linked to democracy and economic development. Economic growth rates are directly correlated with female educational attainment. Societies that discriminate against women have lower economic growth rates and higher rates of armed conflict. Policies that advance gender equality enhance the prospects for peace.

Corruption is the bane of good governance, as we examine in Chapter 6. It exists in many forms, from the petty bribes and payments that are required for daily transactions in many parts of the world, to systems of patronage that dispense benefits to favored clients, to the grand larceny and wholesale diversion of resources that characterize regressive and criminalized regimes. Corruption is especially corrosive when it is linked to violence and enforced through mafia-style gangs and extremist militias. Overcoming corruption requires governance systems that have the qualities of accountability and transparency and the capacity to enforce the rule of law. When state institutions are unwilling or unable to contain corruption, citizens often mobilize under the banner of reform. Civil society campaigns against corruption are common in many parts of the world and in some settings have been effective in curtailing the worst forms of abuse.

The third part of the book looks at the core political and economic dimensions of governance. In Chapter 7 we examine the relationship between democracy and peace. The democratic peace effect between states is thoroughly documented, but the impact of democracy on conflict within states is less certain. Fully mature democratic states are less likely to experience internal armed conflict, but partial democracies or states in the early stages of transition from autocracy tend to be unstable and more prone to violence. Some argue that governance capacity, especially the ability to achieve economic development, is more important

---

[39] Mary Caprioli, "Primed for Violence: The Role of Gender Inequality in Predicting Internal Conflict," *International Studies Quarterly* 49, no. 2 (June 2005).

than democracy in generating peace, but as Norris observes the most stable and peaceful societies are those that combine strong governance capacity with qualities of democracy.[40] Research shows a strong connection between the degree of representation within a political system and the prospects for peace.[41] The ability of citizens to participate fully in political life is essential to making governance more responsive to public needs and helping to reduce the risk of instability and armed conflict.

In Chapter 8 we examine the many deep connections between economic development and peace. Paul Collier and his colleagues trace the root causes of armed conflict to failures of development.[42] Almost every empirical study in the economic literature observes a direct correlation between low per capita income and the likelihood of armed conflict.[43] Raising national income levels is critically important for reducing conflict risk. Peace also depends upon reducing horizontal inequalities of power and wealth among social groups. Research shows that the risk of conflict is greatest when social identity groups are excluded from political power and when their relative economic status is far below that of other groups.[44] Overcoming these conditions requires greater opportunities to participate in development. Amartya Sen has pioneered the concept of development as freedom, the process of social and political empowerment that enables people to gain the assets and capabilities they need to improve their well-being.[45] Development means removing obstacles to freedom and overcoming deprivations related to joblessness, lack of education, ill health and social exclusion. Governance systems promote development when they guarantee economic and political rights and provide equitable opportunities for communities to participate in their own development.

The greatest progress in reducing global poverty rates has come from trade and investment. High rates of economic growth in East Asia, India

---

[40] Norris, *Making Democratic Governance Work*.

[41] Arend Lijphart, *Patterns of Democracy: Government Forms and Participation in Thirty-six Countries* (New Haven: Yale University Press, 1999).

[42] Paul Collier, V.L. Elliot, Håvard Hegre, Anke Hoeffler, Marta Renal-Querol and Nicholas Sambanis, *Breaking the Conflict Trap: Civil War and Development Policy* (Washington, DC: World Bank and Oxford University Press, 2003).

[43] Edward Miguel, "Economic Shocks, Weather and Civil War," *National Bureau of Economic Research, NBER Reporter* 2011 Number 3: Research Summary.

[44] Lars-Erik Cederman, Nils B. Weidman and Kristian Skrede Gleditsch, "Horizontal Inequalities and Ethnonationalist Civil War: A Global Comparison," *American Political Science Review* 105, no. 3 (2011): 487–488.

[45] Amartya Sen, *Development as Freedom* (New York: Anchor Books, 1999).

and other states have lifted hundreds of millions of people out of poverty. As we discuss in Chapter 9, these gains are the result of market reforms and government decisions to guarantee property rights and build human capital through social programs. The market can be a powerful engine for peaceful development, but it functions best within governance structures that include a strong public sector and effective regulation. Capitalism has an inherent tendency toward inequality of wealth, Thomas Piketty argues, which must be tempered by programs of social welfare and income redistribution.[46] China and the Asian tigers achieved economic success with the help of strong state institutions capable of managing development and providing public support for education and training, health care, infrastructure and land reform. Governments in Japan, South Korea and other states liberalized some market sectors but protected others while nurturing nascent industries so that they could become strong enough to compete internationally. Mixed economies that combine market freedom with an active public sector are highly successful in achieving economic growth. They can advance the prospects for peace when combined with systems of accountability and democratic reform.

In Chapter 10 we examine governance at the global level and the increasing number of multilateral institutions, international conventions and transnational civil society networks that are part of globalization. Since the end of the Cold War the United Nations and other institutions have mounted an unprecedented number of diplomatic missions, humanitarian operations and peacekeeping missions to resolve and prevent armed conflict within and between states. As Goldstein and others note, these programs and missions have many limitations and flaws but on balance they have contributed significantly to the declining frequency and severity of armed conflict.[47] Global governance increasingly includes nonprofit groups and civil society networks that advocate for human rights and other global norms, and help to prevent and resolve armed conflict in many countries. New hybrid forms of global governance have emerged in recent decades, with civil society groups, donor states and international agencies cooperating in multi-stakeholder processes to address complex peacebuilding challenges.

In the final chapter we distill some of the key findings of the studies we review to identify core principles for US and international policy

[46] Thomas Piketty, *Capital in the Twenty-First Century* (Cambridge, MA: Belknap/Harvard University Press, 2014).
[47] Goldstein, *Winning the War on War*.

making. Because the various dimensions of good governance are inter-dependent and mutually reinforcing, no single approach by itself is suffi-cient to assure more peaceful outcomes. A comprehensive and integrated approach is needed that mainstreams good governance, emphasizing both security and social capacity and the importance of quality institu-tions that are inclusive, participatory and accountable. Most important is the need to avoid unintended harm, recognize the limits of what can be achieved by external actors, and learn lessons from past experiences and practices.

A recurring theme runs through all the chapters that follow. The pre-vention of armed conflict is linked to stable governance structures that have the capacity to deliver public goods to all stakeholders, provide for public participation and accountability, and manage competing claims to power, resources and territory. Discriminatory policies increase the risk of conflict, while equitable structures of political and economic freedom reduce that threat.[48] Governance systems that are inclusive, participatory and accountable improve the prospects for peace.

In many conflict zones around the world today, these conditions are absent. The governance situation is closer to that of the old Wild West than to modern Europe or North America. The law of the gun prevails, now-adays by Kalashnikov rather than six-shooter, with authority vested in men who command powerful militias or terrorist networks. Women and significant ethnic communities are excluded from power. Transforming these conditions to reduce the prevalence of armed violence requires a greater focus on building the structures of good governance. In the first chapter we discuss the meaning of that concept and define more precisely the institutional capacities and qualities that help to advance the pros-pects for peace.

---

[48] Jeffrey Dixon, "What Causes Civil Wars? Integrating Quantitative Research Findings," *International Studies Review* 11 (2009): 718–719.

I

When Governance Is 'Good'

Governance is about achieving cooperation. It is about the exercise of power and the challenge of persuading and enabling people to work together for common purpose despite differing identities and competing interests. Governance systems exist to solve the 'dilemma of collective action,' as scholars call it.[1] How to convince individuals and groups to follow directives and do what's socially necessary – especially if it means foregoing short-term advantage and requires sacrifice and extra effort? Individuals and social actors have an incentive to be free riders, enjoying the benefits of social cooperation without having to pay the price of making a personal contribution to the collective good.

In his famous essay "The Tragedy of the Commons," Garrett Hardin argues that the pursuit of unrestrained self-interest harms the collective interest and damages the commons upon which all depend.[2] Hardin uses the example of herders grazing cattle in a common pasture. The pasture has limited carrying capacity, but each herder has an incentive to feed and sell more cattle. The ambitious herder gains a benefit from putting more cattle in the field, but all herders pay a price as the pasture deteriorates and becomes less productive. The fractional losses from the depreciating asset are less than the profit from selling additional cows, and are not enough to deter the ambitious herder until it is too late. The commons collapses and the risk of conflict increases. An unmanaged system fails,

---

[1] Mancur Olson, *The Logic of Collective Action: Public Goods and the Theory of Groups*, rev. ed. (Harvard University Press, 1971).
[2] Garrett Hardin, "The Tragedy of the Commons," *Science* 162, no. 3859 (December 1968): 1243–1248.

Hardin writes, because it "rewards individual exploiters for making the wrong decisions – wrong for the group as a whole, and wrong for themselves, in the long run."[3] The herders need a means for managing the shared asset. They need a system of governance.

To overcome the obstacles to social cooperation Hobbes proposed the theory of the Leviathan: the coercive power of the state is necessary to enforce order and prevent the anarchy of unrestrained competition for power. Hardin echoes this approach in arguing that systems of coercive restraint are required to preserve the common good against the pursuit of individual advantage. These are not the only solutions, however, and they are based on understandings of human behavior that are more pessimistic than evidence suggests. The irony of Hardin's example is that village commons were an enduring feature of community life all over the world for hundreds of years, without the collapse he prophesied. The heavy emphasis on top-down enforcement proposed by Hobbes and Hardin ignores the diverse forms of governance and different dimensions of political power that enable communities to work together and solve collective problems. As we examine below, overly coercive forms of enforcement are an expensive and often inefficient way of achieving social cooperation. Easier and more effective ways of maintaining political order are available through systems of voluntary participation based on consent.[4]

Elinor Ostrom and other scholars respond to Hardin by demonstrating that "self-governance is possible" and documenting the ways that humans form systems of collective governance that are able to overcome the problems of advantage-seeking and free-riding.[5] Institutions provide the means for transforming potential zero-sum situations into arenas of cooperation. They embody systems for making and implementing decisions to share available resources for public benefit. Ostrom questions some of Hardin's assumptions. Claims about the efficiency of coercive power assume that rulers have access to accurate information, effective sanctions and low costs of administration.[6] In reality such capacities

[3] Garret Hardin, "The Tragedy of the Unmanaged Commons," in *Evolutionary Perspectives on Environmental Problems*, edited by Dustin J. Penn and Iver Mysterud (New Brunswick: Transaction Publishers, 2007).

[4] Robert Putnam, *Making Democracy Work: Civic Traditions in Modern Italy* (Princeton University Press, 1993), 165.

[5] Elinor Ostrom, James Walker and Roy Gardner, "Covenants with and without a Sword: Self-governance is Possible," *American Political Science Review* 86 (1992): 404–417.

[6] Elinor Ostrom, *Governing the Commons: The Evolution of Institutions for Collective Action* (Cambridge University Press, 1990), 10.

do not always exist, and the result is often ineffective governing institutions. Finding optimal solutions can be a "difficult, time-consuming,
conflict-invoking process," she writes, and is not easily imposed by external authorities. Despite the challenges, Ostrom finds room for individuals and communities to escape the 'tragedy' of Hardin's commons and
develop effective institutions to resolve collective problems.[7]

Through extensive empirical research into the evolution of cooperation strategies in many different countries and cultures, Ostrom identifies
common features that characterize effective systems of collective governance. These principles apply primarily to resource allocation in local
settings, but they have relevance for larger governance systems as well.
Cooperation works best in circumstances where boundaries are clearly
defined and the rules for sharing collective goods are well matched to
local needs and conditions. Governance systems flourish when those who
are affected by the rules have a role in shaping them and can participate
in devising new rules. Cooperation also depends upon community-based
systems for monitoring compliance and a set of graduated sanctions for
violations, along with low-cost mechanisms for resolving disputes. Local
systems ideally are nested within larger systems organized in multiple lay-
ers of coordinated interaction.

Ostrom's principles have parallels in the characteristics of governance that are most conducive to peace. In this chapter we examine these
core dimensions and how they facilitate collective action to achieve
common objectives. We review different understandings of governance
and the challenges of attempting to define 'good governance.' This is
followed by a discussion of the qualities of governance and the necessity of governance capacity for the delivery of essential public goods.
We emphasize the importance of legitimacy and public trust in gaining
social cooperation, and explore the role of social capital and associational linkages that bridge ethnic and social divides. We examine
governance as a system of political power, focusing on consent-based
forms of integrative or 'soft' power that derive their authority more
from society than the state. These more decentralized, horizontal forms
of 'new governance' reflect the increasingly important role of civil society not only at the national level but on the global stage as well. We
argue that governance systems based on consent and social legitimacy
are effective means of achieving collective action and fostering conditions for peace.

---

[7] Ibid., 14.

DEFINING TERMS

Enter the word governance into an Internet search engine and hundreds of different explanations pop up in an almost infinite variety of settings, from corporate governance to the management of medical centers to the workings of global institutions such as the UN. In its broadest context the term refers to systems for determining and regulating social activity. In this volume we examine the role of governance as one of the key factors determining the prospects for peace.

John Ruggie refers to governance as "the constellation of authoritative rules, institutions and practices by means of which any collectivity manages its affairs."[8] James Rosenau sees governance as the opposite of chaos, the act of intentionally creating order or a system of rule.[9] The UN Development Programme defines the term as "the exercise of economic, political, and administrative authority ... comprising the mechanisms, processes, and institutions through which that authority is directed."[10] Governance is exercised not only in and among states but also in the private sector and civil society. It operates both from the top down and the bottom up, with the authority of decision making dependent upon perceptions of legitimacy and degrees of consent among those affected.

It is important to differentiate between governance and government.[11] Government refers to the formal institutions of the state. Governance is the more capacious term and refers to all levels of authority: state, supra-state, private sector and civil society. Governance encompasses the regime or system for making and implementing public decisions, while government refers to the performance of these tasks by the state. In recent decades governance has overtaken government as the preferred term for understanding the challenges of achieving collective action and implementing public policy. Figure 1.1, drawn from a Google Scholar analysis of word usage over time, illustrates the point.

[8] John G. Ruggie, "Reconstituting the Global Public Domain: Issues, Actors, and Practices," *European Journal of International Relations* 10, no. 4 (2004): 504.

[9] James N. Rosenau, *Governance without Government* (Cambridge University Press, 1992).

[10] United Nations Development Program, "UNDP and Governance: Experiences and Lessons Learned," Management Development and Governance Division, Lesson-Learned series #1 (2006). http://204.200.211.31/Publications/Governance/Gov_Prac_doc/UNDP%20and%20Governance-%20Experiences%20and%20Lessons%20Learned,%20Learned%20Series%20No.%201.pdf.

[11] Wolfgang H. Reinicke, *Global Public Policy: Governing without Government?* (Washington, DC: Brookings Institution, 1989); Lawrence S. Finkelstein, "What Is Global Governance?" *Global Governance* 1, no. 3 (1995): 367.

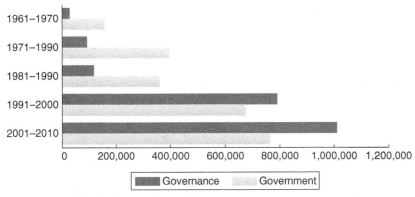

FIGURE 1.1. Scholarly uses of term 'governance' versus 'government'
Source: "State of the World 2014: Governing for Sustainability," Worldwatch
Institute

Governance systems vary according to their jurisdiction, which may encompass activities within a defined physical space or issues related to a particular function or purpose. Scholars categorize these different dimensions as "Type I" and "Type II" governance.[12] Type I regulates activity in a defined physical space and is more typical of government. Type II governance focuses on particular issues or functions and is more characteristic of non-state and networked forms of governance, although functional bodies also exist at national and international levels.

Perspectives on the meaning of governance vary widely but all emphasize institutional authority, domains of responsibility and specific outcomes. Most definitions emphasize the importance of institutions, which include formal legal codes and the organizational structures for their implementation, along with informal behavioral patterns, cultural traditions and social norms.[13] The meaning of governance encompasses formal and informal systems at multiple levels. Our distillation of these definitions is the following:

Governance is the system of rules and procedures used for the purpose of solving collective problems and establishing and maintaining social order. The domain of governance includes norms and policies to guide the system, protection against internal and external threats, and the provision of public goods and services. Essential elements of governance include institutions, mechanisms of compliance, and systems for cooperation and communication among social actors.

[12] Liesbet Hooghe and Gary Marks, "Unravelling the Central State, but How? Types of Multi-level Governance," *American Political Science Review* 97, no. 2 (2003): 233–243.
[13] Douglas North, *Institutions, Institutional Change and Economic Performance* (Cambridge University Press, 1990).

Governance systems function through subsidiary institutional mechanisms that make decisions, coordinate implementation and collective action, and manage and share information.[14] Institutions can be bureaucratic and hierarchical, or informal and loosely structured. The former depend on structural systems for making decisions and shaping behavior. The latter are based on shared understandings of purpose with fewer explicit rules and procedures. At the state level, governance operates mostly through formal institutions, although state activities are also influenced by informal social networks. On the global scale, institutional components can be elaborately structured like the United Nations or the World Bank, or more loosely organized like social movements and civil society networks.

Ideally governance is a means of making and implementing decisions for mutual benefit, but in the real world it is not always so benign. In many settings governance is the exercise of power for domination and exploitation. It is not intended to serve the common good but to benefit particular groups to the detriment of others, to protect the political and economic interests of powerful elites rather than of society as a whole. Governance is intimately tied to the exercise of political and economic power, as we discuss below. When power is unchecked and unaccountable it can lead to exploitation and abuse, exacerbating political grievances and social injustices. The result can be political instability and armed conflict. Authoritarian systems can maintain a degree of social order, but such regimes are by their nature less accountable and more prone to corruption. They tend to be more repressive and bellicose.

The alternative to abusive governance is the concept of 'good governance,' a term that is employed frequently but seldom defined precisely. Many international experts and officials refer to good governance, but there is no consensus on its meaning or universally accepted definition of the term. Good governance is often a catch-all term, Norris observes, "a Humpty Dumpty Rorschach ink plot test meaning whatever the commentator likes it to mean."[15] Our task in this volume is to give the concept greater specificity and define its core components in relation to peace.

The empirical methodologies used to measure governance have only limited value for this purpose. The widely used World Governance Indicators of the World Bank Institute have been criticized for perceptual

---

[14] Kenneth W. Abbott and Duncan Snidal, "Why States Act through Formal International Organizations," *Journal of Conflict Resolution* 42, no. 1 (1998): 3–32.

[15] Norris, *Making Democratic Governance Work*, 9.

biases, limited sample selection and reliance on conceptual models that favor particular neo-liberal economic policies.[16] Many forms of data, such as variances among indicators within countries, are not included. Some of the commonly used categories for defining governance, such as 'rule of law,' have multiple components and are themselves subject to a wide range of interpretation. Scholars have developed rigorous methods for measuring the components of governance and identifying causal relationships among them, but the state of knowledge on these matters remains partial at best.

A consensus exists nonetheless on broad parameters for defining what we mean by good governance. The World Bank and agencies of the United Nations use the term to describe institutional systems that are characterized by qualities of transparency, responsibility, accountability, participation and responsiveness to public need.[17] This approach overlaps well with our understanding of the requirements for sustainable peace and is compatible with general definitions of governance.

Governance is sometimes considered synonymous with democracy, but the two concepts are distinct. Democracy is part of the equation, but so is state capacity. Norris argues that liberal democracy alone is not sufficient for creating peace. Strong institutional capacity is also necessary to provide security and deliver public goods and services. In her "unified theory" of governance, peace is most likely in systems that combine mature democracy with the institutional capacity to deliver public goods and services.[18]

We consider governance 'good' if it ameliorates the conditions and grievances that cause people to fight, and provides mechanisms for resolving and transforming disputes without violence. In the first pathway, governance systems provide socially necessary public goods and deliver services in ways that allow individuals and groups to meet their basic needs. In the second pathway, governing institutions have accessible mechanisms for making decisions and resolving disputes that enable people to voice their concerns. Both dimensions address the underlying conditions that can lead to armed conflict.

---

[16] Ibid., 113.

[17] See the explanations offered by World Bank, "What is Governance?," at http://web .worldbank.org/WBSITE/EXTERNAL/COUNTRIES/MENAEXT/EXTMNAREGTOP GOVERNANCE/o,,contentMDK:20513159~pagePK:34004173~piPK:34003707~theSi tePK:497024,00.html; and the Office of the UN High Commissioner for Human Rights, "Good Governance and Human Rights," at www.ohchr.org/en/Issues/Development/ GoodGovernance/Pages/GoodGovernanceIndex.aspx.

[18] Norris, *Making Democratic Governance Work*, 175–182.

Governance systems help to advance peace when they are inclusive, participatory and accountable. When all significant social and ethnic groups are included and are able to participate in economic and political life, governing systems are more likely to be accountable and responsive to public needs and thus to generate fewer grievances that lead to armed conflict. Governance is 'good' when it is based on strong institutions that guarantee the availability of public services, when it includes mechanisms for effective dispute resolution, and when it offers incentives that facilitate and encourage public use of these pathways.

THE 'POLITICAL GOODS' OF GOVERNANCE

The capacity of governing institutions is often understood as their ability to deliver public goods, a framework of analysis developed by Robert Rotberg. The very purpose of governance, he contends, is to supply "political goods."[19] He bundles these into five categories: (1) safety and security, (2) rule of law and transparency, (3) participation and respect for human rights, (4) economic opportunity, and (5) human development. The effectiveness of a governance system can be evaluated by its ability to provide these goods. They are the deliverables of governance.

This emphasis on governance capacity is shared by Norris, Francis Fukuyama and others. State capacity has two broad components. The first and most important is protecting the safety and security of people, by exercising sovereignty within a given territory, defending against external threats and maintaining social order and stability. The second dimension is the ability to implement public policies, collect revenues and deliver basic goods and services to enhance social welfare and economic growth.[20]

Security is the most important and fundamental political good. It derives from the state's monopoly on the legitimate use of armed force. It can be understood as the duty of ruling authorities to protect citizens from armed attack or predation. Without public safety it is difficult or impossible to provide other political goods. "There can be no economic growth or social elevation, and no societal strength as opposed to failure, without fundamental security," Rotberg argues. "State failure always

---

[19] Robert I. Rotberg, "The Challenge of Weak, Failing, and Collapsed States," in *Leashing the Dogs of War: Conflict Management in a Divided World*, edited by Chester A. Crocker, Fen Osler Hampson and Pamela Aall (Washington, DC: United States Institute of Peace Press, 2007), 83.

[20] Norris, *Making Democratic Governance Work*, 44–45.

leads to civil war."[21] We will have much more to say about security capacity and the control of military force in Chapter 2.

In Rotberg's analysis, the rule of law is closely related to the security
function. For contending social groups to be able to resolve disputes without violence, the governance system must provide predictable, recogniz-
able and systematized methods for adjudicating disputes. This implies an
enforceable body of law, accountable police and security services, and an
impartial and independent judicial system. The courts must be able to dispense justice in a timely and efficient manner while guaranteeing basic legal
rights to all in an equitable manner. When these capabilities collapse or are
lacking, dispute settlement by violence becomes the norm. In such settings
justice is denied, fear increases and security collapses.

In authoritarian regimes the rule of law becomes 'rule by law,' a system for oppressing citizens rather than protecting them. A proper system of
lawful governance requires an independent and empowered judicial system
that can hold political leaders and security forces accountable. Social science indicators for measuring the rule of law have limitations, as noted
above, but the different indices used for this purpose all find a direct relationship between effective systems of legal accountability and a reduced
risk of armed conflict. States with high scores for the rule of law tend to be
more peaceful.[22]

Political freedom entails the ability of citizens to participate in politics
openly and without hindrance. It is characterized by effective political
institutions that have a high degree of accountability and provide mechanisms for the representation of citizen interests. It includes the tolerance
of dissent, the presence of an independent media and the protection of
civil and human rights. These freedoms are guaranteed by an independent and empowered judicial system. Also necessary is a "fearless and un-
self-censored media" that has the ability to criticize and hold ruling elites
accountable.[23] As we note in Chapter 7, states with high ratings for political freedom tend to be more peaceful.

To promote stability and peace, governance systems must create an
enabling environment for economic growth and prosperity. This encompasses protections for the rights of property, guarantees of entrepreneurship and innovation, prudent financial and banking systems, and a sound

---

[21] Rotberg, "The Challenge of Weak, Failing, and Collapsed States," 85.

[22] Institute for Economics and Peace, *Pillars of Peace*, 13–14.

[23] Robert Rotberg, "Governance Trumps Democracy," Africa and Asia: The Key Issues,
blog, http://robertrotberg.wordpress.com/2013/02/01/governance-trumps-democracy/.

currency. Also necessary are critical elements of infrastructure, including effective roads, railways, airports and broadband Internet access.[24] Prosperity and wealth are necessary to supply the fifth category of political goods, human development. Programs for education, social welfare and public health create a skilled and productive workforce and are necessary to sustain and expand economic opportunity.[25] We will explore these themes more thoroughly in Chapters 8 and 9.

Rotberg ranks states according to their ability to supply these political goods, using the categories of strong, weak, failing, and failed or collapsed. The ranking categories are not meant as exact classifications but rather as a guide to understanding the degree to which authorities have the capacity to make and implement decisions related to public order. The categories have direct relevance to national and international security. When a state is failing or failed, Rotberg argues, it is unable to address the needs of its people and is prone to conflict. Failed governance causes hardship and instability for individuals and communities within the state and beyond, especially in neighboring countries. It can give rise to violence and terrorism within and beyond the borders of the affected state.[26] Good governance signals the ability of governing institutions to deliver the key public goods needed to maintain order and stability. It provides outlets for people to voice their grievances and have a say in political decision making.

LEGITIMACY

The capacity to deliver public goods and services helps to generate legitimacy and public trust, which are critically important elements of good governance for peace. Legitimacy can be defined as the popular belief that political authority in a given setting is appropriately constituted and has the right to make public decisions. When governing systems are accepted as legitimate, people abide by public decisions even if they don't agree with or benefit from them. Systems with high levels of legitimacy and trust are based on social consent. They have lower social and economic transaction costs and tend to be more efficient than those that rely heavily on coercion.

The question of legitimacy has featured prominently in debates within the US military over the strategy for defeating terrorism and insurgency.

[24] Rotberg, "The Challenge of Weak, Failing, and Collapsed States," 87.
[25] Rotberg, "Governance Trumps Democracy."
[26] Rotberg, "The Challenge of Weak, Failing, and Collapsed States," 91.

Illegitimate governance has been described as "the root cause and the central strategic problem in today's unstable global-security environment."[27] In the theory of counterinsurgency the political objective of winning popular support for legitimate local governance is the top priority and takes precedence over military considerations. Legitimacy is "the main objective," write the authors of an influential 2006 article for *Military Review*:

> To establish legitimacy, security activities must move from the realm of major combat operations into the realm of law enforcement ... It is best to use the minimum possible force in resolving any situation ... The more force you use, the less effective you are.[28]

Winning the struggle against insurgency and violent extremism requires the establishment of legitimate governance systems that have the support and trust of local populations. This is a long-term process that can be encouraged by external actors but must evolve gradually within affected communities.

When states lack legitimacy and cannot rely on voluntary compliance they need coercive means. They have what Michael Mann calls "despotic power" but not the more important and less costly forms of power that flow from the loyalty and trust of citizens.[29] Trusted and well-governed states can depend upon consent and public cooperation. They are able to rule with a light hand. In states with good governance and high levels of democratic accountability, Fukuyama writes, "the fist is usually hidden behind layered gloves of law, custom, and norms."[30] In these settings trust and public acceptance are the norm, with threats and coercive means more the exception.

High levels of transparency and access to information help to build public confidence in governance and enhance legitimacy. When people have greater information about procedures and processes of decision making, they tend to view systems as fair and legitimate even if they are

---

[27] Eliot Cohen, Lieutenant Colonel Conrad Crane, U.S. Army Retired; Lieutenant Colonel John Horvath, U.S. Army; and Lieutenant Colonel John Nagl, U.S. Army, "Principles, Imperatives, and Paradoxes of Counterinsurgency," *Military Review* 86, no. 2 (March/April 2006): 49.

[28] Ibid., 50–52; quotes in Brooks, *How Everything Became War and the Military Became Everything*, 93.

[29] Michael Mann, "The Autonomous Power of the State: Its Origins, Mechanisms, and Results," *European Journal of Sociology* 25, no. 2 (1984): 185–213.

[30] Francis Fukuyama, *Political Order and Political Decay* (New York: Farrar, Straus and Giroux, 2014), 302.

disadvantaged by the decisions that are made. At the level of larger systems, however, where full information about processes is not available, perceived legitimacy depends more on personal benefit and the ability of governance systems to deliver public goods and services.[31] Public trust is a crucial factor in overcoming corruption. Even the strongest public institutions can be undermined if venality begins to spread and people lose faith in their legitimacy. Anticorruption efforts need to focus on restoring social trust and assuring the integrity of public affairs.[32]

The most important and powerful predictor of legitimacy is the belief that an institution makes decisions in an unbiased and fair manner. This is often referred to as "procedural legitimacy," the acceptance of public authority as impartial and even-handed.[33] Personal interest plays a role, but an individual's assessment of the legitimacy of an institution is distinct from whether he or she benefits from particular decisions. Perceptions of procedural legitimacy are linked to opportunities for public participation and the ability of those affected by policies to have a voice in the decision-making system.[34] This does not mean that governance must be democratic in the fullest sense, or that the voice of participants is always accepted or approved. It is enough simply if governance systems have some level of public participation giving citizens an opportunity to voice grievances and opinions in a manner that will be heard. Also reinforcing perceptions of procedural legitimacy are mechanisms of accountability and transparency and traditional systems of checks and balances. All are included within the common understanding of democracy and political freedom and are necessary for governance to be 'good.'

Another important way of creating legitimacy is to respond to people's social and economic needs by providing basic public services, also known as 'performance legitimacy.' In Rotberg's framework this is the effective delivery of political goods. Other scholars agree that legitimacy is derived

[31] Karen A. Hegtvedt and Cathryn Johnson, "Power and Justice: Toward an Understanding of Legitimacy," *American Behavioral Scientist* 53, no. 3 (2009): 376–399.

[32] Amanda Taub, "How 'Islands of Honesty' Can Crush Corruption," The Interpreter, *New York Times*, December 9, 2016, www.nytimes.com/2016/12/09/world/asia/south-korea-brazil-argentina-impeachment.html?ref=world.

[33] Tom Tyler, "Psychological Models of the Justice Motive: Antecedents of Distributive and Procedural Justice," *Journal of Personality and Social Psychology* 62 (1994): 850–863; Bruce Gilley, "The Meaning and Measure of State Legitimacy: Results for 72 Countries," *European Journal of Political Research* 45 (2006): 499–525.

[34] Daniel Kaufmann, "Rethinking Governance: Empirical Lessons Challenge Orthodoxy," Brookings Institution Working Paper series (2003); Anne-Marie Slaughter, *A New World Order* (Princeton University Press, 2004).

from government performance and effectiveness in fulfilling core state functions. Governments that provide security and improve living standards gain greater legitimacy in the eyes of their citizens. By contrast, the inability or unwillingness of political leaders to provide public goods is a major determinant of state failure and disorder.[35] The prevention of armed conflict depends on the provision of security and essential social services. Combining security protection with programs for human development is a state-building strategy that can contribute to what David Roberts describes as "deeper, more purposive, human-centered positive peacebuilding."[36]

Procedural and performance legitimacy are important but they do not always go together. Authoritarian states such as China and Singapore maintain public legitimacy and social acceptance through their ability to deliver public goods and high levels of economic growth despite little or no democratic accountability.[37] Governments such as Nigeria, Haiti and Afghanistan have elections and the appearance of democratic procedure, but they are highly corrupt and unable to provide the most basic public services. They are more likely to suffer huge legitimacy deficits and problems of instability. As we note in Chapter 6, corruption undermines legitimacy and is a major obstacle to effective governance.

Perceptions of legitimacy are strongly associated with relations of trust between state and society and with networks of political and social integration.[38] Studies in Latin America show that institutions have higher ratings of legitimacy when they incorporate a diverse array of social actors and are perceived as having fair and consistent decision-making procedures.[39] The inclusiveness, participatory nature and accountability of governing institutions, and the degree to which states deliver public goods, are key factors in determining state legitimacy.

Public trust grows with high levels of mutual interaction and interdependence within society. Robert Putnam's research shows that dense networks of civic engagement increase the ability of participating citizens to cooperate for mutual benefit.[40] When people engage in voluntary social activity together, they develop bonds of trust that enhance their mutual confidence

[35] Monica Francois and Inder Sud, "Promoting Stability and Development in Fragile and Failed States," *Development Policy Review* 24, no. 2 (2006): 147, 142.

[36] David Roberts, "Post-conflict Statebuilding and State Legitimacy: From Negative to Positive Peace?" *Development and Change* 39, no. 4 (2008): 551.

[37] Fukuyama, *Political Order and Political Decay*, 211.

[38] Gilley, "The Meaning and Measure of State Legitimacy," 518–519.

[39] T.J. Power and J.M. Cyr, "Mapping Political Legitimacy in Latin America," *International Social Science Journal* 60, no. 196 (2009): 253–272.

[40] Putnam, *Making Democracy Work*, 173, 184–185.

and willingness to cooperate. They are better able to make democracy work. "Individuals are able to be trusting (and not merely gullible) because of the social norms and networks within which their actions are embedded," Putnam observes.[41] High levels of interpersonal trust (as measured by the World Values Survey) predict confidence in government institutions.[42] Indices measuring perceptions of bureaucratic efficiency are also positively related to trust levels, supporting the notion that social capital is related to perceptions of government performance.[43] Social trust, norms of reciprocity, networks of civic engagement and successful cooperation are mutually reinforcing. Governance systems that enhance these characteristics have greater legitimacy and are more effective at gaining public compliance.

Building relationships of trust is essential to the challenge of transforming and preventing armed violence. Communities in conflict often lack the ability to understand and relate to each other, John Paul Lederach observes. The more they are wounded or feel threatened by others, the more insular they become and the less willing to hear or accept alternative perspectives.[44] Breaking the cycle of conflict that leads to violence requires an ability to build bridges and establish relations of trust with the 'other.'[45] Mediation is often needed to facilitate this process and create avenues for dialogue and communication. It takes time and patience for the mediator to gain legitimacy in the eyes of affected societies and for communities in conflict to hear and listen to one another. Through sustained engagement parties in conflict can begin to go beyond immediate differences and identify commonalities that might bring them together. As relations of trust evolve, opportunities emerge for new voices to be heard and for underlying grievances to be addressed. Adversaries can begin to consider options for ending their conflict and reaching mutually beneficial agreement. Peace in this conception is a bottom-up process in which people build new relations of trust to transform conflict into an opportunity for change.[46]

---

[41] Ibid., 177.

[42] Stephen Knack and Philip Keefer, "Does Social Capital Have an Economic Payoff? A Cross-Country Investigation," *Quarterly Journal of Economics* 112, no. 1 (1997): 1275.

[43] Ibid., 1276.

[44] John Paul Lederach, "Addressing Terrorism: A Theory of Change Approach," in John Paul Lederach, Douglas Ansel, Jessica Brandwein, Ashley Lyn Greene, Ryne Clos, Shinkyu Lee and Laura Weis, *Somalia: Creating Space for Fresh Approaches to Peacebuilding* (Uppsala: Life and Peace Institute, 2011), 10–15.

[45] Ryszard Kapuściński, *The Other* (London: Verso, 2008).

[46] John Paul Lederach, *Building Peace: Sustainable Reconciliation in Divided Societies* (Washington, DC: U.S. Institute for Peace, 1997), and *The Moral Imagination: The Art and Soul of Building Peace* (Oxford University Press, 2005).

Trust is not only essential for overcoming armed violence, it is also necessary for facilitating economic exchange. As Kenneth Arrow observes, "virtually every commercial transaction has within it an element of trust, certainly any transaction conducted over a period of time, [or financed on the basis of credit]." It is hard to imagine how any form of constructive economic development can occur without confidence in the reliability of economic agreements. "It can be plausibly argued," Arrow writes, "that much of the economic backwardness in the world can be explained by the lack of mutual confidence."[47]

The degree of trust in society is closely related to economic and social equality, which in turn correlates with lower levels of violence. As Putnam argues, "Community and equality are mutually reinforcing."[48] Empirical studies show that inequality is directly related to social distrust. Higher levels of economic inequality lead to lower levels of social trust and public cooperation.[49] Social equality is the "prime mover" of trust, exerting a stronger impact in generating trust than economic factors.[50] Richard Wilkinson and Kate Pickett concur, arguing that "changes in inequality and trust go together over the years. With greater inequality, people are less caring of one another and there is less mutuality in relationships."[51] As inequality increases, sociability declines and violence becomes more frequent. By contrast, societies with higher levels of income equality have lower rates of homicide and social violence.[52]

SOCIAL COHESION

High levels of social capital are clearly important for enhancing cooperation and public trust, but not all forms of social capital are the same in their impact on the prospects of armed violence. Putnam makes a distinction between "bridging" social capital, which is inclusive and tends to connect disparate groups, and "bonding" social capital, which builds group cohesion by reinforcing exclusive and homogeneous identities. Many groups have both bonding and bridging capacities, but some are

---

[47] Quoted in Putnam, *Making Democracy Work*, 170.
[48] Robert Putnam, *Bowling Alone: The Collapse and Revival of American Community* (New York: Simon & Schuster, 2000), 359.
[49] Bo Rothstein and Eric Uslaner, "All for All: Equality, Corruption and Social Trust," *World Politics* 58 (2005): 45.
[50] Eric Uslaner, *The Moral Foundations of Trust* (Cambridge University Press, 2002).
[51] Richard Wilkinson and Kate Pickett, *The Spirit Level: Why Greater Equality Makes Societies Stronger* (New York: Bloomsbury Press, 2010), 56.
[52] Ibid., 199, 135.

more narrowly focused on a specific identity group. Social capital that fosters exclusivist in-group loyalty is often achieved at the expense of hostility toward out-groups. This can breed group isolation and insularity leading to the marginalization and exclusion of other groups.[53]

Sheri Berman's analysis of social capital in pre-Nazi Germany finds that fragmented and apolitical associational life contributed to the downfall of the Weimar Republic and provided the organizational base from which the Nazi party could rise to power.[54] Professional and trade associations proliferated in 1920s Germany largely in response to the failure of political institutions to channel social needs into effective policy. Weimar-era civic associations were narrow and unable to bridge social divisions. The lack of horizontal integration among different sectors of society "helped lock in the fragmentation of the Reich" and further delegitimized democratic political institutions.[55]

Strong bonds within ethnic groups in the absence of legitimate political institutions can negatively impact economic performance or even lead to violent conflict.[56] A study of the genocides in Rwanda and Cambodia shows that exclusivist forms of social bonding provided networks for survival and rescue, but they also exacerbated ethnic extremism and exclusion, leading to genocide. Intense bonding within a social community may be necessary in times of economic stress or political repression, but it can lead to the exclusion of others and may exacerbate the animosities that lead to conflict and violence.[57]

By contrast, "bridging" social capital builds linkages across ethnic or other identity divides and creates the foundation for peaceful governance. Research produced by the International Institute of Social Studies confirms that high ratings for intergroup cohesion, interpersonal trust and the inclusion of minorities are significantly correlated with a reduced risk of armed conflict.[58] Associational life that contributes to the building of inclusive institutions and decreasing polarization establishes the social trust needed to maintain peaceful societies.

---

[53] Putnam, *Bowling Alone*, 22, 78.

[54] Sheri Berman, "Civil Society and the Collapse of the Weimar Republic," *World Politics* 49, no. 3 (April 1997): 427.

[55] Ibid., 410.

[56] Stephen Knack and Philip Keefer, "Does Inequality Harm Growth Only in Democracies," *American Journal of Political Science* 41, no. 1 (1997): 323–332.

[57] Christiaan Grootaert and Thierry van Bastelaer, "Understanding and Measuring Social Capital: A Synthesis of Findings and Recommendations from the Social Capital Initiative," Social Capital Initiative Working Paper, No. 24, 19.

[58] Institute for Economics and Peace, *Pillars of Peace*, 29–33.

Support for this analysis can be found in Ashutosh Varshney's well-known study of urban riots in Indian cities. Varshney compares three riot-prone cities and three peaceful cities with roughly similar ethnic ratios during the years 1950 to 1995. Cities with well-established interethnic associations were relatively calm, while cities that lacked formal interethnic relationships experienced serious Hindu–Muslim violence. Analysis of these pairs shows that "the preexisting local networks of civic engagement between the two [ethnic] communities stand out as the single most important proximate explanation for the difference between peace and violence."[59] Citizen associations that bridge ethnic communities act as "an institutionalized peace system" that can offset organized political violence. They facilitate open communication, dispel rumors and offer incentives to members of diverse ethnic groups to resolve grievances non-violently.[60] Formal interethnic associations give communities the capacity to withstand national-level shocks – such as India's partition in 1947. Historically, strong associational connections and interethnic cooperation in India emerged from Gandhian mass movements. Broadly based social mobilization helped to foster interethnic networks that later kept the peace. Varshney concludes, "a multiethnic society with few connections across ethnic boundaries is very vulnerable to ethnic disorders and violence."[61] As we shall see in the chapters that follow, empirical studies provide substantial evidence to confirm that ethnically exclusive institutions increase the risk of armed conflict.

Where norms and networks of civic engagement are lacking, the outlook for collective action appears bleak. This may be the fate for much of the developing world today and helps to explain the weakness of governance and the prevalence of armed violence in many societies. In polarized and poorly governed communities, ethnically distinct communities bond mostly with their own kin and distrust the 'other.' Where social linkages are limited or non-existent, the willingness to cooperate with other communities is minimal. By contrast, efforts to promote bridging forms of social capital enhance cooperation, improve governance and facilitate economic development and peace.

Social mobilization can be an important factor in building the foundations of interethnic cooperation. It can strengthen bonds of public trust

---

[59] Ashutosh Varshney, "Ethnic Conflict and Civil Society: India and Beyond," *World Politics* 53, no. 3 (April 2001): 374–375.

[60] Ibid., 380, 394.

[61] Ibid., 380.

and perceptions of legitimacy to bolster systems of effective governance. Social mobilization can also serve as the basis for political contestation and the emergence of new social actors to challenge systems of exclusion and injustice. These expressions of emergent political power can pave the way for new forms of governance that are more inclusive, participatory and accountable.

GOVERNANCE AND POWER

Governance is fundamentally about power, who has it and who does not. It is about who makes and implements decisions, and which interests benefit. In traditional hierarchical models of political authority, power is exercised from the top down, through formal institutional structures that employ sanctions and incentives to gain compliance. Power is commonly associated with the coercive capacity of the state, but as we note in this and subsequent chapters, power is also rooted in society and is based on social consent. Power is relational and requires an interaction between ruler and subject.[62] If people withhold their consent, the power of the authority system begins to erode. Gandhi focused on this dynamic as the basis for his pioneering method of organized mass noncooperation. He fashioned nonviolent civil resistance into a powerful political force for fighting injustice and challenging British rule. The Gandhian method of strategic disobedience, today called 'people power,' has spread throughout the world and has become a significant factor in movements for democracy and human rights in many countries.

Power has multiple forms, which Kenneth Boulding described as destructive, productive or integrative. Destructive power is based on coercion: do what I want or I will hurt you. Productive power is linked to economic exchange: give me want I want and you will receive benefit in return. Integrative power is based on communication and loyalty: do what I want because we trust and respect each other and value our relationship.[63] Boulding considers integrative power the most fundamental and dominant form of power because it achieves results through voluntary cooperation with few social costs.[64] It is self-reinforcing, like exchange power, but is based on deeper and more trusting relationships.

---

[62] Moisés Naím, *The End of Power: From Boardrooms to Battlefields and Churches to States, Why Being in Charge Isn't What It Used to Be* (New York: Basic Books, 2013), 16–17.

[63] Kenneth Boulding, *Three Faces of Power* (Newbury Park: Sage Publications, 1989), 24–25.

[64] Ibid., 61.

An economic transaction is a form of specific reciprocity, while integrative power creates general reciprocity. The expected benefits come from the relationship itself rather than direct payoffs. Economic relationships can grow into integrative relationships. As we note in Chapter 8, sustained networks of economic exchange help to generate greater understanding and trust between communities and can build relationships that create a basis for greater cooperation and peace.

Closely related to the idea of integrative power is Joseph Nye's concept of 'soft power.' Political authority depends less on the capacity to coerce than on the ability to attract, to encourage cooperation and participation.[65] Soft power affects others by framing agendas, using persuasion and eliciting positive responses. It is a form of relational power based on trust and the ability to shape preferences. "Hard power is push; soft power is pull," Nye writes.[66] People cooperate because they want to. They comply with requests because they are attracted to shared values and desire the intended outcomes, not because they are coerced or receive payoffs. Power in this concept is not a process of exercising authority *over* others but of accomplishing goals *with* others.[67] Encouraging rather than forcing people is a more effective and less costly way of achieving public cooperation.

These consent-based forms of power are increasingly relevant in the world today as new social actors enter the political stage and challenge traditional structures of hierarchical authority. Moisés Naím argues that political power is eroding in the face of newer and smaller expressions of what he calls "micropower," the rise of previously unacknowledged social actors who are demanding rights and finding ways to constrain and thwart the options of even the most powerful establishments. While some of these new actors are violent extremists, most of the new challengers are using methods of political engagement and civil obstruction that are generally nonviolent, if not exactly Gandhian. Challenges to established authority are emerging from diverse and unexpected places as the world's population continues to increase and growing numbers of people around the world demand a meaningful role in shaping the decisions that affect their lives. As growing numbers of people enter the middle class and gain literacy and access to the Internet, they become "more difficult

---

[65] Joseph S. Nye, Jr., *Soft Power: The Means to Success in World Politics* (New York: Public Affairs, 2004), 6.

[66] Joseph S. Nye, Jr., *The Future of Power* (New York: Public Affairs, 2011), 20.

[67] Ibid., xvi–xvii.

to regiment and control," Naím argues. The structures of conventional power are "more easily undermined, overwhelmed, and circumvented."[68] Power begins to shift from top-down to bottom-up.

CIVIL SOCIETY AND THE 'NEW GOVERNANCE'

As new forms of political power have emerged from society, the traditional authority of centralized government has diminished. Marx predicted the eventual withering of the state and the rise of more decentralized and cooperative forms of governance. States have not gone away, of course, but the nature of governance has changed in recent decades and is moving toward the decentralized model Marx envisioned – driven ironically by market globalization, the communications and transportation revolutions, and by what Naím terms the "more revolution" – rapid increases in population, literacy, living standards and social aspirations that are challenging traditional power structures throughout the world.[69]

Many dimensions of governance now occur beyond the boundaries of the state and exist within civil society and the private sector. Much attention has focused lately on the role of civil society, which has expanded significantly in recent decades. Civil society can be described as the arena of voluntary collective action for shared interests, purposes, and values.[70] Mary Kaldor defines civil society as the process of autonomous self-organization in which independent groups and individuals "negotiate, argue, struggle against or agree with each other and with the centers of political and economic authority" as they seek to transform society.[71]

The rise of civil society and the spread of Internet-based activism are creating new possibilities for more participatory and inclusive forms of governance for peace. They also provide new means of holding political leaders accountable to the public interest. Transnational civil society networks have played important roles in forging new values and political norms, such as human rights, environmental sustainability and gender equality. They have mobilized nonviolent movements for justice and peace in many countries and have challenged and sometimes removed

---

[68] Naím, *The End of Power*, 9–10, 13, 51, 56–58.
[69] Ibid., 54–58.
[70] Jude Howell, Armine Ishkanian, Ebenezer Obadare, Hakan Seckinelgin and Marlies Glasius, "The Backlash against Civil Society in the Wake of the Long War on Terror," *Development in Practice* 18, no. 1 (February 2008): 91 n. 4.
[71] Mary Kaldor, "Civil Society," in *Encyclopedia of Globalization*, edited by Roland Robertson and Jan Aart Scholte (New York: MTM Publishing, 2007), 104.

autocratic and repressive regimes.[72] Research suggests that the involvement of civil society actors in peace processes increases the prospects for preventing the recurrence of armed conflict.[73] Thania Poffenholz and her colleagues conclude from their analysis of civil society and peacebuilding that "civil society groups have contributed successfully to reducing violence, negotiating settlements, and sustaining peace after large-scale violence has ended."[74]

The connections among civil society groups are often tenuous and may be limited to particular events or activities. They are a form of "structured informality" and are more likely to create temporary collaboration than sustained cooperation.[75] Civil society networks exert influence through what sociologist Mark Granovetter calls "the strength of weak ties."[76] Their power derives from diversity not uniformity. They enable actors among different social sectors and across national boundaries to work together in addressing common challenges and opportunities. They are a form of power that supplants or in some cases challenges the role of bureaucratic state authority.

National governance is no longer the exclusive domain of the state.[77] The process of governance today increasingly depends upon the relationship between state and society and the roles of the private sector, civil society and self-organized social media networks.[78] The meaning of governance has evolved, writes Mark Bevir, to encompass "new processes of governing that are hybrid and multijurisdictional with plural stakeholders working together in networks." Governance increasingly involves "organizational hybrids that cross hierarchy, market, and network, and

---

[72] For the role of antiwar movements see Mary Kaldor, Denisa Kostovicova and Yahia Said, "War and Peace: The Role of Civil Society," in *Global Civil Society 2006/7. Global Civil Society – Yearbooks*, edited by Helmut K. Anheier, Mary Kaldor and Marlies Glasius (London: Sage, 2006); for the power of nonviolent civil resistance see Erica Chenoweth and Maria J. Stephan, *Why Civil Resistance Works: The Strategic Logic of Nonviolent Conflict* (New York: Columbia University Press, 2011).

[73] Anthony Wanis-St. John and Darren Kew, "Civil Society and Peace Negotiations: Confronting Exclusion," *International Negotiation* 13 (March 2008).

[74] Thania Paffenholz, "Conclusion," in *Civil Society and Peacebuilding: A Critical Assessment*, edited by by Thania Paffenholz (Boulder: Lynne Rienner, 2010), 425.

[75] Jan Martin Witte, Wolfgang H. Reinicke and Thorsten Brenner, "Beyond Multilateralism: Global Public Policy Networks," International Politics and Society No. 2 (2000), http://library.fes.de/pdf-files/ipg/ipg-2000-2/artwitte-reinicke-benner.pdf.

[76] Mark S. Granovetter, "The Strength of Weak Ties," *American Journal of Sociology* 78(1973): 1360–1380.

[77] Daniel Kaufmann, "Rethinking Governance: Empirical Lessons Challenge Orthodoxy," in *Global Competitiveness Report 2002–03*, World Economic Forum (2003), 35.

[78] Anne Mette Kjaer, *Governance* (Cambridge: Polity Press, 2004), 11.

embrace multiple actors from the public, private, and voluntary sectors."[79] The new forms of governance are transforming traditional concepts of state sovereignty, David Held argues. Many of the most fundamental economic, social, cultural and environmental forces that determine political outcomes now lie beyond the reach of individual states.[80] The nurturing and enhancement of the public good increasingly requires coordinated multilateral action.

The information revolution has powered many of these transformations and is eroding the ability of states to control public discourse and the policy agenda. Complex adaptive systems and horizontal social media networks are inherently non-hierarchical modes of leadership and collective action.[81] They create new possibilities for governance beyond the state. Virtual communities in all parts of the world cut across territorial jurisdictions to coordinate social action and develop their own unique patterns of interaction. Of course states seek to harness and control social communications, but new forms of expression and patterns of self-governance continue to evolve, reinforcing tendencies toward decentralization and making traditional forms of state hierarchy less relevant to people's lives.[82]

The transformative impacts of the Internet revolution are not always positive. Social media may create new opportunities for bottom-up change, but they can also warp world outlooks.[83] They amply ill-informed amateur voices, allowing anyone to publish and disseminate opinions without regard for fact or scientific evidence. Social media groups can spawn echo chambers and ghettos of communication that encourage group think and reinforce existing prejudices, reducing discourse across political divides and increasing polarization within democratic society.[84]

Civil society engagement and Internet-based activism cannot guarantee beneficial outcomes. Citizen groups can be "uncivil" and xenophobic,

---

[79] Mark Bevir, *Governance: A Very Short Introduction* (Oxford University Press, 2012), 3, 5, 11.

[80] David Held, "Cosmopolitanism: Ideas, Realities and Deficits," in *Governing Globalization: Power, Authority and Global Governance*, edited by David Held and Anthony McGrew (Cambridge: Polity Press, 2002), 307.

[81] Marguerite Schneider and Mark Somers, "Organizations as Complex Adaptive Systems: Implications of Complexity Theory for Leadership Research," *The Leadership Quarterly* 17, no. 4 (2006): 351–365.

[82] Nye, Jr., *The Future of Power*, 114.

[83] Frank Bruni, "How Facebook Warps Our Worlds," *New York Times*, May 22, 2016, Sunday Review, 3.

[84] Shattuck, "Resisting Trumpism in Europe and the United States."

especially when the state is weak.[85] Hate groups are able to use the Internet as easily as peace advocates. Non-governmental groups have no inherent political orientation and can promote reactionary values as well as progressive purposes. Nonetheless, most mass-based civil society networks strive for more participatory and transparent public institutions and policies and on balance help to increase the prospects for peace.

Rosenau sees progressive promise in the new forms of social engagement for global governance. He identifies two important characteristics that enhance the prospects for social cooperation and peace. The first is mass participation. "More than a little truth attaches to the aphorism that there is safety in numbers," he writes. The more pluralistic and crowded the global stage, with multifaceted authority and diverse steering mechanisms, "the less can any one actor, or any coalition of actors, dominate the course of events and the more will all have to be sensitive to the limit of their influence. Every rule system, in other words, will be hemmed in by all the others, thus conducing to a growing awareness of the virtues of cooperation."[86] The great diversity of public actors made possible through social networks constrains the accumulation and abuse of power. This increases the potential for society to monitor and resist trends toward repression and armed violence.[87]

A second beneficial feature is a growing "consciousness of and intelligence about the processes of globalization," a phenomenon of mutual social awareness that is spreading throughout the world. The Internet enables people to be more reflexive and conscious of their mutual interdependence in a world of shrinking dimensions of time and distance. Minds everywhere are turning to global problems and challenges, and many are seeking constructive solutions. "The conditions for the emergence of a series of global consensuses have never existed to quite the extent they do today."[88] The rise of civil society and the emergence of horizontal forms of interaction are changing global consciousness and the nature of political power. In many instances this is a positive trend,

---

[85] Christopher Spurk, "Understanding Civil Society," in *Civil Society and Peacebuilding: A Critical Assessment*, edited by Thania Paffenholz (Boulder: Lynne Rienner, 2010), 18–19.

[86] James N. Rosenau, "Governance in a New Global Order," in *Governing Globalization: Power, Authority and Global Governance*, edited by David Held and Anthony McGrew (Cambridge: Polity Press, 2002), 84.

[87] Mary Kaldor, *Human Security: Reflections on Globalization and Intervention* (Cambridge: Polity Press, 2007), 148–149.

[88] James N. Rosenau, *The Study of World Politics Volume 2: Globalization and Governance* (London and New York: Routledge, 2006), 194.

as reflected in growing awareness and concern about environmental preservation and climate change. Globalized social media can also feed extremism, however, as evidenced by the 'cyber jihad' that glorifies brutality and channels fighters to the so-called Islamic State in Iraq and Syria. The content of what is communicated remains essential and is the most important factor in determining whether globalized awareness leads to peace or war.

GLOBAL GOVERNANCE

The noun 'governance' is often preceded by the adjective 'global.'[89] It is not just alliterative appeal that accounts for the pairing. Global cooperation is indispensable to political, economic and social progress. It is also crucial to the prevention of armed conflict and the building of more peaceful societies, as we examine in Chapter 10. Global governance is unavoidable. Even when states resist the process, they are hemmed in by widening webs of international dependency and collaboration that are essential to their well-being. International institutions play significant roles in shaping the options available to states and local communities.[90] The tasks of national leaders are less to rule their separate domains than to manage complex relationships with other states, international institutions, multinational corporations and multiple civil society actors domestically and internationally.[91] The global stage has become densely packed with new players, all seeking to be heard and to exert influence on international policy.

As Kaldor writes, "The social contract within states is increasingly being supplemented by a social contract at the global level. Rules and laws that apply to individuals as well as states are being negotiated among the family of individuals, groups and institutions that constitute what we call global governance."[92] Decision making increasingly spans borders, diminishing the differences between inside and outside, domestic and external. States are no longer able to provide public goods and assure security solely on their own.

Two seemingly contradictory trends are at work in these developments: globalization, centralization and integration on the one hand; and

---

[89] Rosenau, "Governance in a New Global Order," 71.
[90] Held, "Cosmopolitanism," 306.
[91] Kaldor, *Human Security*, 157.
[92] Ibid., 160.

localization, decentralization and fragmentation on the other. Rosenau describes this as a "shifting balance between hierarchical and network forms of organization," with authority becoming more horizontal and less vertical.[93] As centers of influence have proliferated, elements of governance have become more decentralized. In many arenas of public life, the steering mechanisms of authority are closer to the communities that are most affected by that authority. This process reflects the principle of subsidiarity, which holds that central governments should not decide or do what citizens and local associations can determine for themselves.

The devolution of authority is exemplified in multilevel governance. This is a form of rule in which authority at the local level is enhanced. The European Union applies this model, as do systems of state and local rule in the United States and other countries. Federal bureaucracies and central governments retain significant power, but some forms of authority are redistributed to provincial and municipal systems, or to specialized functional agencies. When governance systems are more responsive to local needs, they are less likely to generate tensions that could lead to violence.[94] The decentralization of public authority can help to build social cohesion and reduce the risk of armed conflict.

CONCLUSION

As we examine in this chapter, governance encompasses multiple dimensions of decision making and implementation to achieve collective action and social order. It involves diverse actors and institutions, multiple realms of policy making, and various levels and jurisdictions of authority. At its heart, governance is about power. It is about who has the political authority to make decisions and influence policy, and how resources and wealth are allocated within society. Contests over these issues are the root cause of many armed conflicts, and the manner in which they are settled is decisive to the prospects for peace. Integrative and consent-based systems of power are better for this purpose than coercive or threat-based forms of governance. By their nature integrative approaches create less social friction and conflict and are less likely to lead to armed violence.

Governance is 'good' and therefore more likely to advance peace when it is inclusive, participatory and accountable, when it is characterized by fair procedures and performs well in delivering necessary public goods.

---

[93] Rosenau, "Governance in a New Global Order," 70, 76–77.
[94] Ibid., 78.

Governance includes not only traditional hierarchical models but also more horizontal network-based forms of social action. Globalization and the rise of the Internet have given voice to a multiplicity of social actors and have added new forms of authority to compete with traditional state-centric models. These developments create greater possibilities for enhancing public awareness and participation and holding officials accountable.

As Rotberg and others emphasize, governance is about delivering public goods and meeting social needs. Governments that are unable or unwilling to provide basic services to their citizens are more likely to experience war and armed conflict. The capacity of governance is thus an essential factor in determining the prospects for peace. We examine questions of capacity in the next two chapters, beginning with a look at the paradox of security. Peace depends upon security and the ability to protect public safety, but an overemphasis on security can be a cause of war and may increase the risk of armed conflict. We turn to these questions in the next chapter.

PART I

CAPACITY

2

The Security Paradox

Security capacity is a foundational element in the relationship between state governance and the prevention of armed conflict. It is the most important political good, according to Rotberg, an essential requirement for stability and peace. Governments cannot maintain public order if they are unable to assure the safety of their citizens and protect against external aggression and internal rebellion. The dynamic between security and peace is complex, however, and fraught with potential contradiction. If keeping the peace requires the threat or use of force, the quality of that peace becomes questionable. Cooperation that is based on social trust and voluntary participation is more efficient than compliance gained through coercive means. Military and police capabilities are necessary for social order, but they have limits, and if they are excessive or unaccountable they can threaten peace and undermine security.

In its broadest sense security refers to being protected or safe from physical harm and danger. In international relations it is understood as the state's ability to use military force against foreign and domestic threats, but this definition is too narrow. It ignores the non-military threats nations, communities and individuals may face and focuses excessively on military capability and the use of force. An integrated approach to security recognizes the full spectrum of risks to public safety and human well-being and seeks to ameliorate the conditions that give rise to armed violence. This approach employs multiple means of preventing and diminishing armed conflict, including diplomacy and political negotiation and the use of economic sanctions and incentives. It also includes longer range strategies such as support for economic development, democracy promotion, the protection of human rights and building institutions of effective governance.

Military capacity is necessary to respond to armed threats, but it is not sufficient by itself to guarantee security. In the absence of an effective system of governance even large well-equipped armies can appear helpless and inept before smaller lightly armed adversaries. In Iraq frontline army soldiers deserted in droves as fighters of the so-called Islamic State routed local defenders and took over Mosul, Ramadi and other cities. In Nigeria an army considered one of Africa's strongest was unable to prevent Boko Haram from terrorizing communities in the northeastern part of the country.[1] The effectiveness of a force depends on whether soldiers believe in what they are fighting for and have trust in their leaders, both military and civilian. Without legitimate and accountable institutions of political governance, even large armies cannot assure stability and genuine security.

In this chapter we explore these issues and review the ways in which security capacity affects the prospects for peace. Our analysis looks primarily at dynamics within states, but we also consider parallel patterns in inter-state relations. We review and critique some of the common assumptions about the meaning of security capacity. We discuss the limits of military power as a means of achieving political objectives. Also examined is the necessity of civilian control of the military and the risks posed by ethnically based security institutions constructed within patronage systems. The chapter concludes with a review of nonviolent means of addressing conflict and an assessment of the human security paradigm as an alternative, more comprehensive approach for protecting individuals and communities and preserving peace.

PEACE THROUGH STRENGTH?

Ronald Reagan had success as a politician through his use of the slogan 'peace through strength.' The concept worked politically because many people naturally equate security with strong military forces. Political leaders in many countries share this belief and seek to build up their armed forces and invest in soldiers and weaponry to bolster security. The relationship between military capacity and security seems obvious, but evidence on the question is mixed, and debate on the value of large military establishments continues.

[1] Adam Nossiter, "Nigerian Army Noticeably Absent in Town Taken From Boko Haram," *New York Times*, March 20, 2015.

Several studies show that states with high levels of military spending and large armed forces are less likely to experience the outbreak of internal armed conflict. In their 2006 review of the empirical literature on the causes of intrastate conflict, Nicholas Sambanis and Håvard Hegre find evidence of a robust connection between military capacity and a reduced risk of conflict onset. Military strength as measured by the number of troops is inversely related to the risk of civil war. As Sambanis and Hegre write, "countries with large militaries may be better able to deter insurgency or repress any opposition before it rises to the level of civil war."[2] These states have greater capacity to prevent or preempt internal conflict.

James Fearon and David Laitin also emphasize the linkage between security capacity and internal peace in their influential 2003 article on the factors associated with the outbreak of civil war. They find a direct association between high levels of state capacity and a reduced risk of civil conflict. Governments with large military and police forces and the capacity to exert authority over all of their territory have greater success in suppressing insurgency. The opposite is also true: "Insurgents are better able to survive and prosper if the government and military they oppose are relatively weak – badly financed, organizationally inept, corrupt, politically divided, and poorly informed about goings-on at the local level."[3] Insurgencies are more likely to emerge and take hold in the absence of effective state governance capacity.

The case for security through military strength may not be as strong as these studies suggest, however. Fearon and Laitin use national income as a proxy for measuring government capacity, but measurements of national income encompass a very broad range of factors and include virtually all forms of activity at every level of government. The finding of a link between national income and reduced conflict risk could be measuring social capacity as much as security capacity. Similarly, the observed connection between military spending and conflict reduction might be measuring levels of economic development and per capita income. As we observe in Chapter 8, income levels are among the strongest independent variables associated with peace and reduced conflict risk.

---

[2] Nicholas Sambanis and Håvard Hegre, "Sensitivity Analysis of the Empirical Literature on Civil War Onset," *Journal of Conflict Resolution* 50, no. 4 (2006): 529.

[3] James D. Fearon and David D. Laitin, "Ethnicity, Insurgency, and Civil War," *American Political Science Review* 97, no. 1 (2003): 80.

While there is undoubtedly some relationship between measures of security capacity and reduced conflict risk, the causal patterns are complex and cannot be reduced to simply measuring income levels. Some countries have very high levels of per capita income, such as Germany or Canada, but relatively low levels of military spending and smaller armed forces and yet are relatively secure and have no recent involvement in internal armed conflict. Other countries have lower levels of per capita income, such as Syria or Sudan, but very large military and police forces and have experienced horrific levels of civil conflict. The size of a country's armed forces is not sufficient by itself to explain the presence or absence of armed conflict. Many other factors also determine the prospects for peace, including the quality of governance institutions and the state's ability to provide the full range of public goods.

In a later background paper for the World Development Report 2011, Fearon reaches a more nuanced conclusion about the relationship between state capacity and the risk of civil conflict. He acknowledges the debate about using national income as a proxy for coercive capability and applies a broader methodology that uses indicators of governance to measure institutional capabilities more directly. He analyzes data for government effectiveness, investment profile, corruption, and the rule of law and finds all to be associated with conflict risk. Within each category higher ratings of good governance are correlated with lower levels of armed conflict. It may be "interesting to learn," Fearon observes, that regardless of which governance indicator one chooses, all show an inverse relationship with the probability of armed violence.[4] This could mean that the different dimensions of governance have similar effects on conflict risk, or, as Fearon puts it, "good governance is like a syndrome and 'all good things tend to go together.' "[5] This suggests that the observed conflict-mitigating impact of state capacity applies to all levels of governance, civilian as well as military, a point we emphasize in the next chapter.

Military capabilities are important for deterring internal armed conflict, but this does not mean that heavily armed states like North Korea are models of peaceful governance. Autocratic regimes with large military establishments tend to be less open and more repressive than their democratic counterparts. They have fewer democratic constraints on the use of force and are usually more ruthless in crushing their opponents.

---

[4] Fearon, "Governance and Civil War Onset," 4.
[5] Ibid., 3–4.

Heavily armed authoritarian regimes may be able to suppress potential adversaries and retain their grip on power for a period, but the order they keep is more like the 'peace of the grave' than a positive human flourishing. The Soviet Union imposed tight political control and maintained a veneer of social order, but the system's supposed stability masked widespread dysfunction and social discontent, leading to its rapid collapse after the reforms of Gorbachev and the Velvet Revolution. In China today the government maintains strict social order through a large security apparatus and a powerful communist bureaucracy, but growing numbers of people demand accountability and many local protests against official abuse have occurred, as we note in Chapter 9.

Authoritarian countries with large military establishments are less likely to experience a transition to democracy. Research shows that a state's military and coercive capacity is inversely correlated with its level of democracy and prospects for democratic transition.[6] As we demonstrate in Chapter 7, states with high levels of institutionalized democracy are more peaceful and are less likely to experience internal armed conflict. To the extent that militarization impedes the transition to democracy, it limits the beneficial impact of the democratic peace effect.

Increases in military spending are associated with reduced human rights, especially in countries that are not fully democratic.[7] A number of studies have found a direct connection between high levels of military spending and repression.[8] This pattern is most pronounced in states with military governments or where the armed forces significantly influence political decision making, as in Pakistan or Egypt.[9] When states rely excessively on repressive power to maintain social order, they exacerbate conditions that can lead to armed conflict. In highly repressive states internal conflicts are more likely to turn into civil war.[10] This was the case

---

[6] Michael Albertus and Victor Menaldo, "Coercive Capacity and the Prospects for Democratization," *Comparative Politics* 44, no. 2 (2012): 151, 157, 166.

[7] Krishna Chaitanya Vadlamannati and K.K. Shakya Lahiru Pathmalal, "Exploring the Relationship between Military Spending and Human Rights Performance in South Asia," *International Journal of Human Rights* 14, no. 2 (2010): 147–165.

[8] Christian Davenport, "Multi-Dimensional Threat Perception and State Repression: Inquiry into Why States Apply Negative Sanctions," *American Journal of Political Science* 39, no. 3 (1995): 683–713.

[9] Robert D. McKinlay and A.S. Cohan, "A Comparative Analysis of the Political and Economic Performance of Military and Civilian Regime," *Comparative Politics* 8, no. 1 (1975): 1–30.

[10] Patrick Regan and Daniel Norton, "Greed, Grievance, and Mobilization in Civil Wars," *Journal of Conflict Resolution* 49, no. 3 (2005): 333–334.

in Syria, where the Assad regime ruthlessly crushed nonviolent protesters in 2011, prompting many to pick up the gun. The repression sparked a brutal civil war that continues to the present. When security capacity is used for domestic repression it can have severe negative impacts. Coercive power in this sense can be a cause of armed conflict rather than a cure.

In post-conflict settings high levels of military spending are associated with a greater risk of renewed armed conflict. Paul Collier and his colleagues find that high levels of military spending in the aftermath of an intrastate civil conflict are "significantly counterproductive" for peace. They observe a direct relationship between rates of military spending and the risk of renewed civil war.[11] As Collier writes in *The Bottom Billion*, "high military spending is part of the problem in post-conflict situations, not part of the solution."[12]

The source of this pattern is partly the signaling effects of different types of government spending. States that prioritize military expenditures in the wake of a peace settlement are hedging their bets and inadvertently signaling an intention to prepare for war and perhaps renege on negotiated agreements. Prioritizing social programs such as education and health care, on the other hand, may signal an intention to focus on peaceful development and economic growth rather than further armed conflict.[13] Spending more on social development rather than the military helps to address socioeconomic grievances and may ameliorate conditions that lead to internal armed conflict. Social development programs that promote economic growth and enhance per capita income reduce the risk of civil war and create greater prospects for peace. The importance of social spending for promoting peace is well established in social science research, as we examine in the next chapter.

Some studies have found that high levels of military spending retard economic growth in developing countries,[14] but the evidence on this question is ambiguous. A comprehensive review of the many studies on the relationship between military spending and economic growth finds mixed results, with some studies showing a negative effect, others a positive impact, and many indicating no net effect either way.[15] Much

---

[11] Collier et al., *Breaking the Conflict Trap*, 86–87.

[12] Collier, *The Bottom Billion*, 132.

[13] Collier et al., *Breaking the Conflict Trap*, 87.

[14] Paul Collier, "War and Military Expenditures in Developing Countries and their Consequences for Development," *Economics of Peace and Security Journal* 1, no. 1 (2006): 10.

[15] In their 2010 survey Paul Dunne and Mehmet Uye examine more than one hundred studies on the economic effects of military spending. More than a third of the studies showed

depends on the characteristics of the countries studied and the econometric models employed. In 1993, the Development Assistance Committee (DAC) of the Organization for Economic Development and Cooperation issued a policy guidance document on participatory development and good governance. It stated:

When military expenditure is excessive, it can result in conflict and repression, contribute to instability in the region, and divert scarce resources away from development needs. DAC members emphasize the importance of establishing and maintaining the primacy of the role of civilians in political and economic affairs and the significance they attach to avoiding or reducing excessive military expenditure.[16]

This is sound advice for any nation, especially for states struggling to overcome armed conflict and facing major development challenges. Military and police capabilities are necessary for security, but an excessive reliance on forceful means increases conflict risk. In the absence of effective institutions of civilian governance and a solid foundation of economic and social development, military forces cannot guarantee peace. Too much security capacity in relation to civilian priorities can be counterproductive. If there is a principle of governance here, it is to keep security capabilities within limits, both of size and mission – a theme we develop further below.

ACCOUNTABILITY

Security depends not only on the capacity of military and police forces but on their relationship to civilian authority. While uncertainties exist about aspects of military capacity, there is no doubt about the central importance of military accountability to civilian rule. In democratic systems of governance the security forces and the state are interdependent and have carefully defined roles and responsibilities. The armed forces and police are entrusted with the authority to use force, maintaining the state's monopoly on the use of force. In return for this privileged status, the security forces are subordinate to civilian political authority and are

negative effects of military spending on growth, 20 percent found positive effects, and more than 40 percent found unclear results. See Paul J. Dunne and Mehmet Uye, "Military Spending and Development," in *The Global Arms Trade*, edited by Andrew Tan (London: Routledge, 2010); see also Aynur Alptekin and Paul Levine, "Military Expenditure and Economic Growth: A Meta-analysis," *European Journal of Political Economy* 28 (2012): 636–650.

[16] Organization for Economic Development and Cooperation, "DAC Orientations on Participatory Development and Good Governance," 1993, para. 53.

bound by laws that limit how and when force can be used. Maintaining this system of accountability is crucial to the prospects for peace.

Civilian control of the military has always been a cardinal principle of democratic governance. The historical evolution of democracy in Europe and other parts of the world was driven substantially by the desire to gain control over the war power and constrain the use of military force. Among the "injuries and usurpations" cited in the American Declaration of Independence was the action of the king "to render the Military independent of and superior to the Civil power." The 'third wave' of democratization that swept through Latin America, the former Soviet states and East Asia in the 1980s and 1990s was a reaction in many countries to dictatorship and in some cases direct military rule. In nearly all of the affected countries, the removal of military regimes had the effect of reducing levels of repression and lowering the risk of armed conflict.

Empirical research confirms the importance of civilian control of the military for preventing internal armed conflict and militarized disputes. A study published in the *Journal of Conflict Resolution* measures the degree of civilian control by placing states in three broad categories: those with strong civilian governance of the military, those with weak governance in which the military exerts major policy influence, and those with direct military rule.[17] The study analyzes the relationship between these regime types and the risk of armed conflict. As expected, fully democratic states tend to have the greatest control over their military forces and the lowest risk of armed conflict. Partially democratic states transitioning from authoritarianism to democracy have weaker civilian control of the military and have the highest risk of internal armed conflict. Autocratic regimes, often military in nature, have relatively strong control over their armed forces, but they are also prone to coups and internal armed conflict, although less so than partial democracies. These findings are compatible with studies showing the varying relationship between different levels and types of democracy and the risk of armed conflict, as discussed in Chapter 7.

States with weak civilian control over their security forces have a much higher probability of initiating war than states with strong governance of the military. When military officers have the authority to initiate militarized conflicts, they tend to do so substantially more often than civilians.[18] Research shows that states with excessive levels of military

---

[17] Sechser, "Are Soldiers Less War-Prone Than Statesmen?"
[18] Ibid., 770.

influence are also more likely to become involved in militarized disputes with other states.[19] Civilian control of the military is not only an essential element of democracy but an important factor in preserving peace. This result has obvious policy implications and confirms the importance of assuring strong civilian control of the military as a strategy for peace and democracy. The link between greater civilian control and reduced conflict risk is another way in which governance enhances the prospects for peace.

The structural foundation of civilian supremacy over the military lies in governmental control of financial and material resources. Military leaders depend upon civilian government not only for political and legal authority but also for the flow of resources needed to maintain their forces. They accept subordination to civilian leadership in exchange for receiving a share of public revenues to maintain their institutional capability. As Michael Desch notes, in return for their submission to civilian authority military leaders also expect a substantial degree of operational autonomy in tactical and technical matters.[20] Yagil Levy describes this relationship as a form of bargaining, an exchange between the state and the citizen, between military and civilian elements of government. When military forces are not dependent on civilian government, Levy notes, "the subordination of the military to civilian control cannot emerge."[21]

In fragile or unstable states that have limited resources and poor governance, military dependence on civilian leaders is often weak or non-existent. Fragile governments often lack the broad tax base and substantial public revenues needed to fund and control military forces. They also have weak parliamentary and judicial institutions and less ability to monitor and discipline military abuses of power. States with limited governance and institutional capacity lack the resources and means to exert control over the military. In some countries – Egypt and Pakistan are prominent examples – the armed forces have their own business enterprises and sources of income and a high level of institutional autonomy that puts them largely beyond the control of civilian political authority.

---

[19] Seung-Whan Choi and Patrick James, "Civil-Military Relations in a Neo-Kantian World, 1886–1992," *Armed Forces & Society* 30, no. 2 (2004): 229, 231–232.

[20] Michael C. Desch, *Civilian Control of the Military: The Changing Security Environment* (Baltimore: Johns Hopkins University Press, 1999), 9–10.

[21] Yagil Levy, "A Revised Model of Civilian Control of the Military: The Interaction between the Republican Exchange and the Control Exchange," *Armed Forces & Society* 38, no. 4 (2012): 537.

Levy notes that military subordination to civilian government is also weak when another state underwrites the cost of the military. The United States and other states train and fund local armed forces in many countries in the belief that they are enhancing security and contributing to state capacity, but these programs can have the opposite effect intended. If civilian governance is weak and the local regime is unable to absorb and manage the external support, the consequences for local security can be negative. When armed forces receive resources and institutional support from external sources, they are less dependent on and thus less accountable to local government. This impedes domestic civilian control and does little to build relationships of trust and dependency between soldiers and society. The balance of power between military and civilian institutions may tip in favor of the former, tempting the armed forces to take independent action. Loyalties to particular ethnic or regional groups may take priority over accountability to the central government.

Security support programs need to be combined with efforts to strengthen the capacity and quality of civilian governance. Building up military forces in the absence of political accountability and civilian capacity will not bring sustainable security. US security assistance programs in Iraq and Afghanistan created large armed forces with sufficient military capability to counter local insurgent forces, but because institutions of civilian governance and political accountability remain weak and riven by sectarianism, neither country has been able to provide for its own security. Iraq has sufficient oil revenues to pay for its armed forces, but Afghanistan is heavily dependent on external funders. Its national revenue base for all functions of government, not counting development aid, is in the range of $2 billion a year. The annual cost of maintaining its security forces is $5 billion, of which the Kabul government pays less than 10 percent.[22] Without international donor support the national government of Afghanistan would collapse. This is not a condition likely to foster sustainable security, no matter how much is spent on the military. Security assistance programs must include efforts to build effective institutions of civilian governance and create a diversified base of sufficient government revenue. Effective systems of civilian governance are the real strength that sustains peace.

[22] SIGAR, Special Inspector General for Afghanistan Reconstruction, *Quarterly Report to the U.S. Congress*, July 30, 2016, 161, www.sigar.mil/pdf/quarterlyreports/2016-07-30qr-section3-economic.pdf.

INCLUSION

The development for peace theory argues that encouraging economic growth and providing equitable opportunity for all reduces the risk of armed conflict. To build peace it is necessary to assure social and economic justice. The reverse of this proposition is also true. To help communities overcome poverty it is necessary to provide protection from war and violent crime. The poor and the vulnerable often suffer most from violence and live in communities where police protection and security systems are inadequate, corrupt or non-existent. Studies show that stability, social cohesion, economic growth and investment all diminish in settings of armed violence and ineffective security systems. As a recent report from the Organization for Economic Cooperation and Development argues, "Security and justice programs are crucial for making inclusive political settlements work, consolidating peaceful transitions, establishing the rule of law and bringing forward development."[23] Too often, however, security systems are abusive and are used to protect the interests of particular ethnic groups in power while ignoring or exploiting the needs of the marginalized. Effective development and stabilization programs depend upon providing security for all in an accountable and impartial manner.

Military accountability depends not only on the capacity of civilian governance but on the social composition and structure of the armed forces. When armies and police forces are organized along ethnically based patronage lines, the risks of armed conflict increase. Such military structures are destabilizing because they pit ethnic groups against one another in competition for a share of military and political power. When posts are awarded to supporters based on ethnicity rather than merit, the orientation of the military changes. Loyalties are to ethnic patrons rather than to the state. Patronage-based systems of governance perform poorly in delivering public goods and may also imperil security.[24] They diminish opportunities for those who are not well connected or part of a favored group. Such systems strengthen and entrench the power of existing elites and impede efforts to expand democratic accountability and participation.

---

[23] *Improving Security and Justice Programming in Fragile Situations: Better Political Engagement, More Change Management*, OECD Development Policy Papers, March 2016, No. 3, OECD publishing, 3, www.oecd-ilibrary.org/docserver/download/5jmov3vd5jgo-en.pdf?expires=1482515245&id=id&accname=guest&checksum=CD3F328EDE6DEF99E4730947963222ED.

[24] Fukuyama, *Political Order and Political Decay*, 86.

When one community holds a disproportionate share of military power at the expense of another, conflict risk increases. In Iraq the government has been dominated by Shia political parties, and military and police forces reflect this sectarian orientation. The strongest fighting forces in the country are Shiite militias that operate beyond government control. Sunni communities and former Baathists have been largely excluded from power and subjected to violent repression, often at the hands of the Shiite militias. As a result some in the Sunni community have taken up arms and turned to the so-called Islamic State for protection.

Ethnically-based patronage systems within the military increase the risk of military coups. In her study of security forces in sub-Saharan Africa, Kristen Harkness finds that ethnically diverse armies situated within larger ethnically based patronage systems are unstable and prone to coups. Countries with these characteristics have experienced coups nearly four times more frequently than those with more balanced military structures and recruitment practices.[25] In a number of African countries leaders have created armies that are staffed by loyalists from their own ethnic community. The practice of ethnic stacking may help to solidify support within one's own community, but it can provoke backlashes from the leaders of excluded ethnic groups. This pattern of building military forces on the basis of ethnic patronage has sparked decades of instability in the affected countries.

States with militaries organized around ethnically based patronage are less likely to experience peaceful political transitions.[26] More than half of all interethnic political transitions in post-colonial Africa have occurred through military coups.[27] African countries that began post-independence with ethnically homogeneous militaries have largely escaped the coup cycle, but states with ethnically based military patronage structures have faced greater instability and conflict risk.[28] Elections are no help with this problem if there are no guarantees for the inclusion of marginalized groups. In fact elections may exacerbate tensions because they create the possibility that leaders from rival ethnic groups may obtain power and attempt to purge ethnic opponents from military leadership. Military leaders who fear the loss of power and patronage often undermine the election process and/or disregard the results. In the African states Harkness

[25] Harkness, "The Ethnic Army and the State."
[26] Ibid.
[27] Philip Roessler, "The Enemy Within: Personal Rule, Coups, and Civil War in Africa," *World Politics* 63, no. 2 (April 2011): 306.
[28] Harkness, "The Ethnic Army and the State."

examines, ethnic militaries staged coups an astounding 75 percent of the time following constitutional transitions that put into power an executive with a different ethnic background than the military leaders.[29]

Fighters expelled from the military and excluded from patronage systems are more likely to form insurgencies. In his study of African cases Philip Roessler finds that purges of rival ethnic groups dramatically increase the risk of armed rebellion by the marginalized community.[30] States that expel ethnic groups from power lose their foothold in the territory of the excluded groups, further weakening state capacity to defend against insurgencies. Lacking contacts within rival ethnic groups, states may resort to the use of indiscriminate violence against insurgents, exacerbating rebel grievances and precipitating full-scale civil war.[31]

The dangers associated with ethnically based patronage systems arise not merely from the existence of ethnic and linguistic differences within the military. The Belgian military, for example, has both French and Dutch speaking soldiers. The Canadian armed forces have a bilingual mandate. Problems arise not from the presence of different languages or identities per se but from the lack of structures for equitable inclusion and accountability to civilian authority. Effective systems of civilian governance are needed to ensure loyalty to the state rather than to a particular ethnic political faction or leader. Genuine security depends upon the development of merit-based military systems in which obedience to civilian authority is obtained through professionalization rather than patronage. Stability and peace depend upon inclusive security forces that are accountable to legitimate institutions of civilian governance.

Attempting to fix the problems of ethnically based military patronage networks may increase the risk of violence in the short run. Armed groups that benefit from such systems are not likely to sit idly and allow their power and privileges to be diminished or removed. The process of creating more accountable armed forces has to come from within. The international community can play a limited role in helping willing governments re-shape their security institutions, but ultimately, as Harkness argues, "lasting military reform is an ordeal that must be grappled with domestically."[32]

At times international intervention can exacerbate the problem. The US invasion of Iraq and decision to disband the Sunni-dominated army

[29] Ibid.
[30] Roessler, "The Enemy Within," 302–303.
[31] Ibid., 316.
[32] Harkness, "The Ethnic Army and the State."

was intended to free the people from tyranny, but it had the effect of substituting one form of exclusion for another. As Shiite forces came to dominate the Iraqi state and gained military clout, Sunnis found themselves subjected to repression and marginalization, as they had done previously against Shiites. Cashiered Baathist soldiers ended up supporting the armed resistance, first with al-Qaida and then with ISIS. US forces re-entered Iraq to train Iraqi recruits to fight ISIS, but the majority of their trainees have been Shiites. This could worsen the underlying sectarian divide that is at the root of the violence.[33]

If security assistance is offered, it should be provided in a manner that ameliorates rather than exacerbates ethnic divisions within the military. Sustainable security depends upon building more inclusive and professionalized military institutions that are accountable to civilian governance. Equitable and balanced relationships within the military and between the armed forces and society are crucial to the challenge of preventing armed conflict.

THE LIMITS OF MILITARY CAPACITY

The value of military force in securing peace and achieving policy goals is often overrated. General Rupert Smith, one of Britain's most highly regarded military leaders, argues in *The Utility of Force* that the era of large-scale industrial warfare is over, and that military interventions often fail to achieve their political objectives. "Most uses of force by the major powers and Russia in recent decades have been unsuccessful," he writes.[34] US military missions in Southeast Asia, Iraq and Afghanistan did not achieve their stated political objectives and produced either outright failure or ambiguous results at best.

When evaluating the effectiveness of military force it is important to keep in mind von Clausewitz's famous observation that "war is a mere continuaton of policy by other means." He refers to "the political object as the original motive" of war.[35] Military force is used for the purpose of achieving political goals, and its effectiveness must be evaluated on that basis. The standard for judging military success is not whether a target is taken or destroyed, but whether the declared political goals are achieved.

---

[33] Tim Arango, "U.S. Troops, Back in Iraq, Train a Force to Fight ISIS," *New York Times*, December 31, 2014.

[34] Smith, *The Utility of Force*, 4.

[35] Carl von Clausewitz, *On War*, in *The Book of War: Sun-Tzu, The Art of Warfare, Carl von Clausewitz, On War* (New York: The Modern Library, 2000), 271, 280.

By that criterion, uses of force often fall short. It is one thing to over-throw an autocratic regime, but quite another to create stable democracy in its place. Armed regime change in Iraq and Libya was considered a military success, but the resulting chaos and violence in each country turned these actions into costly political and human failures.

When judged by the ability to achieve political goals, most uses of military force are ineffective. In his study, *Between Threats and War*, Micah Zenko examines 36 cases of 'discrete military operations' by US armed forces from 1991 into 2009. These are military actions short of full-scale intervention that cause casualties and destruction, consisting of a single strike or series of attacks, lasting just a few minutes or many days. They are intended to compel other states or armed groups to comply with US policy demands. These frequent uses of force have a very low rate of pol-itical success. In Zenko's words, they have been *"tactically successful at meeting most military objectives, but strategically ineffective in achiev-ing specific political goals"* [emphasis in original]. The missions achieved their military objectives half the time, but they fulfilled all their political objectives less than 6 percent of the time.[36]

A more limited form of military involvement is the arming and training of government or rebel forces. The United States has used this approach in Syria to support 'moderate' rebels fighting against the Assad regime, and in Iraq to build armed resistance to ISIS. This form of military inter-vention also has limited impact. A classified CIA report commissioned by the Obama administration found that covert military assistance missions seldom succeed. Past attempts to arm foreign forces have had minimal impact on the long-term outcome of the affected conflicts.[37] One of the few success stories identified in the CIA report was US support for the Mujahideen rebels who battled Soviet forces in Afghanistan in the 1980s. The irony is that some of those fighters later morphed into al-Qaida and the Taliban and became bitter enemies of the United States and the Kabul government.

The United States, Russia and other countries often use military force to counter terrorism, but the record shows that military means are rarely effective in ending terrorist groups. An empirical study by the RAND Corporation published in 2008 shows that terrorist groups end most

---

[36] Micah Zenko, *Between Threats and War: Discrete Military Operations in the Post-Cold War World* (Stanford University Press, 2010), 3, 115.

[37] Mark Mazzetti, "C.I.A. Study of Covert Aid Fueled Skepticism About Helping Syrian Rebels," *New York Times*, October 14, 2014, at www.nytimes.com/2014/10/15/us/politics/cia-study-says-arming-rebels-seldom-works.html?_r=0.

often through political processes and effective law enforcement, and not by the use of military force. An examination of 268 terrorist organizations that ended during a period of nearly 40 years found that the primary factors accounting for the demise of these groups were participation in political processes (43 percent) and effective policing (40 percent). Military force accounted for the end of terrorist groups in only 7 percent of the cases examined.[38]

Many of the reasons that are offered for using military force – countering terrorism, preventing atrocities, promoting democracy – are worthy purposes, but military approaches are often not the most effective means of achieving them. The required tasks are mostly civilian in nature. They evolve through long processes of social, political and economic development, as people establish institutions and struggle for their rights. Security forces can provide protection when needed, but the work of building peace is for civilians, especially those closest to the conflict.

In Afghanistan, the United States and its NATO allies deployed more than 150,000 of their own troops and created large-scale Afghan security forces that eventually numbered more than 350,000 military and police troops. Yet security in much of the country remained precarious, as underlying problems of corrupt and unaccountable governance continued to fuel support for insurgency. As a Defense Department report acknowledged, progress toward achieving security in Afghanistan was impeded by the "lack of sufficient progress in governance and sustainable economic development."[39]

Genuine security is a multifaceted phenomenon that involves not only protection from violence but the presence of conditions that minimize the risk of conflict, including effective governance and opportunities for development. According to the 2006 version of the *U.S. Army/U.S. Marine Corps Counterinsurgency Field Manual*, "the primary objective" of any mission "is to foster development of effective governance by a legitimate government."[40] US Defense Secretary Robert Gates stated in 2008 that military operations "should be subordinate to measures to promote participation in government, economic programs to spur development, and efforts to address the grievances that often lie at the heart of insurgencies and among the

---

[38] Seth G. Jones and Martin C. Libicki, *How Terrorist Groups End: Lessons for Countering al Qa'ida* (Santa Monica: RAND Corporation, 2008).

[39] U.S. Department of Defense, *Report on Progress Toward Security and Stability in Afghanistan*, December 2012, Report to Congress, 9, available at www.defense.gov/news/1230_Report_final.pdf.

[40] *The U.S. Army/U.S. Marine Corps Counterinsurgency Field Manual* (University of Chicago Press, 2007), 37.

discontented from which the terrorists recruit."[41] The prevention of armed conflict and violent extremism requires accountable and inclusive governance systems that meet social needs and facilitate economic development.

THE POWER OF NONVIOLENCE

One of the weaknesses of conventional security policy is the failure to recognize the contributions for peace that civil society can offer. Nonviolent citizen action and civilian peacebuilding practices can make a significant difference in helping communities in conflict move toward reconciliation. Through their support for development and diplomacy rather than war, and through active engagement in conflict transformation processes, peace advocates and peacebuilding practitioners can address the underlying policies and conditions that lead to violence. They can help communities facing repression and marginalization understand that disciplined civil resistance is often more effective than armed struggle in achieving political change and overcoming injustice.

Nonviolent methods have significant capacity for advancing the goals of democracy and human rights. Recent empirical research on the effectiveness of peaceful versus armed methods of resistance indicates that nonviolent means are much more effective than the use of force in achieving political change. In their landmark study *Why Civil Resistance Works*, Erica Chenoweth and Maria J. Stephan examine 323 historical examples of resistance campaigns that occurred over a span of more than 100 years to compare the relative effectiveness of nonviolent and violent methods. Each case involved an intensive political conflict, sometimes lasting several years, in which sociopolitical movements struggled to change regimes or gain major concessions from government adversaries. Overall, nonviolent campaigns were successful 53 percent of the time, compared to a 26 percent success rate when violence was the principal means of struggle.[42] Nonviolent methods were found to be as successful on average in repressive dictatorships as in democratic regimes. Updated research through 2015 shows lower success rates for both violent and nonviolent struggles but a continuing significant effectiveness advantage for nonviolent campaigns.[43]

---

[41] Robert M. Gates, Speech before the U.S. Global Leadership Campaign, Washington DC, July 15, 2008, www.defense.gov/speeches/speech.aspx?speechid=1262.

[42] Chenoweth and Stephan, *Why Civil Resistance Works*.

[43] Erica Chenoweth and Maria J. Stephan, "How the World is Proving Martin Luther King Jr. Right about Nonviolence," *Washington Post*, January 18, 2016, www.washingtonpost .com/news/monkey-cage/wp/2016/01/18/how-the-world-is-proving-mlk-right-about-nonviolence/?utm_term=.f7a9f7b3f811.

Nonviolent action is not only more effective than armed struggle in achieving political change, it is also more likely to expand opportunities for democracy and political freedom. This is the conclusion of an important 2005 study that examined 67 political transitions over the previous decades, many in previously closed or authoritarian governments. The study examined whether violent or nonviolent methods were used to achieve change and evaluated the regimes resulting from these transitions according to the standard Freedom House ratings of free, partly free or not free. The study found that nonviolent civic resistance was a driving factor in 50 of the 67 transitions. In those 50 cases nearly all the resulting regimes (92 percent) were more democratic.[44] Nonviolent movements were three times more likely than armed struggles to produce sustainable political freedom. Chenoweth and Stephan used a different methodology but reached similar conclusions. The use of civil resistance methods is much more likely to produce a democratic society than the use of armed struggle.[45]

These findings on the efficacy of nonviolent resistance challenge traditional realist assumptions about the primacy of military force and the nature of political power. They highlight the significance of political legitimacy and show that the withdrawal of social consent through mass civil disobedience can alter the relations of power. They validate the beliefs of Gandhi and confirm the case study evidence and strategic analysis of Gene Sharp.[46]

The most important factor in the success of nonviolent action, Chenoweth and Stephan find, is the "participation advantage" – the ability to mobilize mass participation in political struggle. "Large campaigns are much more likely to succeed than small campaigns," they argue. As membership increases, so does the probability of success. Mass participation "can erode a regime's main sources of power when the participants represent diverse sectors of society."[47]

Mass participation helps to explain why nonviolent movements are more likely to produce democratic outcomes. Nonviolent movements are by their very nature mass-based, participatory expressions of free will. In Poland, for example, the power of Solidarity flowed from the ten million

---

[44] The findings are presented in Adrian Karatnycky and Peter Ackerman, "How Freedom is Won: From Civil Resistance to Durable Democracy," *International Journal of Not-for-Profit Law* 7, no. 3 (2005).

[45] Chenoweth and Stephan, *Why Civil Resistance Works*, 201–219.

[46] Gene Sharp, *The Politics of Nonviolent Action* (Boston: Porter Sargent, 1973).

[47] Chenoweth and Stephan, *Why Civil Resistance Works*, 39, 30.

members it represented and the support it received from virtually every segment of society. The same was true of the United Democratic Front (UDF) in South Africa in the 1980s. With the participation of churches, trade unions, community organizations and the African National Congress, the UDF was able to mobilize millions and could rightly claim to speak for the majority population in challenging Apartheid.

Nonviolent campaigns are better able to withstand government repression. This is an important factor in explaining their success. In most of the cases studied, opposition campaigns faced violent repression from their government adversaries. When this occurs and the campaign refrains from retaliating in kind, the regime's use of violence is often counterproductive and gives a moral and political advantage to the challengers. The violent repression of unarmed protest often creates a backfire effect, generating a sympathetic reaction among third parties that increases support for the protesters while undermining the legitimacy of the regime. The result is a greater likelihood of loyalty shifts and defections among government officials and within the security forces. As social consent diminishes, political power begins to erode.

HUMAN SECURITY

In the above review, we have argued that a narrow focus on security as protection from armed attack is limited. The traditional national security approach is unable to address problems such as corruption, poor governance, exclusion and failures of development that give rise to violence and instability within countries.[48] What is needed is a broader conception of security that incorporates an understanding of the diverse array of threats people face and that broadens the frame of reference beyond protecting the state to assuring the well-being of communities and people. With the nature of governance changing from state-centric to multi-stakeholder approaches, new understandings of security have emerged to replace the traditional belief in the primacy of state-based military power. The human security framework incorporates human rights, democracy and development into a new paradigm. It is a reframing of security for an age in which the state is no longer the exclusive source of political authority, a world in which the problems of armed conflict are predominantly within rather than between states. It is a way of re-conceptualizing

---

[48] Eamon Aloyo, "Improving Global Accountability: The ICC and Nonviolent Crimes against Humanity," *Global Constitutionalism* 2 (2013): 498–530.

security strategies to meet new realities in a vastly more complex and interdependent world.

The origins of the human security concept can be traced to Franklin Delano Roosevelt's famous Four Freedoms address of 1941. That speech articulated the goals of the world struggle then underway against military aggression and tyranny and provided the foundation for the subsequent Atlantic Charter and many of the ideas that emerged in the UN Charter. Roosevelt defined the Four Freedoms as freedom of speech, freedom of religion, freedom from want and freedom from fear. The fourth, which he described as a worldwide reduction of armaments to the point where no nation could threaten aggression against another, is the closest to the traditional notion of security. It is directly linked to freedom from want, which connotes social and economic development, and the freedoms of speech and worship, which embody civil and human rights.

The idea of human security was popularized by Mahbub ul Haq, special advisor to the UN Development Programme, and was proposed initially in the *Human Development Report 1994*.[49] The report identified economic deprivations, inadequate health and nutrition, and the lack of personal and political freedom as fundamental sources of insecurity. These concepts were developed further in the 2003 report of the Commission on Human Security. The Commission's co-chair, Amartya Sen, described human security as "freedom from basic insecurities."[50] It is a framework for attempting to overcome the insecurities that threaten human survival or the safety and dignity of daily life. In this citizen-centered approach peace is defined as the protection of civilians and the empowerment of people to develop their potential and participate in public decision making. According to the report, "Human security complements state security, furthers human development and enhances human rights."[51] This approach is fully compatible, we believe, with our emphasis on the conditions of governance that are most likely to reduce the risk of war and promote peace.

As a broad concept encompassing diverse understandings of the requirements for peace, human security has been subject to differing interpretations.

[49] United Nations Development Programme, *Human Security Report 1994* (New York: Oxford University Press, 1994).

[50] Commission on Human Rights, *Human Security Now: Protecting and Empowering People* (New York: Commission on Human Security, 2003), 8–9.

[51] Commission on Human Security, Outline of the Report of the Commission on Human Security, 2003, available at www.unocha.org/humansecurity/chs/finalreport/Outlines/outline.html.

One perspective, emphasized by the government of Canada, focuses on responding to threats of political violence and incorporates the principle of the Responsibility to Protect (R2P). This approach acknowledges that the use of military force may be necessary at times to protect people who are threatened by mass atrocities. It obligates international actors to act in order to prevent or end extreme violence. The other interpretation emphasizes the interrelated social, economic and political conditions that give rise to armed violence and focuses on the importance of development as a security strategy. Security is viewed in one approach as protection from physical violence, in the other as protection from economic and social deprivation. The two approaches are sometimes hotly debated for their differences, but they are closely interrelated and are compatible with the holistic vision articulated in the Four Freedoms.[52]

The concept of human security is not without its critics. Roland Paris argues that the term lacks precise definition and is too vague and muddled to provide guidance to international policy makers and scholars.[53] The concept is "normatively attractive but analytically weak," writes Edward Newman.[54] By encompassing so many dimensions of human insecurity it attempts to address everything and in the process becomes meaningless. Andrew Mack agrees that "a concept that aspires to explain almost everything in reality explains nothing," although he emphasizes the importance of the term as "a signifier of shared political and moral values."[55] To be concerned about human security is to be concerned about threats to peace from human rights abuse and economic deprivation as well as from military attack. The importance of human security lies less in its explanatory power than in its role as a broad category of research and policy making that encompasses non-military threats to people and communities, in contrast to traditional security approaches that focus narrowly on threats to the state.[56]

Attempting to define and operationalize such a broad concept is challenging. Strategists in the United States and other countries are beginning to recognize the need for comprehensive approaches to security, as reflected in Gates' 2008 address, but many political leaders remain mired

---

[52] Kaldor, *Human Security*, 183.
[53] Roland Paris, "Human Security: Paradigm Shift or Hot Air," *International Security* 26, no. 2 (2001): 88–89.
[54] Edward Newman, "Critical Human Security Studies," *Review of International Studies* 36, no. 1 (2010): 82.
[55] Andrew Mack, "A Signifier of Shared Values," *Security Dialogue* 35, no. 3 (2004): 367.
[56] Paris, "Human Security," 96.

in outdated thinking. The impetus for developing and specifying the meaning of human security has come from civilian peacebuilding experts, especially those who study civil society. Kaldor has written widely on these subjects and has identified six core principles for human security operations:[57]

1. The primacy of human rights, with the focus on civilian protection rather than defeating enemies.
2. Legitimate political authority, which emphasizes the importance of enabling local communities to establish effective local governance.
3. A bottom-up approach, which requires an inclusive approach in which affected populations have an active role.
4. Effective multilateralism, within the framework of international law and ideally under UN mandate.
5. Regional focus, recognizing that the roots and consequences of conflict cross borders and must be addressed comprehensively.
6. Civilian supremacy over security forces and rules of engagement that are more suitable to police work than armed combat.

These principles provide guidelines for interventions that can enhance the security of people and communities and build a long-term foundation for peace. They overlap significantly with the standards of good governance we examine in this volume. They reflect the need for multifaceted approaches that address the myriad sources of insecurity and the social, economic and political conditions that are necessary for sustainable peace.[58]

Kaldor has provided research and policy guidance to the European Union in operationalizing these principles. Her proposals envision a new type of intervention force that includes not only soldiers but also civilian police officers, human rights monitors, humanitarian aid workers and specialists in civilian peacebuilding and development. These ideas are beginning to be applied in European missions in Mali, South Sudan and other conflict zones, although the coordination of civilian, police and military operations has proved difficult and the results to date have been disappointing. Much more work is needed to develop practical and effective strategies for applying this new concept.

A number of analysts are focusing on the role of civil society in implementing human security principles. Lisa Schirch emphasizes the

---

[57] Shannon D. Beebe and Mary Kaldor, *The Ultimate Weapon is No Weapon: Human Security and the New Rules of War and Peace* (New York: Public Affairs, 2010), 8–9.
[58] Kaldor, *Human Security*.

contributions civil society can make in conducting conflict assessments and accurately identifying the underlying issues that are driving armed conflict.[59] Along with Thania Paffenholz, Erin McCandless and others, Schirch shows how civil society groups can hold security forces accountable to human rights standards and participate in peacemaking and conflict prevention efforts.[60] Schirch has engaged directly with security forces in the United States and other countries and has developed a training and educational curriculum on civil-military interactions within a human security framework.[61] Local peacebuilding groups in the southern Philippines, Central America, West Africa and beyond are engaged in similar efforts to operationalize the concept of human security, working alongside security forces to re-orient military missions toward civilian protection and conflict prevention.

CONCLUSION

Security is the necessary condition for the various dimensions of governance to function effectively. It safeguards opportunities for commerce and investment and allows economic development to flourish. It enables governments to deliver the social services and political goods that are necessary for human development. It is the prerequisite for the 'good things' of governance to exert their influence for peace.

Security is also intimately linked to democracy, which at its core is a means of ensuring public accountability over the use of force. Authoritarian states can maintain security and stability for the nation state, but such regimes lack accountability and are by definition more repressive, especially toward marginalized communities. Repressive security approaches increase tensions between state and society and exacerbate the grievances that lead to armed conflict. Security systems are most conducive to peace when they are inclusive and accountable to all segments of society – when they protect opportunity and freedom for all rather than deny it to some.

---

[59] Lisa Schirch, *Conflict Assessment and Peacebuilding Planning: Toward a Participatory Approach to Human Security* (Boulder: Lynne Rienner, 2013).

[60] Thania Paffenholz, *Civil Society and Peacebuilding: A Critical Assessment* (Boulder: Lynne Rienner, 2010); Erin McCandless, "Wicked Problems in Peacebuilding and Statebuilding: Making Progress in Measuring Progress Through the New Deal," *Global Governance* 19, no. 2 (April–June 2013): 227–248.

[61] Lisa Schirch, ed., *Handbook on Human Security: A Civil-Military-Police Curriculum* (The Hague: Alliance for Peacebuilding, GPPAC, Kroc Institute, March 2016).

Military and police protection is essential but it must be politically subordinate to civilian authority and balanced against other social priorities. The temptations of militarism are powerful and can prompt political leaders to divert resources to unnecessary and excessive operations. Good governance requires maintaining effective security forces, but it also depends upon providing social programs that enhance human development. Social capacity is necessary for human security and helps to create conditions conducive to peace. As we address in the next chapter, the evidence of a link between social capacity and peace is substantial. Effective programs for education, health care and social welfare are strongly associated with peace and a reduced risk of armed conflict. We turn to these findings now.

3

Social Capacity

As we have examined, state capacity is a key dimension of governance in helping to reduce the risk of armed conflict. In the last chapter we focused on security capacity, the ability of states to protect their citizens and prevent aggression and armed rebellion. While security against violent threats is essential, it is only one element of governance capacity. Our definition of governance as presented in Chapter 1 emphasizes the delivery of public goods, following Rotberg's model. This includes not only security capacity but the delivery of vital social and economic development services, providing necessary civilian public goods. The research we explore below shows that this social component of governance is a key predictor of peace.

We examine how the provision of social welfare services, particularly access to education and health care, can encourage peace and stability within a state. We focus on the role of education and review the evidence showing the various pathways through which literacy and learning advance the prospects for peace. We explore how inclusive and equitable access to education and other social services reduces incentives for armed rebellion. Research shows that public goods provision helps to build closer linkages between the state and society while establishing government legitimacy and public trust. We close the chapter with a discussion of possible pathways through which education reduces conflict risk, including Steven Pinker's concept of education as an 'escalator of reason' and evidence linking intelligence and cognitive ability with greater preferences for peace.

"CAN STATES BUY PEACE?"

This was the titular question in an award-winning article showing that governments can increase the prospects for peace if they provide education, health care and other vital social services for their people. Challenging conventional assumptions on the primacy of security capacity for preventing war, Zeynep Taydas and Dursun Peksen argue that by focusing on social programs, states can augment human capital and enhance the capacities local communities need to avoid civil unrest and violent conflict. Their analysis shows that as proportional spending for public welfare increases, the risk of armed conflict declines. They define welfare spending as expenditures for education, health care and social security insurance, including public pensions and unemployment benefits. High levels of spending on these programs are directly related to lower rates of armed conflict within a state. The results offer "convincing empirical support for the argument that the state might buy peace and discourage the use of violent methods via strong social welfare provision."[1] The implications of this finding are significant for broadening how we understand the meaning of good governance.

Political stability and resiliency depend upon social legitimacy and trust. These are enhanced by a state's ability to provide public services and establish and maintain social safety nets. This form of governance capacity strengthens the bonds between state and society. It makes political instability and armed rebellion less likely and alleviates conditions of deprivation that can drive people to violent extremism. Social welfare programs contribute to peace "by improving the living standards of citizens and raising the opportunity cost of insurgency."[2] When governments provide welfare services that directly benefit large numbers of people, they are better able to gain the consent and loyalty of their citizens. The relationship between state and society is solidified, and the incentives for political resistance and armed rebellion diminish.

Spending on social welfare may have a more positive impact on peace than other forms of government spending. Taydas and Peksen test for government spending as a whole and for expenditures on the military. They find that the former has a slightly greater effect in reducing the risk of armed conflict. The authors state, "This finding offers indirect support for our argument that only certain types of public spending (i.e.

---

[1] Taydas and Peksen, "Can States Buy Peace?" 280.
[2] Ibid., 274.

welfare spending) might undermine civil wars." Further study is needed to corroborate this assertion, but the core finding of their study remains valid. Governments that allocate a larger share of their budgets to social welfare policies tend to have greater citizen support and face a lower risk of rebellion.[3] Regarding the impacts of military spending, they note that excessive military spending can divert resources from meeting social needs and in some instances may have a detrimental impact on economic growth.

One reason that social capacity plays an influential role in ensuring peace is that it "can decrease the vulnerability of marginalized citizens." The redistribution of public revenues for the benefit of society strengthens ties between citizens and the state and broadens the political base of the regime. It is a form of government accountability to its citizens. Welfare spending is an indication of the state's interest in the public's well-being. This shapes citizen perceptions in ways that discourage the use of violence to achieve political goals.[4]

Other studies confirm the importance of social welfare provision in minimizing armed conflict and internal unrest. Clayton Thyne uses levels of public investment in health services to measure the quality and effectiveness of governance. He examines World Bank data on child immunization as an indicator of public support for health care and finds a direct relationship with reduced conflict risk.[5] Countries with the highest rates of child immunization have the lowest likelihood of civil war onset. This study shows that states providing basic health care services have a lower risk of internal armed conflict. The Legatum Institute's Prosperity Index corroborates this finding. High national levels of education and health are positively associated with greater prospects for peace.[6]

Government spending for physical infrastructure also may have some beneficial impacts for peace. Roads, ports, reliable electricity, telecommunications and wireless access are essential requirements for economic growth and trade. They contribute to economic development and in that respect enhance the long-term prospects for peace. Little research is available on the direct links between infrastructure spending and peace, but some data suggests a positive connection. The World Economic Forum's index of global competitiveness shows a slight positive correlation

[3] Ibid., 283.
[4] Ibid., 276–277.
[5] Thyne, "ABC's, 123's, and the Golden Rule," 748–749.
[6] Institute for Economics and Peace, *Pillars of Peace*, 41–42.

between infrastructure spending and reduced conflict risk. The association is not strong, but infrastructure may play some supportive role in facilitating peace.[7] The ability to provide basic means of commerce and communication, including roads and bridges, is an indication of quality governance. It fosters economic development and meets the needs of society and increases government legitimacy.

The linkage between social welfare spending and peace raises concerns about the policies of fiscal austerity that governments sometimes adopt in response to financial crises such as the 2008 economic recession. Economists and policy makers debate the pros and cons of reduced government spending as fiscal policy, but they seldom consider the implications of lower social spending for the risk of armed conflict. If the ability to deliver public goods is associated with peace, a curtailment of that capacity could increase conflict risk. Such negative effects are unlikely in fully developed countries, where social safety nets remain strong and intact despite some cutbacks. However, in developing countries where social protections are already weak, the impact of reduced social welfare spending could be worrisome.

Violent conflict can result from the failure of governing authorities to provide public goods and social services on an equitable basis to all communities and ethnic groups within their jurisdiction. Traditionally in Africa and parts of Asia, tribal authorities and locally based institutions provide social services in their communities, albeit often in a rudimentary fashion. When states are formed these patterns are displaced, usually with a process of federation in which the different ethnic groups come together in the emerging state to create a system for the distribution of goods and services. The pattern of distribution within and among these ethnic groups is crucial to creating interethnic solidarity. Peace is more likely when state resources and services flow equitably to all major ethnic groups. Violence occurs when public goods are reserved for elites and particular ethnic groups to the exclusion of others. The cause of many civil wars, Jean-Paul Azam argues, is the failure of the state to distribute public goods and services equitably among major ethnic groups.[8] The equitable distribution of social spending is directly related to a reduced risk of war.

The capacity to provide public goods on an equitable basis is a distinguishing characteristic of good governance. A weak governance system is

---

[7] Ibid., 22.
[8] Jean-Paul Azam, "The Redistributive State and Conflicts in Africa," *Journal of Peace Research* 38, no. 4 (2001): 431.

unable or unwilling to commit credibly to the provision of social services and political goods. Such a system is likely to rely primarily on the threat of force and repression to maintain its hold on power. This increases the risk of armed conflict. By contrast, a strong governance system is one that can commit publicly to equitable and sufficient public expenditures for the provision of social services. In so doing it can gain the confidence and trust of all or most social communities and will have less need to rely on coercive means to maintain its hold on power.[9]

EDUCATION AND PEACE

The provision of public education is the most frequently mentioned and widely studied example of creating social capacity for peace. Many great thinkers have described education as the key to fostering a more tolerant and peaceful world. John Dewey championed universal schooling as the necessary foundation of democracy and peace. He viewed education as the cultivation of critical thinking and the pathway to greater understanding and cooperation.[10] Maria Montessori believed that education helps to build peace by stimulating the moral imagination and encouraging creative thinking.[11] Such ideas are reflected in the Universal Declaration of Human Rights, which states in Article 26 "Everyone has the right to education" and defines the purposes of education as follows:

Education shall be directed to the full development of the human personality and to the strengthening of respect for human rights and fundamental freedoms. It shall promote understanding, tolerance and friendship among all nations, racial or religious groups, and shall further the activities of the United Nations for the maintenance of peace.

The value of education for peace is confirmed in empirical research. Many studies show a direct correlation between higher levels of education and a lower risk of armed conflict within nations. Whether measured as years of schooling, levels of public spending on education or the degree of literacy and learning in a society, educational variables are strongly associated with a greater likelihood of peace. Education is an indispensable element of good governance.

---

[9] Ibid., 435.

[10] Charles F. Howlett, "A Dissenting Voice: John Dewey against Militarism in Education," *Peace and Change* 3, no. 4 (Spring 1976).

[11] Maria Montessori, *Education and Peace* (Oxford: Clio Press, 1992).

Education does not guarantee peaceful behavior of course. History has many examples of educated people perpetrating the most extreme forms of violence. Germany prior to World War II was highly cultured yet many of its people committed unspeakable atrocities. The 'best and the brightest' engineered America's war in Vietnam. Studies of contemporary terrorism show that insurgent leaders and suicide bombers are sometimes better educated than their peers.[12] In some schools, students are taught intolerance and extremist views rather than critical thinking and scientific knowledge. At times education is used as a system of indoctrination in which ideological groups inculcate narrow forms of thinking that dehumanize the other and make it easier to commit acts of violence. In sharply polarized settings schooling may contribute more to the construction of enemy images than to the building of peace.[13]

Madrasas in the Islamic world are sometimes considered breeding grounds of terrorism. Ebrahim Moosa challenges this misperception and shows in his study of madrasas in South Asia that schools for studying the Qur'an and Islamic religious teaching have a long and respectable tradition in Muslim society. Madrasas often play an important role in meeting the educational, religious and cultural needs of working-class and lower-income communities. As Moosa observes, however, the curriculum in many of these schools is narrowly focused on matters of piety and faith, with little or no attention to the knowledge and skills that are necessary for navigating the economic and political challenges of the modern world.[14] Often missing in madrasas are courses in science and technology that can advance development or classes in cross-cultural understanding that foster tolerance and peacemaking.

Education is not a panacea. The content and social context of education matter greatly in advancing social and economy development. The beneficial effects of education for peace work are greatest when

[12] Alan B. Krueger and Jitka Maleckova, "Education, Poverty and Terrorism: Is There a Causal Connection?," *Journal of Economic Perspectives* 17, no. 4 (2003): 131–132.

[13] In Israel, for example, education for Jewish identity and Zionist values has often taken precedence over socializing youth in liberal democratic values. Palestinian textbooks have been criticized for promoting hatred and violence toward Israel. See Esra Çuhadar and Sari Hanafi, "Israel and Palestine: Civil Societies in Despair," in *Civil Society and Peacebuilding: A Critical Assessment*, edited by Thania Paffenholz (Boulder: Lynne Rienner, 2010), 223; and Aaron D. Pina, *Palestinian Education and the Debate over Textbooks*, Congressional Research Service, CRS Report for Congress, May 3, 2005, available at www.fas.org/sgp/crs/mideast/RL32886.pdf.

[14] Ebrahim Moosa, *What is a Madrasa?* (Chapel Hill: University of North Carolina Press, 2015), 11, 140, 184.

combined with other dimensions of good governance such as democracy, gender equality, economic development and political freedom. Education nonetheless has significant independent effects in helping to reduce the risk of conflict.

THE EFFECTS OF SCHOOLING

The most direct way governments can encourage education is by supporting primary and secondary education for all citizens. Empirical studies show that high levels of education are consistently correlated with reduced rates of armed conflict. A 2011 report by the Peace Research Institute of Oslo (PRIO) reviews 30 empirical studies and finds "an emerging consensus in the literature ... that education has a general pacifying effect on conflict." There is "broad empirical evidence of a ... negative relationship between the level of education and conflict," the report concludes.[15] High rates of secondary school enrollment are particularly important in this regard. Jeffrey Dixon's survey of the core social science indicators of peace finds similar results. Almost all existing studies show that high levels of primary and secondary school enrollment are associated with a reduced risk of armed conflict.[16] Raising the level of education in a society increases the prospects for peace.

Improvement in almost any measure of education – spending levels, school enrollment, literacy rates – correlates strongly with greater peace. Thyne correlates government social capacity and the risk of armed conflict by measuring a state's ability to provide educational services. Even when controlling for other major correlates of conflict such as democracy, income per capita and prior war, he finds that higher levels of public education are an independent predictor of peace.[17] Countries above the average level of education have significantly less risk of experiencing armed conflict.

Moses Shayo finds evidence of a link between low education and the risk of armed conflict by testing the hypothesis that poorly educated communities tend to be overly confident in the effectiveness of the military and are more like to support the use of force to resolve differences.[18] This is an important question to test since other scholars have identified it as

---

[15] Østby and Urdal, "Education and Civil Conflict," 2, 12.
[16] Dixon, "What Causes Civil Wars?" 716.
[17] Thyne, "ABC's, 123's, and the Golden Rule," 743.
[18] Moses Shayo, "Education, Militarism and Civil Wars," Hebrew University of Jerusalem, July 2008, 6, 18–22, http://pluto.huji.ac.il/~mshayo/Education_and_Militarism.pdf.

a factor that can lead to war. Seymour Martin Lipset argued that low education, social isolation and economic insecurity are associated with the tendency to seek simplistic solutions and support the use of force to solve complex problems.[19] Geoffrey Blainey wrote in *The Causes of War* that most wars result from overconfidence in one's military strength and misperceptions of the weakness of the adversary.[20] Shayo interrogates the Lipset hypothesis by examining data from 38 national surveys in 32 countries that measure popular confidence in the military and then comparing these results with educational levels. He finds a significant relationship between low education levels and higher confidence in the effectiveness of the use of force.

Of course statistical correlations do not prove causation. Deeper analysis is required to see if causal patterns exist. The *Human Security Report 2012* tests whether the demonstrated linkage between low levels of education and armed conflict is due to the effects of the former or is a matter of reverse causality. It is well known that the social dislocation and physical destruction of war can slow the rise of educational attainment in developing countries. The results of the *Human Security Report* examination show that, even when controlling for the effects of war, low levels of education are directly associated with a higher risk of conflict onset. The principal cause of the educational gap observed in conflict-affected countries is the low level of educational attainment that existed prior to war.[21] The report traces poor educational achievement to weak structures of governance and deep levels of poverty.[22] These conditions of state fragility are strongly associated with an increased risk of war.

THE VALUE OF KNOWLEDGE

Opinions vary on how education exerts its pacifying influence. Some scholars argue that education has the effect of encouraging political participation and channeling conflicts through institutional pathways rather than the use of violence.[23] Lipset believed that education

---

[19] Seymour Martin Lipset, "Some Social Requisites of Democracy: Economic Development and Political Legitimacy," *American Political Science Review* 53, no. 1 (1959): 69–106.

[20] Geoffrey Blainey, *The Causes of War*, 3rd edition (London: Macmillan Press, 1988), 292–294.

[21] Human Security Project, *Human Security Report 2012* (London: Oxford University Press, 2012), 103.

[22] Ibid., 105.

[23] Østby and Urdal, "Education and Civil Conflict," 4.

broadens people's outlook and enables them to understand the value of tolerance.[24] Others emphasize the influence of reason in generating empathy, or the role of science in reducing the prejudices and misperceptions that lead to war.

One of the ways education helps to build peace is through its economic impact. A number of studies emphasize the importance of investing in human capital and the role of educational training in expanding employment and income opportunities. Collier and his colleagues argue that education raises the relative value of labor and creates greater economic opportunity for young people. This lowers the perceived economic benefit of joining armed groups. Secondary school enrollment is particularly important in creating this valuation effect since it involves the age group from which most rebels are recruited. A statistically significant relationship exists between secondary school enrollment and reduced conflict risk.[25] By contrast, young people with low education have fewer economic opportunities, which increases the attraction of joining an armed rebellion as a source of employment.[26] The leaders of insurgent and terrorist groups may have higher levels of education than their peers, but the foot soldiers who join such groups often do so for the pay and have few other options.

Providing adequate secondary education can be an effective way for states to avoid the potential dangers of the so-called "youth bulge." This is the phenomenon of a population age distribution with a disproportionally large percentage of children and young adults. This pattern is common in developing countries in which development advances have reduced the infant mortality rate but birth rates remain high. As we note in Chapter 5, large youth bulges and high fertility rates are associated with increased risk of armed conflict.

Many factors may account for this problem, but low educational levels seem to be one of the most significant. Research shows a robust connection between low education and the heightened risk of conflict in countries with a youth bulge. Policies designed to increase overall educational levels help to limit the pool of potential armed recruits and thus reduce the likelihood of violent conflict.[27] This analysis lends support

[24] Lipset, "Some Social Requisites of Democracy," 69–106.
[25] Paul Collier and Anke Hoeffler, "Greed and Grievance in Civil War," *Oxford Economic Papers* 56, no. 4 (2004): 581, 588.
[26] Østby and Urdal, "Education and Civil Conflict," 10.
[27] Bilal Barakat and Henrik Urdal, "Breaking the Waves? Does Education Mediate the Relationship Between Youth Bulges and Political Violence?" Policy Research Working

to Collier's thesis that economic development increases the opportunity costs of armed rebellion and makes it less beneficial and thus less likely. Better educated youth have more social and economic options and fewer incentives to participate in armed conflict.

Research confirms that a lack of education and the absence of opportunities to earn an income are important reasons why young people, mostly men, join rebel groups.[28] Interviews with more than 50 former fighters in Afghanistan, Sri Lanka, Pakistan, Northern Ireland and several African countries confirm the negative influence of unemployment and a lack of education. Many of the insurgents and militia fighters interviewed were motivated to join armed groups because of a lack of employment and the absence of meaningful education. "The fact of not being physically present in school greatly increases a young person's vulnerability to recruitment," the study concludes.[29] "The young person who is in an educational setting and making satisfactory progress, with the prospect of being able to make a living afterwards, or has already left school and is economically self-sufficient, will require strong incentives to leave to join the armed forces or an armed group."[30]

Education also promotes peace through its broader social effects in facilitating economic development. Economists agree that secondary education and higher levels of learning contribute positively to economic growth.[31] UNESCO's *Education for All* report of 2009 directly links education to development: "When education is broad-based and widely shared by the poor, it can help create economic growth that is also broad-based, with large benefits for poverty reduction."[32] The knowledge and skills acquired through quality education can enhance the productivity of labor and promote economic growth.

Education can help developing nations break out of poverty. Amartya Sen identifies education as an essential dimension of development. The economic successes of South Korea, China and other Asian countries are partly attributable to government decisions to improve social

Paper 5114, World Bank Africa Region Post Conflict and Social Development Unit (November 2009), 4, 15, 24–25.

[28] Østby and Urdal, "Education and Civil Conflict," 12.

[29] Rachel Brett and Irma Specht, *Young Soldiers: Why They Choose to Fight* (Boulder: Lynne Rienner, 2004), 22–23, 44.

[30] Ibid., 80–81.

[31] Robert J. Barro and Xavier Sala-i-Martin, *Economic Growth*, 2nd edition (New York: McGraw-Hill, 2004).

[32] UNESCO, *EFA Global Monitoring Report 2009, Overcoming Inequality: Why Governance Matters* (Oxford University Press, 2008), 9.

opportunity and increase access to basic education, he argues. China was able to achieve rapid economic growth after 1979 not only because of market reforms but because government policies produced high rates of education and literacy. India also made economic advances after turning to marketization in 1991, but its rate of growth has been slower. Sen attributes this difference in part to higher rates of illiteracy.[33] To this day China has much higher levels of education and literacy than India, especially among women. This helps to explain China's comparative economic advantages over India.[34]

The relationship between education and economic development has existed for a long time but has become progressively more important in today's information-based economy. Advances in the processing and packaging of information are increasingly the key to competitiveness and long-term economic development prospects. In a globalized economy where literacy and numeracy are requirements, learning has become indispensable.[35] Knowledge is more than ever the basis of power and wealth. Education and literacy are the basis for economic and social success, and are an important foundation for building more peaceful societies.

It is not just the quantity of education but the quality of learning that determines economic growth prospects. Studies on the impacts of human capital show that indicators of basic math and scientific knowledge are much stronger predictors of economic growth than the number of years of completed schooling.[36] A study in the *American Economic Review* concludes that "Labor force quality has a consistent, stable, and strong relationship with economic growth."[37] The scientific and mathematical skills acquired in quality educational programs enhance the productivity of labor and increase economic growth potential. Studies in countries participating in the International Adult Literacy Survey (IALS) show that higher levels of literacy have a larger effect on earning potential than additional years of schooling.[38] To the extent that these abilities advance the potential for economic development they also increase the prospects for peace.

[33] Sen, *Development as Freedom*, 40–41.
[34] Amartya Sen, "Why India Trails China," *New York Times*, June 20, 2013, A25.
[35] UNESCO, *EFA Global Monitoring Report 2009*, 32.
[36] Eric A. Hanushek and Dennis D. Kimko, "Schooling, Labor-Force Quality, and the Growth of Nations," *American Economic Review* 90, no. 5 (2000): 1184.
[37] Ibid., 1203.
[38] UNESCO, *EFA Global Monitoring Report 2009*, 30.

INCLUSIVE EDUCATION

Equity and inclusive opportunity are crucial to the pacifying influence of education. The beneficial impacts of learning depend upon education being available to all sectors of society, including the poor and marginalized. Discrimination in educational opportunity is likely to exacerbate the risk of armed violence. Several studies show that systematic differences in access to education among ethnic, religious and regional groups are associated with a greater likelihood of armed conflict. Disparities in educational access among social groups are a significant factor in generating the grievances and economic disadvantages that spark armed conflict.[39]

Studies of civil conflict in sub-Saharan Africa show a strong relationship between unequal access to education and a higher likelihood of armed violence.[40] The interviews with former combatants cited above also found that ethnically based school segregation was a factor that generated grievances and exacerbated social tensions.[41] Some research suggests that educational inequalities may be more conflict-provoking than economic disparities.[42] Different forms of inequality often go together and are mutually reinforcing, but it is possible through regression analysis to isolate the effects of educational inequality while controlling for other factors.[43] Studies applying these methods confirm the conflict-inducing effect of educational discrimination based on ethnic, religious or linguistic differences. The risk of violence increases when significant ethnic, linguistic, religious or regional groups are excluded from opportunities available to similarly situated groups.[44] This is a form of horizontal inequality, which we identify in Chapters 4 and 8 as an important driver of armed conflict.

Limited access to education often stems from state weakness and is related to inadequate governance capacity. Educational inequality also results from deliberate government policies that favor particular social groups over others. Ethnically based regimes often steer available resources toward their own community, while marginalizing others. The Apartheid governments of South Africa spent 14 times more per pupil

---

[39] Østby and Urdal, "Education and Civil Conflict," 15.
[40] Marie L. Besancon, "Relative Resources: Inequality in Ethnic Wars, Revolutions and Genocides," *Journal of Peace Research* 42, no. 4 (2005): 405.
[41] Brett and Specht, *Young Soldiers*, 126.
[42] Cited in Østby and Urdal, "Education and Civil Conflict," 16.
[43] Wilkinson and Pickett, *The Spirit Level*.
[44] Østby and Urdal, "Education and Civil Conflict," 5.

on the education of white students than native Africans.[45] In Northern Ireland, Sri Lanka and other conflict settings, demands for more equitable access to education (and employment) have been principal factors driving social mobilization and armed revolt. In Nepal districts with extreme inequalities in access to education have the highest levels of conflict intensity.[46] In these and other settings educational discrimination combines with other forms of social inequality to increase the risk of conflict.

AN ESCALATOR OF REASON?

Over the centuries educational attainment and scientific advancement have greatly enlarged human knowledge and understanding, with multiple implications for life and society. The spread of literacy and learning that accelerated with the Enlightenment now extends to populations in nearly every corner of the world. The global explosion of communications and the creation of the World Wide Web make vast stores of learning available to anyone with a computer or smart phone, creating possibilities for immediate access to information and images from every part of the world. The spread of education and literacy have profoundly altered human consciousness and social relations. According to Pinker they are broadening human sensibilities and have contributed to what he calls the 'humanitarian revolution.'

Education helps to inculcate traits of rationality and empathy toward others, Pinker contends, contributing to the declining legitimacy of armed violence. Over the course of the twentieth century, children and now even adults have come to spend a substantial portion of their lives in school. In the process they gain greater knowledge and acquire technical and cognitive skills that incline them toward greater engagement with the world and preferences for cooperation. The growth of education has raised average levels of intelligence in many societies. Pinker argues that this 'escalator of reason' carries humans "away from impulses that lead toward violence" and creates expanding circles of empathy and sensitivity toward others.[47] Thyne agrees that the

[45] Frances Stewart, "Horizontal Inequalities and Conflict: An Introduction and some Hypotheses," in *Horizontal Inequalities and Conflict: Understanding Group Violence in Multiethnic Societies*, edited by Frances Stewart (New York: Palgrave Macmillan, 2008), 16.

[46] S. Mansoob Mershed and Scott Gates, "Spatial-horizontal Inequality and the Maoist Insurgency in Nepal," *Review of Development Economics* 9, no. 1 (2005): 125–126, 132.

[47] Pinker, *The Better Angels of Our Nature*, 656.

pacifying effects of schooling result in part from the greater empathy and understanding for others that advanced learning and literacy make possible.[48]

Not all scholars are convinced of Pinker's sweeping generalizations about the evolution of culture and society. Some of the claims are not provable scientifically, although parts of his argument about the role of reason have empirical grounding. Studies of intelligence as measured in IQ tests indicate that persons with sophisticated reasoning abilities tend to be "more cooperative, have larger moral circles, and are less sympathetic to violence." This form of cognitive ability is characterized by logic, clarity, objectivity and proportionality. In game theory tests of the Prisoner's Dilemma, Pinker reports, persons who score highest in measures of these traits are more likely to respond affirmatively rather than negatively to an initial act of cooperation.[49]

Studies of public opinion in the United States show that people with higher levels of education are less supportive of the use of military force. Polls show a relationship between years of completed schooling and opposition to specific war policies. In his study of public opinion from Vietnam to Iraq, Vallon Burris observes a consistent pattern of less support for military action among respondents with higher education. In the wake of Vietnam, he reports, highly educated persons were more likely to change their views toward "greater distrust of government or wariness of military intervention." People with high levels of education were less likely than other Americans to favor the invasion of Iraq or subsequently judge it as the "right thing."[50] The evidence suggests that more highly educated segments of society generally have a more skeptical and critical view of large-scale military interventions.

High levels of education and literacy are significantly linked with prosperity, democracy and the rule of law, conditions that are strongly associated with a lower risk of armed conflict.[51] A study of cognitive ability as measured by educational attainment and scores on national tests of academic achievement and intelligence shows a significant correlation with conditions of good governance. High scores for cognitive ability among school children are strongly associated with levels of democracy, rule of

---

[48] Thyne, "ABC's, 123's, and the Golden Rule," 733.

[49] Pinker, *The Better Angels of Our Nature*, 660–661.

[50] Val Burris, "From Vietnam to Iraq: Continuity and Change in Between-Group Differences in Support for Military Action," *Social Problems* 55, no. 4 (2008): 467, 469.

[51] Cited in Pinker, *The Better Angels of Our Nature*, 664–665.

law and political freedom – conditions that are strongly associated with tolerance and peace.[52]

Measures of intelligence turn out to be more significant statistically than years of schooling in predicting the likelihood of democracy and rule of law. This confirms findings from other studies. The positive social impacts of education result more from the quality of learning than the number of years spent in a classroom. Measures of educational output such as literacy and basic mathematical ability are the strongest indicators of economic and social success, and therefore of peace. This fits with Pinker's emphasis on the role of reason and his argument that "an education-fueled rise in reasoning ability" paves the way for democracy, which leads to less violence and war.[53] This is just as Dewey and Montessori would have expected.

CONCLUSION

Public education is the clearest and most thoroughly documented example of how social governance capacity advances more peaceful and prosperous societies. A very large body of research confirms these positive impacts. The advanced cognitive skills and in-depth knowledge that are acquired through quality education have social and economic benefits for individuals and society that make war less likely. They also have deeper impacts that increase understanding and empathy for others and reduce the inclination to support armed violence.

Education is the quintessential public good and a necessary ingredient of effective governance. It is also a core dimension of state capacity, the ability to deliver basic services and meet public needs. States must be able to provide services such as education, health care and public welfare to ensure social well-being and stability. As Fukuyama observes, political order is not just about the control or use of state coercive power. It is also about delivering the public goods citizens expect, such as education and public health services, the protection of property rights, and the maintenance of public infrastructure.[54] Governments that provide these services have stronger bonds with society and enjoy greater legitimacy and public

---

[52] Heiner Rindermann, "Relevance of Education and Intelligence for the Political Development of Nations: Democracy, Rule of Law and Political Liberty," *Intelligence* 36, no. 4 (2008): 316–317.

[53] Pinker, *The Better Angels of Our Nature*, 665.

[54] Fukuyama, *Political Order and Political Decay*, 54.

trust. They are more stable and resilient and less prone to violence. Social capacity is an indispensable component of governance, helping to define what it means to have a strong and impartial state. For purposes of fostering peace, it may be as or more important than providing security.

The significance of state social capacity is seldom recognized in international policy making. State-building missions usually focus on strengthening the security capacity of local governments, with less attention to enhancing social capacity. In Mali, South Sudan, Somalia and other international interventions little effort is made to enhance the capacity of local authorities to deliver essential social services. Demands for austerity and privatization conditions attached to aid and loan programs can worsen the situation by reducing the funding of public education and health programs. Although many political leaders acknowledge the necessity of establishing legitimate governance as a counterweight to violent extremism, the allocation of resources to these purposes in international missions often takes a back seat to security assistance programs. In Afghanistan, Iraq and other countries, tens of billions of dollars have been spent to train and equip local security forces, while programs to help local communities train teachers, create health clinics and generate sustainable employment have received far fewer resources. Until these priorities are reversed and the building of social capacity receives greater attention, the struggle against insurgency and violent extremist groups will falter.

PART II

QUALITIES

4

Inclusion and Social Equity

The core argument of this volume is that governance systems support peace when they have the capacity to ensure security and provide a wide array of public goods, and when they are organized in ways that are inclusive, participatory and accountable. In Chapters 2 and 3 of the previous section, we addressed the first two points: the role of security and social capacity in supporting peace. In this chapter and those that follow in Part II, we examine the qualities of governance structures and how they affect the prospects for war or peace. We focus on the qualities of inclusion, participation and accountability as essential conditions for building peace. We begin in this chapter with a discussion of the most frequent causes of armed conflict and the importance of inclusive institutions for preventing those conflicts.

Many factors contribute to war, but scholars generally agree on two interrelated conditions that play a significant role in most armed conflicts: (1) grievances based on the exclusion and repression of specific ethnic or identity groups; and (2) competing claims for political power and resources in a particular regime or territory. Struggles for greater power and control of resources by groups self-defined by ethnic or religious identity are a common feature in many of the world's armed conflicts. Many wars and militarized disputes stem from competition for political power and the control of territory and may become wars for self-determination or independence. Within these broad categories conflicts can be categorized according to differing rebel objectives: controlling or gaining a major share of state power, or gaining territorial autonomy or secession from the state. Ethnically based groups are active in both types

of conflict, especially in separatist struggles.[1] We argue that questions of
social inclusion are important for understanding these conflicts and how
to prevent them. Reducing the risk of armed violence requires effective
institutions of governance that are fully inclusive and participatory and
that deliver public goods equitably across all parts of society.

Ethnic grievances and territorial claims often reinforce one another
and together fuel the flames of armed conflict. In struggles over access to
resource wealth, ethnic grievances and disputes over boundaries and territory overlap. When these conditions are combined with weak or corrupt
governance, the result is a persistent threat of armed violence and seemingly intractable conflict. One factor reinforces another as the affected
communities descend into a downward spiral of insecurity and lawless-
ness from which it is extremely difficult to recover. Refugee flows, criminalized economies and other spillover effects from these conflicts disrupt
neighboring countries and sometimes entire regions. The result can be a
widening vortex of self-perpetuating instability and armed conflict.

Would-be peacemakers have learned over the decades that short-term
attempts to address one source of conflict without resolving others are
not effective. Interventions that emphasize security without equal or
greater efforts to address grievances and governance needs are not sufficient. Comprehensive approaches that address all factors simultaneously
are required to overcome violence and instability in these settings. Most
important are efforts to empower local communities in establishing governance systems that provide voice and opportunity for all relevant stakeholders and that have equitable institutional mechanisms for assuring
accountability and the rule of law. These are daunting challenges, but
they are necessary and unavoidable steps for building sustainable peace.

In this chapter we examine these interrelated dimensions of conflict
and how they are affected by the capacity and quality of governance
and the presence of inclusive political institutions. We focus on the need
for governance structures that address the needs of all social groups and
provide equitable opportunities for participation. We begin with a look
at the greed versus grievance debate and identify the factors that underlie
both economic and political causes of war. This is followed by a summary
of research on the role of territorial disputes as a cause of armed conflict,
and an examination of the conflict-inducing impact of ethnic grievances
rooted in marginalization and exclusion. Advances in the measurement

---

[1] Halvard Buhaug, "Relative Capability and Rebel Objective in Civil War," *Journal of Peace
Research* 43, no. 6 (2006): 694.

of ethnic exclusion provide new insights into the importance of equitable structures of governance for preventing armed conflict. The chapter concludes by contrasting outcomes of ethnic conflict in countries with different levels of inclusive and participatory structures of governance.

GREED AND GRIEVANCE

At the end of the Cold War an intense debate developed among scholars and researchers on the causes of civil conflict. Two main schools of thought emerged, oversimplified as greed versus grievance. One approach focused on the economic causes of war, the other on sociopolitical grievances. The continuing debate about these approaches is useful for examining the underlying factors that give rise to armed conflict, but the notion of a sharp dichotomy between the two is unhelpful. In the real world economic factors and political grievances reinforce one another as drivers of conflict. It is not either/or, but both, with each dimension subsumed under the broader framework of governance. The causes of war include not only economic factors and political grievances but also failures and problems of governance, including inadequate state capacity and a lack of accountability and opportunities for inclusive participation.[2]

Collier was a leader of the economic school and in his earlier works stressed the importance of labor market explanations for war. He and his colleagues emphasized economic explanations for the causes of armed conflict. Rebellion often has an economic motive. It is a means of gaining wealth and income from predation and looting. Insurgents fight because they are paid, and in some cases are more like bandits and pirates than liberation fighters. According to this formulation, armed conflicts are motivated by greed, by the desire for profitable opportunities to gain income and resources.[3] To test these hypotheses, Collier and his colleague Anke Hoeffler examined indicators of political grievance (including repression, ethnic polarization, political exclusion, level of democracy, economic inequality) and economic opportunity (including measures of income, dependence on natural resources, donations from diasporas, secondary school enrollment, subventions from foreign governments). In their regression analyses they found that the variables most

---

[2] David Sobek, "Masters of their Domains: The Role of State Capacity in Civil Wars," *Journal of Peace Research* 47, no. 3 (May 2010): 268.
[3] Collier and Hoeffler, "Greed and Grievance in Civil War."

strongly associated with the onset of civil war are economic, including low scores for economic growth, income per capita, secondary school enrollment, and high dependence on primary commodity exports. They concluded that variables related to the economic viability of rebellion provide considerably more explanatory power than political and social factors.[4]

Collier's work is very influential in global policy circles and has made an important contribution to understanding the economic causes of war and the benefits of economic development as a strategy for peace. Many scholars and policy makers agree that low levels of income and high rates of youth unemployment increase the risk of armed conflict. Such conditions reduce the opportunity costs of armed rebellion and create a ready 'market' for the recruitment of militants. Development, if balanced and equitable, can help to ameliorate these conditions. Economic growth creates opportunities for those who might otherwise be inclined toward militancy and minimizes the incentives for participating in armed rebellion.[5] Development and trade policies that help to raise living standards and increase per capita income reduce the likelihood of armed conflict, as we discuss in Chapter 8.

It is important to go beyond a narrow or exclusive focus on economic causes of war, however, and to address the complex web of interconnecting dynamics that often cause armed conflict and make it so difficult to prevent and resolve. Econometric models face inherent limitations and ambiguities in the data being analyzed. As Laurie Nathan notes, some of the proxy indicators scholars use for testing economic factors could just as well be indicators of political grievance.[6] Low scores for economic growth or secondary school enrollment, for example, could reflect political grievances resulting from corrupt governance or exclusionary policies toward particular ethnic communities. Dependence on primary commodity exports is indeed a factor in many civil wars, but violence results not from the existence of commodity exports per se but from political disputes over how the resulting revenues are distributed and who benefits, a point we examine below. Financial factors are important but they are not the whole picture.

---

[4] Ibid., 563.

[5] Paul Collier, "Doing Well Out of War: An Economic Perspective," in *Greed and Grievance: Economic Agendas in Civil Wars*, edited by Mats Berdal and David M. Malone (Boulder: Lynne Rienner, 2000), 94.

[6] Laurie Nathan, "The Causes of Civil War: The False Logic of Collier and Hoeffler," *South African Review of Sociology* 39, no. 2 (2008): 262–275.

An economic model of conflict cannot explain why thousands of young people in Europe (and to a lesser extent in North America) have left lives of relative comfort to risk death fighting with the so-called Islamic State in Iraq and Syria. Poor schooling and underemployment are factors in generating social resentments, but many who join insurgent movements are also strongly motivated by identity issues and political grievances. They fight to overcome injustice and oppression and perceived humiliations. As a young Afghan recounted in a report by Mercy Corps, "I did not join the Taliban because I was poor ... I joined because I was angry. Because they (the West) wronged us."[7] An understanding of political grievances and how they motivate people toward violence is crucial to the challenge of preventing armed conflict.[8]

In his classic book *Why Men Rebel*, Ted Gurr emphasizes the political dimensions of conflict and points to the importance of unresolved grievances and unmet social needs. He and his colleagues trace the causes of war to social and economic conditions that produce frustration and humiliation among marginalized ethno-national communities, leading to militant mobilization.[9] At the core of this theory is the concept of "relative deprivation," which is the perceived discrepancy between what people think they deserve and what they have or believe they can get. It is the disparity between aspirations and achievements. When specific ethnic groups or communities are systematically denied access to political power and economic resources, the resulting resentment and anger can lead to conflict. If social groups experience marginalization and humiliation, they may be tempted to resort to violence. This is especially true when groups experience targeted discrimination and an abrupt downgrading of power and wealth.

The experience of humiliation is one of the most important but least acknowledged ways in which grievances can lead to armed conflict. Humiliation is the act of making another person feel ashamed and foolish, of dishonoring and denying the dignity of an individual and her community. As Nelson Mandela observed, to humiliate another is to make that person suffer "an unnecessarily cruel fate."[10] Neuroscientific research

---

[7] Mercy Corps, "Youth and Consequences: Unemployment, Injustice and Violence," (2015), 23, at www.mercycorps.org/sites/default/files/MercyCorps_YouthConsequencesReport_2015.pdf.

[8] Ted Robert Gurr, "Introduction," *Why Men Rebel* (Boulder: Paradigm Publishers, 2011, 40th anniversary edition).

[9] Ted Robert Gurr, *Why Men Rebel* (Princeton University Press, 1970).

[10] Nelson Mandela, *Long Walk to Freedom* (New York: Back Bay Books, 1995), 10.

shows that humiliation is a painful and pathogenic experience that can cause severe personality and behavioral changes.[11] The regions of the brain that become active during physical pain are also activated when we experience or witness humiliation. The perception of humiliation is closely linked to feelings of mistreatment and injustice. People have a visceral negative reaction to unfairness. A preference for equal treatment seems to be hardwired into our brains. Recent neuropsychological studies show that when subjects witness people being treated equitably, the reward centers of the brain respond positively. Subjects respond more favorably when a poor person receives a financial reward than when a rich person does. This pattern holds true even if the person responding is rich.[12] When subjects witness others being treated unfairly, negative emotions and anger increase.

Public humiliation is particularly harmful. When humiliation is experienced collectively it can exert an influence on group identity and increase the collective sense of grievance that drives conflict. "The single most underappreciated force in international relations is humiliation," wrote Thomas Friedman a few months after the US invasion of Iraq. Friedman quotes former Malaysian Prime Minister Mahathir Mohamad saying that all Muslims feel humiliated at being "treated with contempt and dishonor" and are increasingly angry.[13] Patterns of perceived humiliation poison the mind and create feelings of alienation and hopelessness. They make it difficult to establish relationships of trust and cooperation between individuals and social groups.[14] They are often the root cause of political instability and violent conflict. Feelings of shame and humiliation also motivate criminal violence. James Gilligan concludes that perceived threats to pride and personal dignity are the primary triggers of criminal violence.[15] Among individuals as in society, humiliation and feelings of marginalization can generate resentments and grievances that lead to violence.

[11] Walter J. Torres and Raymond M. Bergner, "Humiliation: Its Nature and Consequences," *Journal of the American Academy of Psychiatry and the Law* 38, no. 2 (2010): 195–204.
[12] Elizabeth Tricomi, Antonio Rangel, Colin F. Camerer and John P. O'Doherty, "Neural Evidence for Inequality-averse Social Preferences," *Nature* 463 (February 25, 2010): 1089–1091.
[13] Thomas Friedman, "The Humiliation Factor," *New York Times*, November 9, 2003, www.nytimes.com/2003/11/09/opinion/the-humiliation-factor.html.
[14] L.M. Harling, E. Lindner, U. Spalthoff and M. Britton, "Humiliation: A Nuclear Bomb of Emotions?" *Psicología Política* 46 (2013): 55–76.
[15] James Gilligan, *Violence: Our Deadly Epidemic and its Causes* (New York: G.P. Putnam, 1996); James Gilligan, *Preventing Violence* (New York: Thames & Hudson, 2001).

Greed and grievance are regarded as competing paradigms for understanding the causes of armed conflict, but in many instances they reinforce one another, with economic factors contributing to political grievances and vice versa. In case studies of conflict in Asia, Africa and Latin America, Karen Ballentine and her colleagues find that economic factors "are not the only or even the primary cause" of armed violence, although they acknowledge that poverty and joblessness contribute to the grievances that trigger armed violence.[16] In many of the cases studied, the sources of conflict are "grievances and insecurity bred by the systematic exclusion of ethnic minorities from political power and an equitable share of economic opportunities and benefits."[17] Leaders of insurgent movements exploit these grievances and use ethnically based nationalist rhetoric and ideology to attract political support and recruit followers.

Even where political factors and grievances are the major drivers of armed conflict, economic factors play a significant role in prolonging armed conflict. In the Colombian and Angolan civil conflicts, financial opportunities from illicit trade in narcotics and gemstones did not cause the violence but helped to prolong the conflict once it was underway. The same has been true in Sierra Leone and the Democratic Republic of Congo, where the exploitation of diamonds and other resources helped to sustain militia groups and rebel movements but was not the key factor causing them to go to war. These insurgencies are "rooted in decades of political misrule and corruption by a parasitic state elite and exacerbated by ensuing socioeconomic deterioration and institutional decay," Ballentine writes.[18] Economic factors combine with political grievances to drive communities toward war and sustain armed conflict once it begins.

Greed and grievance co-exist and are important factors in driving communities toward conflict, but they are not sufficient on their own to explain the outbreak of armed violence. Some societies remain peaceful despite high levels of poverty or strong feelings of injustice. In these settings inclusive, participatory mechanisms exist for resolving disputes and institutions are capable of meeting public needs. When governance is weak or dysfunctional, however, the ability to manage economic and political disputes is diminished, and conflicts over political power and

---

[16] Karen Ballentine, "Beyond Greed and Grievance: Reconsidering the Economic Dynamics of Conflict," in *The Political Economy of Armed Conflict: Beyond Greed and Grievance*, edited by Karen Ballentine and Jake Sherman (Boulder: Lynne Rienner, 2003), 260.

[17] Ibid., 260.

[18] Ibid., 261.

access to land and resources are more likely to lead to armed violence.[19] Ballentine emphasizes the importance of governance and state capacity issues in many of the cases she and her colleagues examine. Problems of institutional weakness and ineffective governance contribute to the conditions that lead to armed violence. One of the most common problems is the failure of institutions to incorporate ethnic minorities into full economic and political citizenship.[20] In the absence of inclusive and accountable institutions of governance economic deprivation and unresolved social and political grievances combine to increase the risk of armed conflict. Exclusion and marginalization exacerbate the conditions that can lead to identity-based ethnic conflicts. To counter this risk it is necessary to address both economic factors and political grievances, and to work for improvements in the inclusiveness and capacity of governing institutions.

CONTROLLING TERRITORY

Disputes over territory and political secession historically have been a frequent cause of war within states. Nils Petter Gleditsch observes that territorial disputes are the number one cause of armed conflict in the modern era. Of 277 armed conflicts in the period 1946–2004, 60 percent were fights over the control of territory.[21] Some of the most intractable intrastate military conflicts in recent decades – in the Balkans, the Congo, Sudan, Kashmir and beyond – have been fought by communities over contested claims to territory. They are the result of attempts by distinct ethnic groups to realign or break away from existing states and/or form new states[22] They are settings in which boundaries are in dispute and aggrieved communities are striving for greater autonomy and in some cases sovereign independence.

[19] Syed Mansoob Murshed and Mohammad Zulfan Tadjoeddin, "Revisiting the Greed and Grievance Explanations for Violent Internal Conflict," *Journal of International Development* 21, no. 1 (2009): 87–111.

[20] Ballentine, "Beyond Greed and Grievance," 264.

[21] Niles Petter Gleditsch, "Environmental Change, Security and Conflict," in *Leashing the Dogs of War: Conflict Management in a Divided World*, edited by Chester A. Crocker, Fen Osler Hampson and Pamela Aall (Washington, D.C.: United States Institute of Peace, 2007), 180; John A. Vasquez and Marie T. Henehan, *Territory, War, and Peace: An Empirical and Theoretical Analysis* (London: Routledge, 2010).

[22] Barbara Harff and Ted Robert Gurr, *Ethnic Conflict in World Politics*, 2nd edition (Boulder: Westview Press, 2004), xii, 1.

These conflicts over territory and the demarcation of borders are often the most difficult to resolve. They are matters of supreme significance for a state's identity and even its existence. They are existential issues for ethno-national groups seeking to assert their identity and achieve recognition and autonomy. Territorial claims often acquire symbolic and transcendent meaning. They are highly emotive and tend to arouse intensive and broadly based political mobilization.[23] These wars for self-determination rarely achieve outright independence – South Sudan being an exception – but they often lead to legal or de facto autonomy for the contending rebel groups. Many of the civil wars since 1960 have resulted in "increased autonomy for the groups that fought them," according to Gurr.[24] Of the 57 conflicts studied by his team, 30 led to greater regional autonomy, power sharing, or independence for ethnic and national groups.[25]

Over the centuries states in Europe and other parts of the world consolidated structures of governance within relatively stable borders. Before achieving national coherence, however, the states of Europe passed through many wars, revolutions and rebellions. In southeastern Europe that process of defining national territory and borders was more recent. The wars in former Yugoslavia during the 1990s were partially internal civil conflicts, as Slovenians, Croatians, Serbians, Bosnians and Kosovar Albanians battled for political autonomy and independence. These were conflicts within the state of Yugoslavia, but they also had the characteristics of inter-state wars, as newly emergent countries fought against each other and with Serbia over who would control what territory. The Balkan wars ended with international interventions of the 1990s, but underlying disputes and irredentist claims remain unresolved. In many parts of the contemporary world, struggles for autonomy or state formation are far from complete, and in some areas have barely begun.

Competing territorial claims lead to armed violence when governance is weak and excludes important social groups from power. Many regions have fragile authoritarian states that claim to rule territory over which they have little actual control. These are states and regions where governance barely exists or is undermined by impunity, bureaucratic inertia, and

---

[23] John A. Vasquez, *The War Puzzle Revisited* (Cambridge University Press, 2009), 209–210, 231.

[24] Ted Robert Gurr, *People versus States: Minorities at Risk in the New Century* (Washington, DC: U.S. Institute of Peace, 2000), 197.

[25] Ibid., 197, 223, 203.

ethnic and religious fragmentation and marginalization.[26] When these failings of governance overlap with economic and political grievances, the affected communities may take up arms to seek self-governance and claim territorial autonomy.

Disputes over territory are often struggles between distinct ethnic groups. Communities united by ethnicity, language and/or religion tend to reside together in contiguous settlements within a common territory. They form social bonds among themselves in the context of a particular geographic setting, which acquires meaning as the 'homeland' of that community. In most settings these ties to the land and bonds within ethnic communities are not a source of conflict. Individuals of different ethnicity and place of origin are able to interact normally without violence. When governance systems weaken or break down, however, conflicts between ethnic communities can intensify and turn violent. In pre-war Yugoslavia it was not uncommon for Croatians and Serbs to live together peacefully and inter-marry. When the Tito regime unraveled and economic conditions worsened, ethnic and territorial differences became increasingly important and were exploited by unscrupulous politicians like Slobodan Milosevic. The result was horrific violence between communities that previously co-existed peacefully.

In ethnically based conflicts, fighters seek to preserve their communities and control a particular territory by getting rid of people who have a different identity. Their goal is not to win hearts and minds, Kaldor observes, but to force their ethnic antagonists to flee – often referred to as ethnic cleansing.[27] Combatants seek to drive out the unwanted 'other' through methods of terror and intimidation, using violence to sow fear and force resettlement. This helps to explain the greatly increased number of refugees and displaced persons in recent armed conflicts.

Overcoming this form of armed violence requires governance systems that have effective mechanisms for addressing grievances of exclusion and managing polarized claims over the control of territory. States must have the capacity and the will to resolve territorial claims through inclusive political means rather than violent repression. When governments respond to ethnic or territorial grievances with military repression, support for insurgency often grows within the affected community. As we

---

[26] Kalevi J. Holsti, *The State, War, and the State of War* (Cambridge University Press, 1996), 116, 16–17, 41, 147, 150–151, 183, 185; Goldstein, *Winning the War on War*, 278.

[27] Mary Kaldor, *New and Old Wars: Organized Violence in a Global Era*, 2nd edition (Stanford University Press, 2007), 8–9.

note in Chapter 7, the result can be full-scale civil war.[28] The risk of government repression and ethnic brutality is reduced when governance systems are perceived as fair and responsive to the grievances of all communities, when they maintain security in a balanced and even-handed manner.

ETHNIC EXCLUSION

At the end of the Cold War, as ethnic strife erupted in Yugoslavia and other regions, political commentators identified ethnic differences among distinct social groups as a major cause of armed conflict. Multiethnic countries were thought to be at greater risk of war. Subsequent research failed to confirm this assumption, however. In their influential 2003 article, Fearon and Laitin found that ethnically or religiously diverse countries are no more likely to experience significant civil violence than other countries.[29] Hegre and Sambanis (2006) came to a similar conclusion in their review of the literature on causes of civil war: there is no causal link between ethnic fractionalization and conflict onset.[30] This does not mean that ethnicity has no relation to war. Distinct social groups obviously engage in armed conflict, but they do so for complex reasons that go beyond the mere fact of ethnic diversity. Violence results not from the number of different identity groups in a country but from the way they are governed and the political and economic relations among them. Especially significant in causing conflict is the sharp degree of polarization that can result when one group feels exploited by or disadvantaged in relation to another. When substantial social communities are marginalized and excluded from political power and economic resources, the likelihood of violence increases.

The marginalization of one social group by another is a form of structural or "categorical" inequality, to use Charles Tilly's term.[31] It is the result of governance structures that privilege certain groups at the expense of others, in which specific social groups are denied access to political power and economic opportunity. Frances Stewart and her colleagues define this as horizontal inequality, which they describe as differences of

[28] Regan and Norton, "Greed, Grievance, and Mobilization in Civil Wars."

[29] Fearon and Laitin, "Ethnicity, Insurgency, and Civil War," 75.

[30] Sambanis and Hegre, "Sensitivity Analysis of the Empirical Literature on Civil War Onset."

[31] Charles Tilly, *Durable Inequality* (Berkeley: University of California Press, 1998), 170–180.

status and wealth among subgroups within a society that are based on ethnic, religious or linguistic identity, without regard for the subgroup's social needs or capacities. Their research shows that horizontal inequalities can be conflict-promoting, and that policies designed to ameliorate such inequalities can reduce the likelihood of conflict.[32] Other studies have come to similar conclusions on the links between structural inequality and violence. When people within specific communities are excluded from power and denied assets and resources that are available to others, the risk of armed conflict increases.[33]

New research tools have emerged in recent years to measure how horizontal inequality and ethnic marginalization cause violent conflict. Lars-Erik Cederman and his colleagues have constructed sets of variables that measure the proportion of distinct ethnic groups in government decision-making positions and their per capita income in relation to other groups and the national average. They find that when the share of "ethnic groups in power" (EGIP) is small and the share of "marginalized ethnic groups" (MEG) is high, the risk of armed conflict is significant. In their book *Inequality, Grievances, and Civil War*, Cederman et al. deepen the analysis by employing geo-coded data to measure subnational social configurations in relation to a particular group's access to power.[34] Their studies provide empirical confirmation of the link between social exclusion and the likelihood of violence.[35] The probability of armed conflict within a state increases significantly when the representatives of a significant social group are excluded from power.[36]

Cederman et al. offer corroboration for Stewart's thesis that structural asymmetries in access to power and wealth increase the risk of civil war. They employ a broad concept of horizontal inequality, measuring both political exclusion and lack of access to economic wealth. The authors measure the degree of political marginalization by determining whether large ethnic groups are politically dominant, share power with other groups, or are excluded. They also measure relative wealth among these

---

[32] Frances Stewart, ed., *Horizontal Inequalities and Conflict: Understanding Group Violence in Multiethnic Societies* (Hampshire: Palgrave Macmillan, 2008).

[33] Wilkinson and Pickett, *The Spirit Level*, 134–135.

[34] Lars-Erik Cederman, Kristian Skrede Gleditsch and Halvard Buhaug, *Inequality, Grievances, and Civil War* (Cambridge University Press, 2013), 3–4.

[35] Lars-Erik Cederman and Luc Girardin, "Beyond Fractionalization: Mapping Ethnicity onto Nationalist Insurgencies," *American Political Science Review* 101, no. 1 (2007).

[36] Lars-Erik Cederman, Andreas Wimmer and Brian Min, "Why Do Ethnic Groups Rebel? New Data and Analysis," *World Politics* 62, no. 1 (2010): 88.

groups. They find that "excluded groups are much more likely to experience conflict than included ones."[37] The risk of conflict is greatest when social groups are excluded from political power and when their relative wealth level is far below the national average. The data suggest that political exclusion is the more important conflict-inducing factor and that "the impact of economic horizontal inequality on conflict risk hinges on the group in question being politically excluded."[38] The empirical results show that political exclusion and significant wealth disparity increase the likelihood of civil war. This reinforces the point made earlier that greed and grievance go together. Resentments resulting from political exclusion and sharp differences in levels of wealth motivate affected groups to rebel and can increase the risk of armed conflict.

It is not merely a group's lack of power or wealth that generates conflict-inducing grievances but the experience of intentional marginalization and discrimination. The risk of armed conflict is greater when specific social groups are subjected to systematic and targeted discrimination that blocks their access to political power and economic resources. The impacts of exclusion are greatest when a group has experienced a recent downgrading of its access to state power.[39] Political reversals in the absence of consensual institutions for transferring power are often destabilizing and tend to increase the risk of armed conflict.

Political and economic marginalization can be a factor in motivating ethnic separatist conflicts or struggles for control of the state. Small ethnic groups are more likely to seek autonomy or secession, while larger groups may have the resources to contend for control or a major share of state power.[40] When groups with a common heritage and identity are systematically repressed and denied opportunities, they may be attracted by the idea of self-determination and the lure of creating their own state. They seek to gain political freedom and greater access to power and economic resources, but in the process of forming their own state they may violate the rights of other groups. As Tilly notes, nationalist sentiment is often linked to efforts by one social group to exclude others in the name of the nation. When the dominant national group hoards power and resources for itself, this intensifies the risk of armed conflict.

---

[37] Cederman et al., "Horizontal Inequalities and Ethnonationalist Civil War," 487–488.
[38] Cederman et al., *Inequality, Grievances, and Civil War*, 117.
[39] Ibid., 68, 91.
[40] Ibid., 166–167.

This pattern is evident in the agony of South Sudan. The marginalized people of the south fought a bitter war for autonomy against the repressive government in Khartoum and finally won national independence in 2011. The new state quickly descended into civil war, however, as the Dinka and Nuer communities battled each other over access to political power and resources. Rivalry between political leaders representing the two communities combined with competition for dwindling and degraded sources of water and grazing land to generate armed violence. Impoverished and lacking even the most elementary structures of effective governance, the new state of South Sudan sundered in the throes of civil war.

Sectarian exclusion has also been a cause of violence and war in Iraq. Prior to 2003 the Baathist regime of Saddam Hussein monopolized power for the Sunni minority while ruthlessly suppressing the Shia majority and the Kurdish-dominated north. After the overthrow of the Hussein regime the Shia majority took power and turned the tables on the Sunni population. Shia-led militias terrorized Sunni communities, which retaliated in kind, leading to horrific sectarian killing. The Kurdish zone became increasingly autonomous amidst growing pressures for political independence and control of the region's oil resources. Sunni demands for an enhanced role in government and greater access to oil revenues were met with violent repression, intensifying sectarian violence. These pervasive insecurities and unmet political and economic grievances provided fertile ground for the so-called Islamic State, which gained a foothold in the Sunni majority communities of western Iraq. The continuing armed conflicts in Iraq are essentially struggles over governance. They are challenges by ethnic communities to the capacity and authority of the state in relation to local communities. Until these disputes are settled, armed violence will likely continue.

INCLUSIVE INSTITUTIONS

The degree of marginalization and exclusion in a society is directly related to the structures of political authority. The more inclusive and representative the system of decision making and implementation, the lower the likelihood of civil war. Research shows that consensus-based or power-sharing systems of governance lower the risk of armed conflict in deeply divided multiethnic societies.[41] Polarized political systems are

---

[41] Donald L. Horowitz, *Ethnic Groups in Conflict* (Berkeley: University of California Press, 1985); Arend Lijphart, *Thinking about Democracy: Power Sharing and Majority Rule in Theory and Practice* (New York: Routledge, 2008); Andrew Reynolds, *Designing Democracy in a Dangerous World* (Oxford University Press, 2011).

prone to armed conflict, while those characterized by inclusiveness and consociationalism have a lower likelihood of civil war onset.[42] Cederman et al. argue that political inclusion and a more equitable distribution of public goods are essential for conflict prevention.[43]

Gurr observes that ethnically based conflict is usually settled "by some combination of the policies and institutions of autonomy and power sharing."[44] Group autonomy means that distinct identity groups have authority to run their own internal affairs, especially in education and culture. Power sharing denotes the participation of representatives of major communal groups in political decision making, especially at the executive level.[45]

Studies on civil war recurrence reach similar conclusions. Peace agreements that specify multiple power-sharing arrangements among former combatants are more likely to endure, although this depends on how fully these arrangements are implemented.[46] Military and territorial power-sharing arrangements are particularly important for preventing armed conflict.[47] Peace agreements and governance systems based on consensus models and power-sharing arrangements perform well in reducing the risk of armed conflict.[48]

Arend Lijphart has examined the different forms of power-sharing governance and famously observes that consensus-based systems generate "kinder, gentler" policy outcomes. He finds that closed list proportional representation systems perform better than other political models in providing participation for all major stakeholders and reducing the risk of armed conflict.[49] Proportional representation provides the greatest

[42] Marta Reynal-Querol, "Ethnicity, Political Systems, and Civil Wars," *Journal of Conflict Resolution* 46 (2002): 35, 45, 48.

[43] Cederman et al., *Inequality, Grievances, and Civil War*, 224.

[44] Ted Robert Gurr, *Minorities at Risk: A Global View of Ethnopolitical Conflicts* (Washington, DC: U.S. Institute of Peace Press, 1993), 292.

[45] Arend Lijphart, "Constitutional Design for Divided Societies," *Journal of Democracy* 15, no. 2 (2004): 97.

[46] Melani Cammett and Edmund Malesky, "Power Sharing in Post Conflict Societies: Implications for Peace and Governance," *Journal of Conflict Resolution* 56, no. 6 (2012): 982–1016; see also Caroline Hartzell and Matthew Hoddie, "Institutionalizing Peace: Power Sharing and Post-Civil War Conflict Management," *American Journal of Political Science* 47, no. 2 (2003): 318–332.

[47] Anna K. Jarstad and Desirée Nilsson, "From Words to Deeds: The Implementation of Power-sharing Pacts in Peace Accords," *Conflict Management and Peace Science* 25, no. 3 (2008): 206–223.

[48] Esteban and Ray, "Polarization, Fractionalization and Conflict," 174, 180.

[49] Lijphart, "Constitutional Design for Divided Societies," 96–109.

opportunity for diverse voices to be heard. Such systems are the most inclusive and representative form of conventional political decision making. They promote stability by incentivizing negotiation among political parties, placing checks on executive power, and reducing the influence of demagoguery and personalistic voting. In post-conflict settings within divided societies, power-sharing models are more likely to be accepted by local populations and have the best chance of preventing the onset and recurrence of armed conflict. Consensus-based systems guarantee greater inclusion and representativeness. They are the very opposite of exclusion and marginalization and help to mitigate the conditions that lead to violence.

The evidence reviewed here indicates that unequal social relations and ethnic group discrimination increase the risk of civil conflict.[50] These findings corroborate the analysis of Gurr et al. that armed conflict often results from marginalization and perceptions of relative deprivation – from the sense that others have unfair privileges of power and wealth relative to the aggrieved community. These grievances are rooted in perceptions of injustice and discrimination among specific social groups in relation to the control of territory and access to economic resources. These forms of inequality can be considered a failure of governance, the result of decision-making structures that are not sufficiently inclusive and that lack mechanisms for sharing access to power and resources. When political structures are discriminatory and polarized they generate resentments and grievances that can lead to violent conflict. On the other hand, representative systems that incorporate substantial ethnic, national or religious communities are more likely to have the capacity to contain and resolve disputes peacefully.

Where governments are well-established and have inclusive, participatory mechanisms for managing ethnic disputes, political settlements can be reached without the risk of armed violence. Stable states with strong and inclusive political systems are able to deal with territorial and ethnic disputes through political means. Consider the examples of independence movements in Quebec and Scotland. In both cases, substantial locally based movements seek greater autonomy or complete political independence. Central governments in Ottawa and London vigorously oppose calls for secession and seek to preserve their territorial integrity. In the past such disputes might have led to civil war, but in these struggles the contending parties have relied largely on political means to

---

[50] Fearon, "Governance and Civil War Onset," 19.

assert their differences. Examples include the 1980 and 1995 independence referendum votes in Quebec and the 2014 independence referendum in Scotland. Ottawa and London work against the independence movements not with armed repression but through political concessions, such as the bilingual mandate in Canada and economic and financial inducements for Scotland to remain part of the United Kingdom. Mechanisms of democratic governance provide avenues for addressing these contentious issues through political means rather than armed violence.

Mature democratic institutions are no guarantee of sustainable peace if the grievances of a marginalized community are not addressed and no mechanisms exist for resolving ethnic political differences. In Northern Ireland the grievances of the Catholic community boiled to the surface in the later 1960s with civil rights protests and increasing violence from Irish Republican Army paramilitaries. The conflict intensified with the 'Bloody Sunday' massacre by the British Army in 1972, prompting a gruesome wave of terrorist attacks by the IRA, counter-violence from pro-British loyalist paramilitaries, and harsh internment and policing practices by British security forces. The 'Troubles' continued for 30 years and left more than 3,600 dead.[51] The 1998 Belfast (or 'Good Friday') agreement that ended the conflict did not resolve the underlying tensions between pro-British Protestants and pro-Irish Catholics, but it provided mechanisms for the two communities to share political power and elect their own representatives to the reconfigured new Northern Ireland Assembly. Many challenges remain and occasional incidents of violence flare from dissident spoiler groups, but the two communities generally are now able to express their differences through political channels rather than with bombs and bullets. Power sharing and inclusive political institutions that enable communities to negotiate their grievances can play a crucial role in resolving and preventing armed violence.

CONCLUSION

Conflict prevention and peacebuilding policies require linked actions that address the core conditions that are most often associated with the outbreak of violence. Building effective political capacity to manage disputes is clearly relevant to this challenge. So is increasing the inclusiveness and participatory nature of governance. Some of the most important causes

[51] BBC History, "Violence in the Troubles," www.bbc.co.uk/history/topics/troubles_violence.

of war – ethnic conflict and border disputes – are related to the capacity and quality of governance. Competing territorial claims and ethnic exclusion are at the heart of many armed conflicts. The ability to manage ethnic grievances and territorial disputes is crucial to the prevention and resolution of armed conflict. Preventing and resolving such conflicts requires governance systems that are inclusive and that can provide equitable access to political power and economic and social opportunity.

As we have documented in earlier chapters, states with higher ratings on governance quality indicators are more likely to experience political stability and have lower risks of armed violence. States that can provide security and the full range of public goods are better able to address these challenges. As the World Bank 2011 Development Report emphasizes, "security, justice, and economic stresses are linked: approaches that try to solve them through military-only, justice-only, or development-only solutions will falter."[52] Effective peacebuilding requires policies that incorporate security, diplomatic and development activity within the rubric of good governance. The more complete the capabilities of a state, the more options it will have for meeting the needs of its citizens and preventing and co-opting armed violence.

It is especially important for governance systems to be equitable and inclusive so that all significant communities have a voice in decision making and have opportunities for gaining access to economic resources and addressing political grievances. Governance systems with these qualities reduce the risk of violent conflict by offering a stake in society to groups that might otherwise be tempted to resort to armed violence. They help to advance the prospects for peace by incorporating the contributions of previously marginalized parts of society. This applies particularly to the role of women and the value of gender equality as a foundational aspect of good governance affecting conflict across all contexts – a subject to which we now turn.

[52] World Bank, *World Development Report 2011*, 22.

5

Gender Equality

When we consider inclusion as a quality of governance, the role of women has obvious importance. Half of the human population, marginalized and excluded over the centuries from public participation in government and society, women around the world have asserted their right to equality and in many countries are assuming a greater role in political, economic and social life. Women's progress is incomplete and uneven, of course, but it is a reality in many societies, especially in the most prosperous and well-governed states. In this chapter we discuss the significance of this greater participation of women in public life for peace and development and consider its implications for our theory of governance.

Virginia Woolf argued decades ago that women's advancement is a pathway for peace.[1] War can be prevented, she believed, through the social, economic and political advancement of women. Education and employment would enable women to achieve greater social influence, which would lead to positions in parliament and government. She urged programs to promote women's education, to support women's employment outside the home, and to encourage greater female participation in political decision making. The rising status of women, Woolf wrote, would transform the social structures associated with war and help to create a more cooperative, peaceful world.

Extensive research has corroborated Woolf's insights on the importance of women gaining equitable social, economic and political access. Many studies find that the status of women in society strongly predicts

---

[1] Virginia Woolf, *Three Guineas* (New York: Harcourt, Brace & World, 1938).

the likelihood of peace between and within states. While competing theories explain this phenomenon, the evidence shows that higher levels of gender equality are strongly associated with reduced rates of armed conflict. Gender equality enhances the prospects for peace directly through social impacts explained below and indirectly by strengthening conditions that mitigate conflict, such as economic development, good governance and democracy. These findings led UN Secretary-General Kofi Annan to state in 2006:

There is no policy more effective [in promoting development, health, and education] than the empowerment of women and girls. And I would venture that no policy is more important in preventing conflict, or in achieving reconciliation after a conflict has ended.[2]

Below we review the evidence linking gender empowerment with political preferences for peace and the prospects for economic and social development. We highlight control over fertility as an essential dimension of women's empowerment and a proxy for female education, employment and social standing.[3] The World Bank's 2012 World Development Report on gender equality and development finds that fertility rates are linked to poverty levels and reflect complex social patterns related to women's educational and social status.[4] They serve as an indicator of violence against women and of the likelihood of armed conflict in society.[5]

All four dimensions of women's status are interconnected. Higher education for women tends to delay the onset of childbearing years, which reduces fertility rates. Having fewer children frees women to participate in economic and political life. Women's participation in the work force tends to reduce birth rates, and reinforces the value of girls' education.[6] Indicators of progress in fertility, education, political agency and employment are not only interrelated but also mutually reinforcing.[7] Women

[2] Kofi Annan, "No Policy for Progress More Effective Than Empowerment of Women, Secretary-General Says in Remarks to Woman's Day Observance," United Nations press conference, March 8, 2006, www.un.org/News/Press/docs/2006/sgsm10370.doc.htm.

[3] Caprioli, "Primed for Violence," 169.

[4] World Bank, *Gender Equality and Development*, *World Development Report* (Washington, DC, 2012), 75.

[5] Mary Caprioli, Valerie M. Hudson, Rose McDermott, Bonnie Ballif-Spanvill, Chad F. Emmett and S. Matthew Stearmer, "The WomanStats Project Database: Advancing an Empirical Research Agenda," *Journal of Peace Research* 46, no. 6 (November 2009): 10.

[6] Caprioli, "Primed for Violence," 169–170.

[7] World Bank, *Gender Equality and Development*, *World Development Report*, 12.

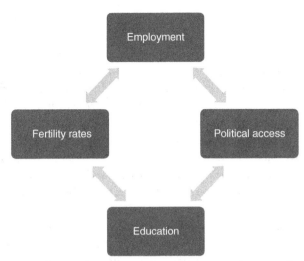

FIGURE 5.1. Reinforcing dimensions of women's status that contribute to peace

who are educated and employed have greater social independence and are better able to participate in political life and exert influence in government decision making.[8] As we review below, greater empowerment in each dimension supports peace (see Figure 5.1).

POLITICAL PARTICIPATION

When women participate in political decision making, the risk of armed conflict decreases. Several empirical studies show an inverse relationship between the proportion of women serving in a state's legislature and the probability of that government experiencing armed conflict. A landmark 2001 article in the *Journal of Conflict Resolution* measures the degree of violence used by states from 1945 to 1994 and compares it to the percentage of women in the upper legislative house and the length of time women have held the vote. The study shows that states with higher levels of women in the legislature have a reduced likelihood of using extreme violence in crisis situations.[9] This effect is especially strong in mature democratic countries, where gender equality in the legislature correlates significantly with a reduced risk of armed conflict and lower levels of

---

[8] Caprioli, "Primed for Violence," 169–170.
[9] Mary Caprioli and Mark A. Boyer, "Gender, Violence, and International Crisis," *Journal of Conflict Resolution* 45, no. 4 (August 2001): 503–518.

military spending.[10] Higher rates of female political representation have a pacifying effect on the risk of armed conflict.

Women's political representation is not a straightforward variable, however. In many countries, the presence of women in the legislature is due to quotas or external factors rather than direct democratic election of women. Many of the women legislators who serve as part of the 25 percent reserve quota in Afghanistan's lower house of parliament are aligned with male warlords and vote according to sectarian interests rather than as a cohesive bloc for female empowerment.[11] In some countries voters choose among political parties rather than candidates, with women and men representing party interests. The correlation between more women legislators and reduced military funding is substantially greater in electoral systems where legislators have greater autonomy and are not bound to represent party interests by strict party discipline.[12] Otherwise, if male-dominated political party structures dictate voting patterns, the peace effect is diminished.

A related finding suggests the importance of institutional and systemic contexts in influencing the pacific impact of women's representation. Women's political representation is related to the degree of state repression and violence against its own citizens. A higher percentage of women in parliament is associated with fewer instances of human rights abuse. This finding holds even when controlling for other factors that influence human rights behavior, such as the level of democracy, GNP per capita and ethno-linguistic fractionalization. Political gender equality is an important determinant of state respect for human rights and personal integrity.[13] In the absence of democracy, however, the benign impact of women's political representation disappears. This suggests that the presence of democracy and female political representation are mutually reinforcing mechanisms in decreasing state repression and human rights abuse.

---

[10] Michael Koch and Sarah Fulton, "In the Defense of Women: Gender, Office Holding, and National Security Policy in Established Democracies," *Journal of Politics* 73, no. 1 (2011): 2, 6.

[11] Interview, Sara Smiles Persinger, with Arsila Wardak, Kabul, May–June 2010; see David Cortright and Kristen Wall, *Afghan Women Speak: Enhancing Security and Women's Rights in Afghanistan*, Kroc Institute for International Peace Studies, August 2012, http://kroc.nd.edu/sites/default/files/Afghan_Women_Speak_Report.pdf.

[12] Koch and Fulton, "In the Defense of Women," 9.

[13] Erik Melander, "Political Gender Equality and State Human Rights Abuse," *Journal of Peace Research* 42, no. 2 (2005): 162.

A study of the onset and severity of militarized disputes between states finds that fertility rates are the best predictor of the use of force.[14] Country dyads with low birthrates or high levels of women in the workforce are less likely to use military force in disputes. This finding holds when controlling for other factors such as democracy and level of economic development. Disputes are more likely to escalate to greater intensity when one member of a dyad has high fertility rates (over 4.5 children per woman).[15] These results are linked to the ability of women to participate in politics at the local level. Women are better able to engage in political activity when they have fewer children and greater personal income as a result of employment. Countries in which women engage more actively in political life are less likely to experience an onset of conflict.[16]

The evidence confirms that when political systems enable women's meaningful, rather than 'showpiece,' representation, states are more peaceful within and without. As noted, the peaceful impact of women's representation is strongest in fully mature democracies, especially in proportional representation systems, which do the best structural job of representing the distribution of opinions in the public. Power-sharing institutions are especially significant in explaining gender differences in political engagement.[17] Political institutions with the greatest degree of inclusion have the highest rates of female representation and are least likely to experience armed conflict.[18]

The importance of proportional representation systems for enhancing the political role of women reinforces the positive impact of inclusive and participatory governance systems for reducing the risk of armed conflict. As we have observed in other chapters and explore more thoroughly in Chapter 7, findings from a range of studies on various aspects of governance confirm the beneficial impacts of representative political institutions. Higher levels of political inclusion and participation are associated with more effective state capacity and fully mature democracy. These conditions are strongly associated with a reduced risk of armed conflict and state repression. They are also associated with women's political

---

[14] Patrick M. Regan and Aida Paskeviciute, "Women's Access to Politics and Peaceful States," *Journal of Peace Research* 40, no. 3 (2003): 288.

[15] Ibid., 297.

[16] Ibid., 292.

[17] Miki Caul Kittilson and Leslie Schwindt-Bayer, "Engaging Citizens: The Role of Power-Sharing Institutions," *Journal of Politics* 72, no. 4 (October 2010): 990–1002.

[18] Marijke Breuning, "Women's Representation and Development Assistance," *Women & Politics* 23, no. 3 (2001): 48.

empowerment. All of these factors come together in helping to define good governance for peace.

THE EXCEPTION: FEMALE EXECUTIVES

Evidence of a gendered peace effect due to higher women's political participation is robust and comprehensive – with one striking exception. Female political executives are likely to promote more, rather than less, militarized violence. Studies show that the presence of women in the legislature decreases state violence in crisis situations, but that the presence of a female executive *increases* the likelihood of severe violence.[19] Female executives are also more likely than their male counterparts to increase military spending and resort to the use of force.[20] The number of national female political leaders is very small, so caution is needed in drawing conclusions from such limited data. It is also important to note that many of the female executives in recent history have been able to assume power on the basis of their family's political legacy.[21] Nonetheless the evidence suggests that female executive leadership is associated with greater state bellicosity.

The reasons for this apparent anomaly are unclear. Mary Caprioli and Mark Boyer attribute it to the extra pressures female leaders face to prove themselves in masculine environments.[22] They write:

From a social and interpersonal level ... female leaders who have risen to power through a male-defined and male-dominated political environment may well need to be more aggressive in crises than their male counter-parts ... women may also work harder to "win" in crises for the same reasons, because to appear and act feminine (and therefore weak) would be political suicide both domestically and internationally.[23]

Others note that women in executive office have a "credibility challenge" due to stereotypes that women are less capable of handling security issues.[24] In masculinized leadership positions, like executive office, the challenge to gain credibility may lead women to present themselves as more masculine, in an attempt to combat the stereotype of being soft on security issues.[25] Women executives in the male-dominated political environment

[19] Caprioli and Boyer, "Gender, Violence, and International Crisis," 506.
[20] Koch and Fulton, "In the Defense of Women," 3.
[21] Melander, "Political Gender Equality," 155.
[22] Caprioli and Boyer, "Gender, Violence, and International Crisis," 515.
[23] Ibid., 507.
[24] Koch and Fulton, "In the Defense of Women," 4.
[25] Ibid.

that surrounds security issues adopt more bellicose responses than they would in more gender-equal environments in order to overcome cultural gender biases.

SOCIAL AND ECONOMIC STATUS

Women's empowerment means more than political representation. It also involves socioeconomic status, including opportunities for education and employment, and lower fertility rates. In this sense women's empowerment is a function of governance capacity, especially the state's ability to deliver public goods and provide equitable access to education, public health services, and opportunities for economic development. All are crucial to the empowerment of women and are essential elements of good governance for peace.

Research shows a connection between women's socioeconomic status and the prevention of armed conflict between states. A study of three interrelated indicators – the percentage of women in democratic legislatures, the proportion of women in the labor force, and fertility rates – shows a direct link to the likelihood of war. The risk of militarized international disputes diminishes significantly in states where fertility rates are low, women participate fully in the work force, there is a longer history of female suffrage, and women hold a substantial percentage of seats in parliament.[26] The political, economic and social empowerment of women helps to encourage more peaceful foreign policies.[27] A related study using a composite gender equality index confirms that states with lower fertility rates and more women in the labor force are less likely to initiate the use of force in international disputes.[28]

The pacifying impact of gender equality on inter-state conflict is matched by a similar effect on the risk of internal conflict. In a 2005 study Caprioli examines the impact of women's socioeconomic status on civil violence within states. She finds that countries with high fertility rates (3+ children per woman) are much more likely to experience civil conflict than those with low fertility rates. Lower birth rates are consistently related to a lower risk of deadly violence. Similar patterns exist in relation to employment rates. States with low female participation in the

---

[26] Mary Caprioli, "Gendered Conflict," *Journal of Peace Research* 37, no. 1 (2000): 63.
[27] Ibid., 63.
[28] Mary Caprioli, "Gender Equality and State Aggression: The Impact of Domestic Gender Equality on State First Use of Force," *International Interactions* 29 (2003): 205.

labor force (10 percent) are many times more likely to experience internal armed conflict than states with a high proportion (40 percent) of women in the labor force.[29]

The identified links between conflict risk on the one hand and high fertility rates and low female participation in the workforce on the other could be measuring the level of economic development rather than an independent peace effect. Countries with high levels of poverty are likely to have higher birth rates as well as higher rates of armed conflict. As we will see in Chapter 8, economic development is the strongest predictor of peace. Studies that have attempted to examine these questions point to interrelated and mutually reinforcing impacts of both development and women's empowerment. The World Bank's 2012 report argues that "the links between gender equality and development go both ways."[30] While economic development certainly can increase gender equality, gender equality also increases a country's productivity and economic development. The impacts of gender equality contribute to and reinforce the pacifying effects of development.

Part of that peace effect is related to levels of female educational attainment. Low levels of schooling for girls are directly associated with the prevalence of intra-state violence. This finding holds true even when controlling for economic development or the degree of democracy in a county. A relative increase in girls' enrollment at all levels of education reduces the risk of armed conflict.[31] Women who are educated also tend to ensure that their children are educated, creating a cascade effect for peace since educated boys are less likely to be recruited to rebel causes.

Gender equality in education is strongly correlated with indicators of good governance. An analysis by Margit Bussmann compares measures of gender equality with governance indicators for more than 100 countries. To measure governance she uses the international country risk guide (ICRG), based on 22 components that gauge political, economic and financial risk factors. High rankings in the ICRG are significantly correlated with reduced risk of armed conflict. Female educational levels have the strongest direct link with reduced conflict risk, but other gender variables are also associated with improved governance and lower rates of armed conflict. All the major gender indicators – the number of years

---

[29] Caprioli, "Primed for Violence," 172.

[30] World Bank, *Gender Equality and Development, World Development Report*, 46.

[31] Margit Bussmann, 2007, "Gender Equality, Good Governance, and Peace," paper presented at the General Polarization and Conflict (PAC) Meeting, Gaillac (France), June 7–9, 10: 12.

women have had suffrage, female labor force participation rates, educational enrollment and female literacy rates – are significantly correlated with good governance and peace.[32]

Gender equality in education also promotes peace through its beneficial effects on democracy. A study of more than 100 countries finds a strong relationship between women's educational status and the likelihood of democracy. In countries where the gap between male and female primary education is narrow, the prospects for democratic governance are higher.[33] Others have reached similar conclusions. A study of Muslim-majority countries links the democratic deficits in these regimes to the lower status of women, arguing that this is a more significant factor than religious systems in explaining the lack of democracy.[34] Lower rates of democracy in these regimes are most strongly associated with gender indicators, especially the literacy gap that exists between men and women.

Gender equity in education also promotes peace indirectly through its beneficial effects on economic growth and development. A World Bank paper notes that female education increases human capital and spurs economic growth, concluding that "female education is a good investment that raises national income."[35] This is especially important in societies at or above middle levels of development that are dependent on skilled labor. The same study measures other indicators of gender equality in addition to educational attainment and finds that all are positively correlated with levels of per capita income.[36] Gender equality and higher levels of economic development are mutually reinforcing.

Education has the greatest beneficial impact on development when it goes beyond primary school. Partial female education may inadvertently contribute to population growth and falling per capita income. A study of the impacts of various levels of education in 52 countries in sub-Saharan Africa found that education for girls up to 9th grade was associated with lower infant mortality rates but little change in fertility. As demographers note, lower infant mortality rates can lead to an increase in population growth if fertility rates remain high. In the absence of general economic

[32] Ibid., 11–12.
[33] Robert J. Barro, "Determinants of Democracy," *Journal of Political* Economy 107, no. S6 (December 1999): S158–S183.
[34] M. Steven Fish, "Islam and Authoritarianism," *World Politics* 55, no. 1 (October 2002): 37.
[35] David Dollar and Roberta Gatti, "Gender Inequality, Income and Growth: Are Good Times Good for Women?" Mimeograph, World Bank, Washington, DC, 1999, 3.
[36] Ibid., 5.

growth and productivity gains, this can lower per capita income.[37] When girls complete secondary education, fertility rates are substantially lower, which helps to offset increases in population. This research indicates that school enrollment for girls helps to lower fertility rates, but only if the educational process is sustained through high school and if public policies support access to family planning.[38]

The economic development prospects of lower income nations are strongly linked to gender equality. Global development patterns show that inequalities in male and female education and employment rates are associated with slower rates of economic growth. Imbalances in the number of years of schooling for boys and girls have a negative effect on growth. As a major study of the subject concludes, "the challenge of increasing the economic growth of a country is ... to a considerable extent linked to the role played by women in the society. The costs of discrimination towards women in education and employment not only harm the women concerned but also impose a cost for the entire society."[39] The wide gender male and female employment gaps in South Asia help to explain why that region continues to lag behind East Asia in economic growth rates. Barriers to female employment are not only disadvantageous to women, but also reduce national economic growth rates. Conversely, countries with a greater proportion of women in the labor market achieve higher economic growth. Gender equality in employment is particularly important in countries with high levels of international trade.[40]

Taken together these and other studies confirm that higher levels of gender equality, as measured by educational attainment and socioeconomic status, are directly correlated with development, improved governance and reduced rates of armed conflict. States characterized by gender equality are less likely to engage in militarized international disputes, have lower rates of military spending, and are less likely to experience internal armed conflict, repression and human rights abuse. Even when controlling for a state's level of democracy and economic growth rate, gender equality stands out as a significant factor in its own right. Societies in which women are empowered politically, participate in the

---

[37] Elizabeth N. Appiah and Walter W. McMahon, "The Social Outcomes of Education and Feedbacks on Growth in Africa," *Journal of Development Studies* 38 no. 4 (2002): 37.

[38] Ibid., 37, 49.

[39] Stephan Klasen and Francesca Lamanna, "The Impact of Gender Inequality in Education and Employment on Economic Growth: New Evidence for a Panel of Countries," *Feminist Economics* 15, no. 3 (July 2009): 117.

[40] Ibid., 113–114.

workforce, are well educated and have low fertility rates are more likely to be peaceful in relations with other states and internally.

FERTILITY AND DEMOGRAPHICS

A number of studies show that lower rates of fertility and population growth enhance economic growth and thereby reduce the risk of armed conflict. Decreases in birth rates raise a country's median age, which generates potential economic dividends. Lower fertility rates enhance economic growth when the working-age population is growing and savings rates are rising. As fertility nears the replacement level, small families become common and working-age adults assume a larger proportion of the population. In East Asia this "demographic bonus" has played a significant role in facilitating rapid economic growth. Governance programs for public education, improved health care and family planning have provided a major boost for economic development and in the process increase the prospects for peace.[41]

Approximately a third of the world's countries are in the last stages of a transition from higher birth rates and shorter lives to lower birth rates and longer lives. Societies that have not started this transition or are in its early stages are characterized by high rates of fertility, higher levels of infant mortality and large youth populations. These are all factors associated with a greater risk of violent conflict. A Population Action Council report found that nearly half of the countries with birthrates higher than 45 per 1,000 people experienced an outbreak of civil conflict, while countries with falling birth rates have a lower conflict risk.[42] Movement along the demographic transition from high to low birthrates corresponds with a decreased risk of internal armed conflict. According to the report, "Countries in the earlier stages of the [demographic] transition are at greater risk [of conflict] than those near its end, and most importantly ... moving through the transition gradually reduces that risk."[43] The report attributes declining birthrates to education for girls, marriage at a later age, employment outside the home, and greater availability and use of contraceptives.

As noted in Chapter 3, societies with large bulges of uneducated and unemployed youth are prone to violence. A comprehensive study

---

[41] Richard P. Cincotta, Robert Engelman and Daniele Anastasion, *The Security Demographic: Population and Civil Conflict After the Cold War* (Washington, DC: Population Action International, 2003), 33, 36.

[42] Ibid., 30–31.

[43] Ibid., 27.

of population patterns in every country of the world finds that youth bulges significantly increase the risks of armed conflict, terrorism and riots.[44] Countries in which youth comprise 35 percent or more of the population have a higher risk of armed conflict than countries with normal population distributions.[45] This pattern holds regardless of regime type. Youth bulges increase the risk of conflict in both highly autocratic and democratic countries. Policies that reduce birthrates can help to mitigate this problem.

A 2011 Council on Foreign Relations report, *Family Planning and U.S. Foreign Policy*, highlights the profound influence of demography on development and peace. A high level of population growth "has the potential to jeopardize international poverty reduction measures, exacerbate security threats already present, and threaten the sustainable use of the world's natural resources."[46] The report argues that an increased prioritization of family planning measures will help to advance economic development, international security, and environmental sustainability. Policies that lower birthrates and flatten the population curve empower women and thereby help to promote economic growth and reduce the risk of armed conflict. As girls have the opportunity to learn and stay in school, they are more likely to delay having children. As they gain access to productive employment they tend to have fewer children.[47] Fostering greater social and economic opportunity for women encourages these trends and helps to advance the prospects for peace and prosperity.

EXPLAINING THE GENDER PEACE EFFECT: THE "WOMEN'S VALUES" THESIS

Some feminists of the early twentieth century believed that women are inherently more peaceful than men. Jane Addams argued that women are by nature more nurturing and caring than men. She believed that feminism and militarism are in "eternal opposition" and that women's suffrage would create more pacific governments.[48] Feminists and social

---

[44] Henrik Urdal, "A Clash of Generations? Youth Bulges and Political Violence," *International Studies Quarterly* 50 (2006): 624.

[45] Ibid., 618.

[46] Isobel Coleman and Gayle Tzemach Lemmon, *Family Planning and U.S. Foreign Policy: Ensuring U.S. Leadership for Healthy Families and Communities and Prosperous, Stable Societies* (New York: Council on Foreign Relations, April 2011), 15.

[47] Appiah and McMahon, "The Social Outcomes of Education," 38.

[48] Addams in Jean Bethke Elshtain, *Women and War* (University of Chicago Press, 1995 [1987]), 235.

analysts today offer more nuanced views. Sara Ruddick argues that the unique demands of women's roles as mothers cultivate the potential for peacefulness. While Ruddick acknowledges that many mothers have historically embraced militarism, she writes "the promise of maternal peacefulness lies in the work and love to which mothers are committed ... [b]y virtue of her mothering she is meant to be an initiator of peace and a witness against war."[49] Some psychologists argue that women have a different sense of moral sensibility. Carol Gilligan's important book, *In A Different Voice*, describes an "ethic of care" among women, as opposed to an ethic of justice found in men.[50]

These perspectives are based on the assumption that women possess unique values rooted in biologically determined reproductive roles and capacities.[51] Proponents assert that women are more naturally inclined toward cooperation and peaceful behavior, and thus women's empowerment promotes more peaceful and cooperative social values in the public sphere. These "essentialist" theories predict, following Woolf, that foreign policy will become more peaceful as a result of women gaining decision-making power through political office. When women achieve political power, their values are translated into policies which tend to promote peace. A variant of this theory is that a critical mass of female leaders must be present before a change in governmental values will be discernible.[52]

There is strong evidence that women do indeed hold different attitudes about the use of force and have different public policy priorities than men. Opinion polls in the United States consistently find that women are less supportive of war and the use of force than men.[53] Researchers find similar results in New Zealand, Denmark and the United Kingdom.[54]

[49] Sara Ruddick, *Maternal Thinking: Toward A Politics of Peace* (Boston: Beacon Press, 1995 [1989]), 221.
[50] Carol Gilligan, *In a Different Voice: Psychological Theory and Women's Development* (Cambridge, MA: Harvard University Press, 1982).
[51] Caprioli, "Gendered Conflict," 52.
[52] Melander, "Political Gender Equality," 152.
[53] Richard C. Eichenberg, "Gender Difference in American Public Opinion: Evidence from Before and After the Wars in Iraq and Afghanistan, 1980–2013," Paper prepared for the workshop on New Approaches to Gender Roles in Peace Making, Leonard Davis Institute for International Relations, Hebrew University of Jerusalem, June 16–18, 2014, www.researchgate.net/publication/264707090_Gender_Difference_in_American_Public_Opinion_on_the_Use_of_Military_Force_Evidence_from_Before_and_After_the_Wars_in_Iraq_and_Afghanistan_1980-2013.
[54] Lise Togeby, "The Gender Gap in Foreign Policy Attitudes," *Journal of Peace Research* 31, no. 4 (November 1994): 375–392.

A study of attitudes about the use of force in 37 countries finds that "the direction of gender differences is *always and everywhere* that women are less supportive of using military force than men" [emphasis in original].[55] A survey of 300 parliamentarians from 110 countries finds that women officeholders are perceived as viewing issues differently. They are assumed to have different policy agendas. They are more likely than men to prioritize social issues, gender equality and development, and are less likely to focus on security issues.[56] A study of women legislators in OECD nations shows that when women comprise 30 percent or more of the parliament, states are more likely to allocate additional funding for development assistance.[57] When women achieve a significant presence in government decision making, public policies tend to reflect different social values.

GENDER EQUALITY AS NORMATIVE CHANGE

While evidence supports the notion that women hold different policy preferences than men, especially concerning the use of force, feminists have warned against essentializing women and men. Critics of essentialist positions dispute the notion that women are innately peaceful and men inherently warlike. Jean Bethke Elshtain argues that unidimensional portrayals of women serve to reinforce war narratives that depend upon a dichotomy between men and women.[58] Ruddick writes of the "myth of maternal peacefulness" that persists despite ample historical evidence that "everywhere men fight, mothers support them."[59]

Scientific evidence disputes the claim that women are biologically programmed to be inherently more peaceful. A study of 14,000 twins, opposite and same sex, surveyed political and social attitudes to determine whether differences on political issues were due to genetic or environmental factors. The results showed that sex differences did not significantly influence attitudes relating to use of force and

---

[55] Richard C. Eichenberg, "Gender Differences in Support for the Use of Military Force in Cross-National Perspective: The War System, Modernization, and the Universal Logics of Military Action," Unpublished paper, October 2, 2007, 7, http://as.tufts.edu/political science/sites/all/themes/asbase/assets/documents/eichenberg/genderDiffsSupport.pdf.

[56] *Equality in Politics: A Survey of Women and Men in Parliaments: An Overview of Key Findings*, Inter-Parliamentary Union (2009).

[57] Breuning, "Women's Representation and Development Assistance," 46.

[58] Elshtain, *Women and War*, 171.

[59] Ruddick, *Maternal Thinking*, 219.

militarism, although they did affect social issues related to mating and reproduction.[60]

Some writers trace differences between men and woman on issues of violence to conditioning and socialization. Woolf famously wrote, "to fight has always been the man's habit, not the woman's."[61] By this she meant that men traditionally were socialized through education and social custom to accept war as a natural and valued part of life, while women were kept apart from society and were not subjected to this conditioning. Western societies have changed since then, and women now also experience socialization for war, but distinctive social and cultural processes continue to shape boys and girls toward gendered patterns of thinking.

A survey of attitudes of men and women in the United States at the time of the first Gulf War found evidence of a significant gender gap in support for the use of force. The authors of the study explain this difference as the result of "a pervasive, gendered pattern of early learning of cognitive and especially affective orientations toward the use of violence, particularly as a form of conflict resolution."[62] They highlight empirical research showing that in early childhood girls and boys develop different ways of thinking about the use of violence.[63] "The point is not that women learn early in life never to engage in conflict nor use violence, but rather that they learn to put off the use of violence until later in the course of a conflict than do men, to escalate its use more slowly, and to be more emotionally upset by it."[64]

Other public opinion studies suggest that the difference in men's and women's policy preferences may be the result of attitudes about gender equality rather than gender identity itself. Surveys among urban men and women in Israel, Palestine, Egypt and Kuwait in the late 1980s and mid 1990s showed that women were not more pacific than men in their attitudes about the Arab–Israeli conflict. However, in all four countries, respondents who favored the principle of gender equality were

---

[60] Peter K. Hatemi, Sarah E. Medland and Lindon J. Eaves, "Do Genes Contribute to the 'Gender Gap'?" *Journal of Politics* 71, no. 1 (2009): 270.

[61] Virginia Woolf, *A Room of One's Own and Three Guineas* (Oxford University Press, 1992), 158.

[62] Pamela Johnston Conover and Virginia Sapiro, "Gender, Feminist Consciousness, and War," *American Journal of Political Science* 37, no. 4 (November 1993): 1096.

[63] P.M. Miller, D.L. Danaher and D. Forbes, "Sex-related Strategies for Coping with Interpersonal Conflict in Children Aged Five and Seven," *Developmental Psychology* 22 (1986): 543–548.

[64] Conover and Sapiro, "Gender, Feminist Consciousness, and War," 1096.

significantly more pacific and supportive of diplomacy and compromise in the conflict.[65]

Alternative explanations for the gender peace effect also focus on social values and norms. One variant of this approach is social dominance theory, which explains hierarchies of status and social norms as based on the dominance of certain groups over others. According to this theory political attitudes and values regarding violence are more likely to reflect views on social equality than a person's sex.[66] This suggests that broader social values and norms are more important than gender differences in explaining policy choices. Preferences for gender equality may thus be part of a broader normative framework of social equality.[67]

Support for this theory is found in surveys of college students and voters in the United States showing differences in political attitudes based on whether respondents favor or disfavor equality between social groups.[68] Those with a higher social dominance orientation tend to support military programs and punitive policies, while those with a greater preference for group equality rather than hierarchy show stronger support for equal rights and social programs. While a greater number of men fall into the former category and a greater number of women fall into the latter, the determining variable is the belief system of the respondents, not their sex. Research in other developed countries reveals similar results. The study concludes, "men and women seem to hold different political attitudes largely to the extent that they differ in social dominance orientation."[69] Caprioli and Boyer also attribute support for gender equality to "a norm of equality among individuals ... [which] translates into equality and more restrained treatment for other political communities and countries."[70] Women (and men) hold more peaceful attitudes to the extent that they embrace a more egalitarian worldview.

Some social scientists hypothesize that the trend toward women's empowerment in mature democratic societies is the result of a larger cultural shift towards more cooperative and deliberative forms of conflict

---

[65] M. Tessler and I. Warriner, "Gender Feminism, and Attitudes Toward International Conflict," *World Politics* 49 (January 1997): 275.

[66] Felicia Pratto, Lisa M. Stallworth and Jim Sidanius, "The Gender Gap: Differences in Political Attitudes and Social Dominance Orientation," *British Journal of Social Psychology* 36 (1997): 56.

[67] Tessler and I. Warriner, "Gender Feminism, and Attitudes Toward International Conflict," 281.

[68] Pratto et al., "The Gender Gap," 52.

[69] Ibid., 56.

[70] Caprioli and Boyer, "Gender, Violence, and International Crisis," 509.

resolution. It is a reflection of deeper social norms shared by both men and women. As societies embrace equity as a core value, women's participation in politics naturally gains support.[71] Gender equality is linked to the evolution of democratic norms and vice versa. In this sense the gendered peace may be a deeper form of the democratic peace.

A study by Monty Marshall and Donna Ramsey supports the proposition that egalitarian norms promote peace and democratic values. They study state behavior in 88 countries, correlating the tendency to use force with levels of gender empowerment and democracy. Their research shows that gender equality, democracy and nonviolence are closely intertwined. Gender equality is directly linked to greater democracy and peace.[72] Gender empowerment "allows for the inclusion of the broadest range of values and options in political analysis and collective action ... [I]t is the perfectly *inclusionary* and the most deeply entrenched democratic state and society that is the most civil, responsible, and accommodative neighbor in the global community of states" [emphasis in original].[73]

Genuinely democratic systems are based on a broad power-sharing formula that values dialogue and cooperation over dominance and the threat of force. Democracy is fundamentally incompatible with gender inequality and patriarchal social structures. Equalizing the power relations between women and men deepens democracy and undermines the legitimacy of violence as a mechanism for maintaining social cohesion. As societies become more gender balanced, cooperation gains over social dominance and governance begins to reflect a more inclusive range of interests.[74]

CONCLUSION

As this chapter indicates, the empowerment of women is strongly associated with more peaceful and cooperative means of resolving conflict. Societies in which women are educated, employed and politically active, and have lower fertility rates are less likely to experience armed conflict.

---

[71] Breuning, "Women's Representation and Development Assistance," 48.

[72] Monty G. Marshall and Donna Ramsey Marshall, *Gender Empowerment and the Willingness of States to Use Force*, Center for Systematic Peace Occasional Paper Series 2 (February 12, 1999), 32.

[73] Ibid., 36.

[74] Valerie Hudson, Mary Caprioli, Bonnie Ballif-Spanvill, Rose McDermott and Chad F. Emmett, "The Heart of the Matter: The Security of Women and the Security of States," *International Security* 33, no. 3 (Winter 2008/2009): 20–21.

This gendered peace effect flows along multiple pathways, directly influencing policy preferences for less use of force and lower levels of military spending, but also reinforcing conditions for democracy, economic development and good governance. Lower birthrates mean more stable societies that enhance the prospects for peace.

The policy implications of these findings are obvious. Policies for enhancing security and avoiding armed conflict should focus more on the empowerment of women. One of the unconventional implications of this research is that international family planning should have greater priority in the foreign policy toolbox. Many gender experts agree in recommending a stronger emphasis on the impact of population dynamics for security and development. As Caprioli notes, "Foreign policy goals to ensure peace ... should concentrate more on supporting organizations aimed at improving the status of women, including those aimed at lowering fertility rates and offering credit to women for business enterprises, especially in developing countries."[75] Other scholars agree that policy makers should focus more on family planning and the inclusion of women in political and economic decision making as an effective way to encourage peace.[76]

Changing population dynamics is a complex and long-term task. It requires increasing educational attainment and literacy levels for girls, encouraging equitable employment opportunities for women, and enhancing female political participation and legislative representation. All of these are fundamental governance issues that affect the basic structures and mechanisms of social decision making and implementation. Because of the interdependence of educational, employment, political and reproductive influences, governance policies should simultaneously address all four dimensions. Assuring that girls have at least a secondary education, facilitating employment-intensive growth strategies that enhance women's economic participation, training and supporting women for greater access to political decision making, and strengthening international family planning programs – all should be advanced together as means of reducing armed violence and promoting peace.

Creating genuine gender equality involves a profound transformation in the very nature of society, away from previous male-dominated structures toward more inclusive systems of interaction in which women and men share power and opportunity. Some societies are moving in

[75] Caprioli, "Gendered Conflict," 64.
[76] Regan and Paskeviciute, "Women's Access to Politics and Peaceful States," 291.

this direction, particularly in northern Europe, charting a novel course with social policies and political mechanisms that enhance state capacity, expand democratic representativeness and maintain economic prosperity, while reinforcing preferences for peaceful and cooperative relations with other states. These trends confirm that gender equality is an essential element of good governance and a vital means of creating a more prosperous and peaceful future.

6

Countering Corruption

In the previous two chapters we discussed the importance of inclusion and participation as essential qualities of governance and described some of the ways in which they contribute to development and peace. In this chapter we address the equally important quality of accountability, which is crucial for good governance and necessary to counter the acidic effects of corruption. Nothing does more to erode public trust and the legitimacy of government than public officials abusing their authority for illicit gain. Corruption exists when government decisions serve the interests of the privileged few rather than the general public. It is present when institutions lack accountability and officials can abuse their access to resources to steal what belongs to the public. It violates the foundational principle of equality before the law, the belief that justice should be provided dispassionately across all groups without bias or variability.

Corruption undermines the conditions that favor peace: economic development, stable governing institutions and social trust. Through its negative effects on economic growth and government performance, corruption diminishes the foundations of stability and weakens the essential pillars of peace and security. When corruption is endemic and deeply embedded in government and society, the prospects for peace diminish.

As observed in Chapter 1, people are more likely to accept public authority if they believe governing institutions operate according to rules of fairness and objectivity and if their interests and perspectives are treated with respect.[1] In societies with pervasive corruption, this essential

---

[1] Tom R. Tyler, "Psychological Perspectives on Legitimacy and Legitimation," *Annual Review of Psychology* 57 (2006): 375–400, http://dx.doi.org/10.1146/annurev.psych.57.102904.190038.

bond of social trust is missing. Those who experience corruption and see the theft and misuse of public resources are likely to develop a jaundiced view of governing institutions. This is true not only in authoritarian states but in democratic systems as well. In the United States, according to surveys by Gallup and the Pew Center, many people are dissatisfied with the practices of government and corporations and believe that public policies unfairly benefit favored groups at the expense of average citizens.[2] A study of thousands of citizens in four Latin American countries found that exposure to corruption erodes confidence in government and reduces interpersonal trust.[3] An analysis of reactions to public fraud and abuse in Nigeria reached similar conclusions.[4] People lose faith in government if they see it as a means of benefiting officeholders and favored elites rather than serving society as a whole.

Corrupt systems are built on disparities of power and access to resources and tend to widen the inequalities that can lead to conflict. If the governing system is perceived as unfair and corrupt, the willingness of citizens to comply with public decisions that go against their self-interest diminishes. Some groups may be prompted to fight for what they consider rightfully theirs. When corruption is severe it allows violent criminals to gain access to public resources and offices. This destroys the credibility of governing institutions and undermines their ability to provide goods and services, especially security. Society becomes more vulnerable to the predation of armed gangs and militias and instability increases. Overcoming these conditions is essential to the broader challenge of establishing good governance and reducing the risk of armed conflict.

In this chapter we examine the meaning of corruption and explore some of its manifestations, both grand and petty, from hard systems of criminalized violence to softer, more pervasive forms of patronage and clientelism. We assess the harmful impacts of corruption on government and society and explore its relationship to the prospects for peace and security. In the latter part of the chapter we examine the conditions that help to overcome corruption and explore different approaches for

[2] Pew Research Center, "Distrust, Discontent, Anger and Partisan Rancor: The People and Their Government," April 12, 2010,www.people-press.org/2010/04/18/distrust-discontent-anger-and-partisan-rancor/; Gallup, "U.S. Satisfaction with Gov't, Morality, Economy Down Since '08," January 24, 2011, www.gallup.com/poll/145760/satisfaction-gov-morality-economy-down.aspx.

[3] Mitchell A. Seligson, 'The Impact of Corruption on Regime Legitimacy: A Comparative Study of Four Latin American Countries," *Journal of Politics* 64 (2002): 408–433.

[4] Omololu Fagbadebo, "Corruption, Governance and Political Instability in Nigeria," *African Journal of Political Science and International Relations* 1 (2007): 028–037.

countering criminality and strengthening the rule of law. Chief among these are systems of accountability and transparency. We review the impacts of top-down anticorruption agencies and bottom-up civil society campaigns, concluding that the combination of the two approaches offers the greatest potential for overcoming the curse of corruption.

UNDERSTANDING CORRUPTION

People around the world often complain about corruption, but it is not always clear what they mean when using the term. Corruption is a catch-all word that covers a multitude of institutional sins and acts of public malfeasance. It comes to mind frequently when citizens describe what's wrong with their government, but it is used more often as a general category for wrongdoing rather than a description of specific behaviors. Corruption is usually thought of as a problem with governments, but it also occurs in the private sector and within nonprofit organizations. A common definition employed by scholars is "the misuse of public office for private gain."[5] Corruption is driven not only by the desire for economic gain, but can also serve political and ideological purposes. It is illicit behavior in violation of the public trust by those in authority for the benefit of perpetrators and their clients.

Corruption is fundamentally about inequality and the abuse of power, a process for maintaining privilege for some and marginalization for others. It exists at the pinnacles of political and economic power, where elites cling to privileges for themselves and their clients, and at the lowest rungs of public bureaucracy, where underpaid officials demand bribes to perform basic services that should be freely available to all. An anticorruption activist in India described it as "the external manifestation of a denial of a right."[6] It undermines the ability of institutions to serve public needs and perpetuates asymmetries of wealth and power.[7] To challenge corruption is to confront "the myriad injustices to which it is linked," writes Shaazka Beyerle.[8]

---

[5] Daniel Treisman, "The Causes of Corruption: A Cross-National Study," *Journal of Public Economics* 76 (2000): 399–457.

[6] Shaazka Beyerle, *Curtailing Corruption: People Power for Accountability and Justice* (Boulder: Lynne Rienner, 2014), 26.

[7] Michael Johnston, *Public Officials, Private Interests, and Sustainable Democracy: When Politics and Corruption Meet* (Washington, DC: Institute for International Economics, 1997), 63.

[8] Beyerle, *Curtailing Corruption*, 8.

Many different forms of corruption exist. Four common types are bribery, extortion, embezzlement and nepotism. It is also helpful to define corruption in relation to patronage and clientelism as we do in the next section. Bribery is the offer of money or favors to gain a benefit from a public official or someone in authority, for example when corporations offer secret payments to government leaders to obtain a lucrative contract. Extortion is the demand of public officials for payment to perform their duties, as when officials request money to provide a license.[9] Embezzlement is the diversion of public funds for private gain, seen when political leaders use public funds for personal expenses. Nepotism is the giving of jobs or lucrative positions to relatives or personal connections, without regard for competence and professionalism. These categories can be divided into petty or grand corruption. The former refers to everyday behaviors, such as the need in India to pay a bribe for attention at a hospital, while the latter involves vast criminal acts that can affect an entire nation, such as the diversion of billions of dollars of oil revenues in Nigeria while basic public services decay. No listing can include all the different types of corrupt and abusive behavior by those in power, but these are some of the main categories.

This typology assumes that corruption is driven by self-interest and is maintained through the manipulation of institutional power and the dispensation of rewards and benefits. A more pernicious category of corruption involves the use of coercion and the threat or use of violence, often by criminal gangs and/or security forces. In some countries, offers of a bribe or payoff are combined with threats of violence and physical harm if the bribe isn't taken. If economic inducements aren't enough, violence is used. In South America the practice is known as "*plata o plomo*" ("silver or lead").[10] Linking financial payoffs with the threat of death or injury places targeted officials and individuals in impossible situations. The choices are to engage in corruption and accept the structures of coercion, abandon public office and flee, or take the risk of attempting to fight the system. In settings of entrenched corruption candidates enter politics not to serve the public interest but to accumulate wealth and power. The criminalization of politics leads to an increased use of criminal gangs and organized violence, often linked to the mobilization of

---

9 James Lindgren, "Elusive Distinction between Bribery and Extortion: From the Common Law to the Hobbs Act, The," *UCLA Law Review* 35 (1987): 815.

10 Ernesto Dal Bó, Pedro Dal Bó and Rafael Di Tella, "'Plata o Plomo?': Bribe and Punishment in a Theory of Political Influence," *American Political Science Review* 100, no. 1 (2006): 41–53.

sectarian politics.[11] The result is a maelstrom of misery and impunity for affected communities.

This corrosive combination of financial payoff and violent coercion exists in many weak or fragile states. Corruption thrives in settings of uncertainty, scarcity and disorder. It emerges in governing systems that lack sufficient institutional capacity for security and the rule of law. It also arises where public institutions have been hijacked for personal or sectarian gain by criminal elements and/or armed factions. In countries where economic and social opportunities are limited, control of the state provides one of the few available avenues for gaining wealth and power. The state is "as an asset to be grabbed and exploited for narrow partisan benefit," Fukuyama writes, rather than a means of serving the common good.[12] State structures and security forces become instruments for enriching and enhancing the power of privileged elites, to the detriment of society and the prospects for lawful governance.

PATRONAGE AND CLIENTELISM

Softer but more pervasive forms of political corruption also exist. These are patronage and clientelism, which are closely related terms that refer to the granting of favors to specific individuals and constituencies. In some instances the interaction involves not only material advantage but shared political and ideological interests, based on bonds of common identity. Kinship and ethnic affinity are frequent bases for patronage networks.[13] These forms of corruption are often rooted in an exchange: the patron delivers rewards and political goods in return for the support of the favored clients. Some argue that patron–client relationships based on reciprocity can maintain a degree of social order, as we discuss below. But most forms of clientelism sustain patterns of inequality – not only between patron and client, but between favored constituencies and less fortunate groups.

These forms of corruption emerge not only in poor countries that lack mature institutions but also in wealthier democratic countries. In Italy corruption persists despite decades of struggle against it. Previous systems of patronage based on the control of land and resources have

---

[11] Philippe Le Billon, "Buying Peace or Fuelling War: The Role of Corruption in Armed Conflicts," *Journal of International Development* 15, no. 4 (2003): 422.

[12] Fukuyama, *Political Order and Political Decay*, 107.

[13] James A. Robinson and Thierry Verdier, "The Political Economy of Clientelism," *The Scandinavian Journal of Economics* 115, no. 2 (2013): 263.

given way to more institutionalized patterns that operate through bureaucratic organizations, mass political parties and control of the media.[14] A financial form of corruption exists in the United States, according to Fukuyama, where "interest groups are able to effectively buy politicians with campaign contributions and lobbying. Most of this activity is perfectly legal, so in a sense the United States has created a new form of clientelism, only practiced at a much larger scale and with huge sums of money at stake."[15]

Some analysts consider clientelism a normal system for serving constituent interests, a way in which governments deliver public goods to specific clients. This can benefit communities and facilitate overall economic growth.[16] In newly emerging democracies citizens and pressure groups generate demands on politicians for patronage benefits. Voters increasingly become 'transactional,' assessing candidates mainly on their ability to deliver cash, goods or other tangible benefits to their communities.[17] Political candidates face pressures from their constituents for direct assistance and payoffs.[18] Providing services to constituents is expected in politics, but clientelism can exacerbate inequalities if benefits flow disproportionately to one community at the expense of another. Problems also arise if the emergent state is not capable of delivering the services newly empowered voters demand. Horizontal inequalities and unmet social demands can generate grievances that may lead to conflict.

MEASURING THE COSTS

Significant methodological challenges exist in trying to measure corruption and assess its impacts.[19] Indicators of corruption are uncertain and difficult to quantify. Most do not measure actual corruption but rather perceptions about its severity drawn from surveys in

---

[14] Mario Cacliagi and Frank Belloni, "The 'New' Clientelism in Southern Italy: The Christian Democratic Party in Cataria," in *Political Clientelism, Patronage, and Development*, edited by S.N. Eisenstadt and Reneé Lamarchand (Beverly Hills, CA: Sage Publications, 1981).

[15] Fukuyama, *Political Order and Political Decay*, 208.

[16] Nathaniel H. Leff, "Economic Development through Bureaucratic Corruption," *American Behavioral Scientist* 8 (1964): 8–14.

[17] Edward Aspinall, "Parliament and Patronage," *Journal of Democracy* 25 (2014): 96–110.

[18] Ibid.

[19] Paul M. Heywood and Jonathan Rose, "'Close but No Cigar': The Measurement of Corruption," *Journal of Public Policy* 34 (2014): 507–529.

multiple countries.[20] Commonly used sources of data are Transparency International's (TI) Corruption Perceptions Index (CPI), the corruption index of the International Country Risk Guide, and the World Bank's control of corruption indicator. These sources are based on perception surveys among country, governance and business experts. Transparency International also produces a periodic Global Corruption Barometer, which seeks to measure corruption experience through surveys that ask respondents if they or family members have paid a bribe in the past year.

Perception indicators inevitably reflect observer biases and are based on particular normative assumptions about approaches to government and business. Findings derived from household surveys come closer to observing actual corruption experience, but they also have limitations because the behavior in question is illegal and respondents may be reluctant to respond accurately. The challenge of defining corruption and differentiating among its different forms adds to these dilemmas. The line between patronage systems and the legitimate representation of constituent interests, for example, can be blurry. Despite the methodological challenges, the available indices offer an approximation of the extent of the problem and provide a useful baseline for assessing trends and comparing corruption in different countries. The evidence drawn from the different perception surveys is consistent, and their ratings correlate significantly. The diverse country, governance and business experts surveyed for these indices basically agree on corruption ratings.[21] The perception surveys also have the benefit of measuring levels of trust and legitimacy, which as noted are closely related to the performance of governmental institutions and their ability to deliver public goods. When legitimacy is low, governance is weak and ineffective, and the risks of corruption and armed conflict are higher.

According to the 2015 Transparency International perceptions index, Somalia and North Korea rank as the most corrupt countries in the world, scoring a meager 8 points out of a possible 100. Next to them near the bottom is Afghanistan with 11 points.[22] These ratings mean that functionally almost every aspect of the government of these countries is driven not by

---

[20] Daniel Treisman, "What Have We Learned About the Causes of Corruption After Ten Years of Cross-National Empirical Research," *Annual Review of Political Science* 10 (2007): 215.

[21] Treisman, "The Causes of Corruption," 438.

[22] Transparency International, *Corruption Perceptions Index 2015* (Berlin: Transparency International, 2016), www.transparency.org/cpi2015#results-table.

formal rule of law and an emphasis on the public good, but by illegality and the diversion of resources for benefit of narrow interests. This scoring confirms the status of these and other countries at the bottom of the list as fundamentally lacking the conditions of good governance. It is no coincidence that Somalia suffers from endemic violence, that North Korea poses a deadly threat to neighboring states while its citizens suffer hardship and political imprisonment, and that the war in Afghanistan drags on with no apparent end in sight.

Corruption undermines governance in multiple ways. It comes at the cost of lost political choices and inferior public services.[23] When senior office-holders are selected on the basis of political loyalty or ethnic kinship rather than competence and honesty, governments tend to perform poorly. As Fukuyama notes, increased levels of corruption are directly associated with poor governmental performance and lower economic growth.[24] Payoffs and protection payments add to the problem. The excessive bureaucracy created by patronage systems inflates government expenditure and can be a major source of fiscal deficit. Some analysts contend that corruption can 'grease the wheels' of economic development, but careful econometric analysis shows a strong negative relationship between measures of corruption and sustainable economic growth.[25] Innovation and productivity suffer when economic incentives are allocated on the basis of favoritism rather than ability.

According to studies for the World Bank, corruption "imposes a significant tax on foreign direct investment."[26] A 1 percent increase in perceived levels of corruption (as measured by Transparency International's perceptions index) reduces the economic growth rate of a country by 0.72 percent.[27] Corruption lowers economic growth by increasing levels of political instability and reducing the confidence of and opportunities for potential investors and entrepreneurs. Systems of patronage and nepotism "tend to fill the ranks of the civil service with inept and incompetent individuals, thereby lowering the productivity of public bureaucracies."[28] This diminishes the capacity of government to

[23] Johnston, *Public Officials*, 63.
[24] Fukuyama, *Political Order and Political Decay*, 87–88.
[25] Toke S. Aidt, "Corruption, Institutions, and Economic Growth," *Oxford Review of Economic Policy* 25, no. 2 (2009): 271–291.
[26] Cheryl Gray and Daniel Kaufman, *Corruption and Development* (Washington, DC: World Bank, 1998).
[27] Pak Hung Mo, "Corruption and Economic Growth," *Journal of Comparative Economics* 29 (2001): 66–79.
[28] David J. Gould and Jose Amaro-Reyes, *The Effects of Corruption on Administrative Performance: Illustrations from Developing Countries*, World Bank Staff Working

facilitate economic growth and deliver public goods and quality social services.

THREATS TO SECURITY

In her book, *Thieves of State*, Sarah Chayes describes corruption as a matter of national security. Offering incisive analysis and numerous examples of the deeply rooted corruption in Afghanistan and other countries, she argues that "acute government corruption may lie at the root of some of the world's most dangerous and disruptive security challenges." Afghanistan's system of "kleptocratic governance" is driving people to revolt, she writes, and provides "fodder for an expanding insurgency." Public anger at the pervasive fraud and abuse in the country has the effect of "manufacturing Taliban."[29] An Asia Foundation survey in 2011 found that 76 percent of Afghans consider corruption a major problem for the nation and 87 percent regard it as a challenge in their daily lives.[30]

Corruption has a deep and pervasive relationship to armed conflict in former colonial countries. In many African states, Chayes observes, post-independence elites inherited corrupt colonial-era administrations and simply adapted them to their purposes, redirecting systems of resource extraction to benefit themselves and their ethnic kin, while excluding other communities.[31] In West Africa this pattern led to the domination of Western-oriented elites in southern coastal regions, and the continued marginalization and oppression of animist or Muslim populations in northern inland areas. The result has been frequent discontent and occasional armed rebellion within affected communities. The rise of Boko Haram was motivated in part by anger and resentment at the corruption of Western-educated elites – those perceived as reading Western books to become administrators of corrupt legal systems and post-colonial oppression. The insurgents have gained support by attacking these systems and promising to establish clean government and Islamic courts that they claim will be free of corruption.

Papers (Washington, DC: World Bank, 1987), wwwwds.worldbank.org/external/default/WDSContentServer/WDSP/IB/1983/10/01/000009265_3980716172221/Rendered/PDF/multi_page.pdf.

[29] Sarah Chayes, *Thieves of State: Why Corruption Threatens Global Security* (New York: W.W. Norton & Company, 2015), 6–7.

[30] Cited in Hassan Abbas, *The Taliban Revival: Violence and Extremism on the Pakistan-Afghanistan Frontier* (New Haven: Yale University Press, 2014), 173.

[31] Chayes, *Thieves of State*, 129–130.

Attempts to build national security forces in Afghanistan and Iraq have exacerbated corruption. Massive programs to recruit, train and equip government military and police forces have foundered as vast sums are squandered on overpriced equipment, 'ghost soldiers' who exist on paper but not in the barracks, and other scams for profiteering and the enrichment of senior officials and their suppliers in the United States and the host countries. The corrupted client armies created through such programs have performed poorly in combat and shown a tendency to flee rather than fight. By contrast, rebel forces often portray themselves as fighting against government abuse and gain support from local communities through their reputation for being less corrupt.[32]

Research confirms the link between corruption and insecurity. Quantitative studies comparing corruption ratings and levels of political violence indicate a strong relationship between the two. Regions and countries with pervasive corruption experience higher rates of political violence.[33] Studies prepared for the World Development Report of 2011 show that countries with lower ratings for government effectiveness, rule of law and control of corruption have a higher risk of civil war recurrence.[34] A 2015 report by the Institute for Economics and Peace shows a direct correlation between perceptions of widespread corruption and the risk of armed conflict.[35] This risk is especially significant when corruption is coercive and associated with criminal violence.

When governance systems are weak and dependent on structures of patronage, attempts to root out corruption may increase instability. If alternative avenues for economic and political opportunity are absent, disrupting existing payoff patterns can cause hardship for affected communities.[36] Domestic or external shocks sometimes exacerbate these dynamics and increase the risk of conflict. Examples of such precipitating events include the collapse of communist regimes at the end of the Cold War, and the overthrow of the Gadhafi regime and subsequent disintegration of Libya in 2011. The removal of authoritarian regimes may bring

[32] William Maley, *The Afghanistan Wars*, 2nd edition (New York: Palgrave Macmillan, 2009), 254.

[33] Paulo Mauro, "Corruption and Growth," *Quarterly Journal of Economics* 110, no. 3 (1995): 681–712; see also Le Billon, "Buying Peace or Fuelling War," 417.

[34] Walter, "Conflict Relapse and the Sustainability of Post-Conflict Peace."

[35] Institute for Economics and Peace, *Peace and Corruption 2015* (Sydney: Institute for Economics and Peace, 2015), www.visionofhumanity.org.

[36] Matthew Simpson, "Terrorism and Corruption: Alternatives for Goal Attainment Within Political Opportunity Structures," *International Journal of Sociology* 44, no. 2 (2014): 87–104.

benefits in the long run, but the near-term consequence can be harmful. New and more violent forms of predation may arise as former elites ally with criminal elements to seize or maintain power.[37] This was the pattern in former Yugoslavia in the 1990s. Slobodan Milosevic used militarized nationalism with support from criminal networks to control state institutions and assert Serbian hegemony in the region, with devastating human costs.[38]

The conflict-inducing effects of corruption are especially evident in what Kaldor calls the globalized 'war economy,' the shadowy world of black marketeering, arms and human trafficking, oil and commodities smuggling and financial crime that emerges from and nurtures the outbreak of intrastate armed conflict and extreme violence.[39] Rebel insurgencies and militias often finance their operations through criminality. Armed groups engage in fraud, bribery, smuggling and criminal activities to acquire weapons and supplies and maintain the functioning of the war system.

War provides fertile ground for illicit enrichment. Looting, predation and impunity offer many opportunities for accumulating power and wealth. The reports of UN sanctions committee expert panels provide ample documentation of the criminal networks and illicit revenues that are used to fund political violence in the Democratic Republic of the Congo and other conflicts.[40] Militias and armed rebel groups, sometimes backed by foreign allies, plunder resources to finance atrocities, enriching those for whom war is a business and an end unto itself. The economy of corruption that often surrounds armed violence becomes self-perpetuating and creates incentives for those who profit from war to keep it going. The resulting concentration of power and self-interest makes it harder to end the violence and restore regular trade and governance.

Violent corruption undermines security and the rule of law in multiple ways.[41] In Central America and Colombia narcotics trafficking has fueled violence and armed conflict as transnational cartels and pro-government

---

[37] Le Billon, "Buying Peace or Fuelling War," 414.
[38] V. Bojicic and M. Kaldor, "The Political Economy of the War in Bosnia-Herzegovina," in *Restructuring the Global Military Sector*, Vol. 1, edited by M. Kaldor and B. Vashee (London: Pinter, 1997), 137–176.
[39] Kaldor, *New and Old Wars*, 95–118.
[40] For example, a listing of the many expert panel reports produced for the UN Security Council Committee Established Pursuant to Resolution 1533 (2004) concerning the Democratic Republic of Congo can be found at www.un.org/sc/suborg/en/sanctions/1533/work-and-mandate/expert-reports.
[41] Beyerle, *Curtailing Corruption*, 10–11.

militias fight to gain control of the lucrative drug trade. Organized criminal interests are able to infiltrate and shape politics and warp the functioning of state institutions and the economy. In Guatemala the civil war ended with the peace accord of 1996, but drug-related criminal violence continued, taking thousands of lives and generating additional roadblocks to development and good governance – although hope for better outcomes emerged in the fall of 2015 when corrupt political leaders were forced from office by public pressure, as noted below.

'BUYING' PEACE?

Some analysts contend that payoffs to aggrieved constituencies can be used to end armed conflict and prevent criminal violence. Philippe Le Billon argues that a redirection of patronage payments can be used to buy off belligerents and their supporters.[42] Armed conflict is caused more often by changes in the pattern of corruption than by corruption itself, he asserts. When existing patronage relationships are disrupted, groups that lose benefits may experience relative deprivation, generating grievances that lead to armed violence. This interpretation draws from the analytic framework developed by Gurr et al., as noted in Chapter 4. The solution may be to provide economic rewards and incentives to aggrieved communities as part of a negotiated peace agreement. Political and economic payoffs and the redirection of patronage benefits to previously excluded groups can ameliorate the conditions that give rise to conflict, according to Le Billon.[43]

A number of successful peace processes have employed this approach. In Mozambique, the UN-led international peace mission offered financial and political rewards to the RENAMO rebel movement as encouragement for its participation in the peace process and agreement to transform itself from a guerrilla movement into a political party. This was perceived as 'buying out' the rebel movement.[44] The package of incentives offered to RENAMO included access to an international trust fund, the ability to tax businesses in its areas of control, and the right to hold political office in provincial administration and in the new national government. Similar uses of financial and political inducements for rebel groups exist in other negotiated peace accords.

---

[42] Le Billon, "Buying Peace or Fuelling War," 413–426.
[43] Ibid., 424.
[44] Ibid., 420.

Incentives for cooperation are an essential element of the art of diplomacy and can include payoffs that closely resemble or reinforce patterns of patronage and clientelism. This can be controversial, however, and is open to criticism for rewarding bad behavior. If the process is negotiated transparently and has the consent of affected communities, the positive peacebuilding benefits may outweigh the negative effects, and could be preferable to the greater hazard of continued war. Ambiguities abound, however, and questions arise about the quality of the resulting 'peace' if it must be purchased at the price of reinforced corruption.

The use of payoffs to buy peace may be a temporary measure to reduce the risk of direct violence, but it is not a strategy for generating stable security. Building sustainable prosperity and peace over the long run depends on good governance and the creation of professionalized and impartial institutions that treat all citizens on an objective basis without favoritism. Effective governance for peace depends on inclusive and participatory systems of accountability and transparency that preserve the rule of law and provide equitable access to all.

CONDITIONS FOR REDUCING CORRUPTION

Some countries are relatively free of corruption, and it is important to know why. Empirical studies show that the problem is lowest in countries that are highly developed economically and open to international trade, and that have a record of sustained democracy and press freedom and a higher proportion of women in government.[45] By far the strongest and most consistent factor associated with reduced corruption is economic development and high per capita income.[46]

Empirical analyses confirm that corruption is lowest in countries that are the most economically advanced. The correlation between per capita income and low levels of perceived corruption is "extremely robust," Daniel Treisman observes, and is found in every region of the world.[47] Even when controlling for other factors that are related to low corruption, such as democracy, trade, equity and low inflation, researchers find that economic development is the dominant factor.[48] The question of causality is more complicated, but the data suggests that higher development

---

[45] Treisman, "What Have We Learned About the Causes of Corruption," 211–244.
[46] Ibid., 223.
[47] Gabriella R. Montinola and Robert W. Jackman, "Sources of Corruption: A Cross-Country Study," *British Journal of Political Science* 32 (2002): 147–170.
[48] Treisman, "What Have We Learned About the Causes of Corruption," 225.

does indeed cause lower perceived corruption. After extensive parsing of the data and controlling for multiple factors, Treisman concludes that there is "a causal pathway from development to perceptions of cleaner government."[49] Progress toward economic development is the single most important factor in reducing corruption and creating good governance.

Empirical studies also show an association between mature democracy and low levels of corruption. Institutions of political participation, such as competitive elections and representative parliamentary structures, are strongly associated with reduced corruption.[50] Bruce Bueno de Mesquita points to the important role of political accountability mechanisms in supporting the human rights record of mature democracies.[51]

States with a history of consistent democratic governance are most likely to have reduced levels of corruption.[52] The influence of democracy holds even when controlling for economic development and openness to trade, but the statistical significance of democracy is less than that of economic development. Countries that have been continuously democratic for more than 40 years have lower levels of perceived corruption. In countries with less than 20 years of sustained democracy, however, the democratic effect is negligible.[53] The results confirm that higher income states with institutionally mature systems of democracy experience the lowest levels of corruption.

The beneficial effect of democracy in reducing corruption stems in part from the mechanisms of accountability that are built into the structures of democracy. World Bank indicators combine democratic voice and accountability into a single factor to measure good governance.[54] Democratic political systems enable citizens to voice their concerns and hold decision makers accountable. They allow for the regular review of the performance of government officials and the replacement of those who violate the law or fail to meet voter expectations. Voice and veto are the essential ingredients of democratic accountability.

---

[49] Ibid., 228.

[50] Daniel Lederman, Norman V. Loayza and Rodrigo R. Soares, "Accountability and Corruption: Political Institutions Matter," *Economics & Politics* 17 (2005): 1–35.

[51] Bruce Bueno De Mesquita, George W. Downs and Alastair Smith, "Thinking inside the Box: A Closer Look at Democracy and Human Rights," *International Studies Quarterly* 49 (2005): 439–457.

[52] Treisman, "The Causes of Corruption," 399–457.

[53] Ibid., 433–435.

[54] Daniel Kaufmann, Aart Kraay and Massimo Mastruzzi, *Governance Matters III: Governance Indicators for 1996–2002* (Rochester: Social Science Research Network, June 30, 2003), http://papers.ssrn.com/abstract=405841.

For democracy to function effectively, voters must have access to information about the functioning of government and the actions of political leaders. The availability of information and the presence of a free press are essential. Scholars have found substantial evidence of a direct connection between free access to information and reduced corruption.[55] Studies of access to electoral information show that "the presence of a well-informed electorate in a democratic setting explains between one-half and two-thirds of the variance in the levels of governmental performance and corruption."[56] A free press, releases of public data, audits of government performance and other means of disclosing public information are crucial to the effective functioning of government institutions.

Taming corruption requires quality public institutions of the type Max Weber envisioned. He emphasized the importance of professionalized bureaucracies and strong institutions of state authority for national development. His observations on the subject were drawn from the experience of his native Germany in the nineteenth century, as Prussia led the country to unification and the creation of technically skilled and autonomous institutions of state governance.[57] A similar pattern of bureaucratic professionalism emerged in Victorian Britain at the time.[58] The Weberian concept of bureaucracy involves disciplined and well-resourced institutions that enforce laws and deliver services impartially, treating all citizens in an even-handed manner without favoritism. Institutions have the specialized knowledge and skills needed to provide services fairly and comprehensively. They rely on systems of recruitment and promotion for civil servants that are based on competence and performance rather than kinship or political loyalty. Government bureaucracies are supposed to operate autonomously, carrying out tasks and serving goals that are set for them by responsible political authorities.[59] A properly functioning professional institution structured in this manner is necessary for delivering public goods efficiently and avoiding corruption. It is difficult to

---

[55] Aymo Brunetti and Beatrice Weder, "A Free Press Is Bad News for Corruption," *Journal of Public Economics* 87 (2003): 1801–1824.

[56] Alícia Adserà, Carles Boix and Mark Payne, "Are You Being Served? Political Accountability and Quality of Government," *Journal of Law, Economics, and Organization* 19 (2003): 445–490.

[57] Fukuyama, *Political Order and Political Decay*, 66–80.

[58] William D. Rubinstein and Patrick von Maravic, "Max Weber, Bureaucracy, and Corruption," in *The Good Cause: Theoretical Perspectives on Corruption*, edited by Gjalt de Graaf, Patrick von Maravic and Pieter Wagenaar (Opladen: B. Budrich, 2010), 21–35, www.ssoar.info/ssoar/handle/document/36876.

[59] Fukuyama, *Political Order and Political Decay*, 23, 75, 511.

establish effective, trustworthy and impartial institutions in societies torn by violent civil conflict. When political, ethnic and/or religious factions are at war with one another, few people remain neutral or can be trusted to be genuinely impartial.[60]

International engagement in post-conflict settings can help to establish professional institutions and build bonds of social trust. In Kosovo institutions managed by the international community in the years after the war were buffered from corruption and enjoyed higher public trust, compared with institutions that were given back to local control more quickly.[61] In several countries the deployment of external election monitors has helped to ensure impartial and fair voting procedures, offering models that local officials can employ in future elections. A similar external support function has been utilized in the management of natural resources in conflict settings. In Liberia, where illegal lumbering helped fund the war, the UN Security Council initially imposed sanctions on timber sales to prevent further conflict. These measures were maintained and adapted in the post-war transition to help the new democratically elected government in Monrovia establish a transparent and more accountable system for managing forestry resources for public benefit. The lifting of Security Council sanctions was tied to government progress in establishing accountable resource management systems.[62] External capacity building and the use of sanctions for post-conflict peacebuilding combined to help establish more effective governance.

TRANSPARENCY

Justice Louis Brandeis famously said that "sunshine is the best of disinfectants, a remedy to problems of social disease and corruption."[63] The public disclosure of information about the operations and decisions of government is necessary for good governance and public accountability.[64] A 2005 UN report described accountability as operationally equivalent to transparency: "Accountability refers to the obligation on the part of public officials to report on the usage of public resources and answerability for failing to

---

[60] Bo Rothstein, "What is the Opposite of Corruption?" *Third World Quarterly* 35, no. 5 (2014): 737–752.

[61] Elton Skendaj, *Creating Kosovo: International Oversight and the Making of Ethical Institutions* (Cornell University Press and Woodrow Wilson Center Press, 2014).

[62] Le Billon, "Buying Peace or Fuelling War," 423–424.

[63] Louis D. Brandeis, *Other People's Money and How the Bankers Use It* (US: Seven Treasures Publications, 2009)

[64] Ann M. Florini, "Increasing Transparency in Government," *International Journal on World Peace* 19 (2002): 3–37.

meet stated performance objectives."[65] Governments that do not release public information about their operations are much less accountable and more likely to engage in corrupt and criminal behavior.

Research shows that the release of public information can be a tool against corruption. A study in Brazil found that the dissemination of audit information strongly affected the re-election prospects of corrupt mayors.[66] Under an anticorruption program initiated in 2003, the Brazilian government each year randomly audited 60 municipalities applying for federal funds, releasing the information to local broadcast and news media. The study found that reports of corruption violations significantly reduced the re-election prospects of the implicated mayors. The results show that when voters are informed about corruption they are able to discipline responsible officials at the polls.[67] More general forms of transparency also help to reduce corruption. A statistical examination of programs using Internet-based release of data on government operations finds that e-government policies for the dissemination of public information help to reduce levels of perceived corruption.[68]

Achieving transparency is difficult in authoritarian regimes that control and suppress the media and silence critics. Even in these settings, though, local activists may be able to gain access to the press through what Margaret Keck and Kathryn Sikkink call the "boomerang effect" – utilizing transnational networks to release information in other countries that can reverberate back home.[69] Activists from repressive regimes have learned to use the United Nations and other international fora as alternate routes for distributing information that is censored in their countries. Reports released at international gatherings are picked up by media at home and disseminated through social media and other outlets.[70] With

---

[65] Elia Armstrong, "Integrity, Transparency and Accountability in Public Administration: Recent Trends, Regional and International Developments and Emerging Issues" (United Nations, Department of Economic and Social Affairs, 2005), 1–10.

[66] Claudio Ferraz and Frederico Finan, *Exposing Corrupt Politicians: The Effects of Brazil's Publicly Released Audits on Electoral Outcomes* (Rochester: Social Science Research Network, June 1, 2007), http://papers.ssrn.com/abstract=997867.

[67] Ibid., 4.

[68] Dong Chul Shim and Tae Ho Eom, "E-Government and Anti-Corruption: Empirical Analysis of International Data," *International Journal of Public Administration* 31 (2008): 298–316.

[69] Margaret Keck and Kathryn Sikkink, *Activists Beyond Borders: Advocacy Networks in International Politics* (Ithaca: Cornell University Press, 1998).

[70] Alexandru Grigorescu, "International Organizations and Government Transparency: Linking the International and Domestic Realms," *International Studies Quarterly* 47 (2003): 643–667.

the increasing pace of global information exchange, this transnational effect may be an important pathway to greater transparency at all levels, making it more difficult for repressive states to limit access to information.

There is some evidence of a link between transparency and peace, although only under certain conditions. In his study of international crises involving the UN and multinational security negotiations, Dan Lindley finds that increased transparency can be an important part of successful peace operations, particularly in the context of multifaceted and well-resourced UN peacekeeping missions.[71] In these settings information programs can dispel false rumors, encourage cooperation and facilitate elections. Lindley cautions, however, that transparency may not be effective for peacebuilding purposes when conflict-related biases are deeply entrenched and local adversaries do not have effective information dissemination capabilities. Kristin Lord also notes that while transparency may lead to the dissemination of information about peace preferences, it can also give voice to extremists and the purveyors of violence.[72]

Information dissemination alone is not enough to counter corruption. The content of the information being released matters greatly. Just as the right of free speech can be a license for some to spread hatred and intolerance, information campaigns by governments and insurgent groups can be a significant factor in exacerbating armed conflict.[73] For groups such as the so-called Islamic State, the cyber-jihad of hate and extremism on the Internet is a vital component of their political military strategy. In this case the challenge becomes one of developing and disseminating counternarratives against the glorification of violence and intolerance, while simultaneously exposing and countering corrupt practices that may drive communities toward extremism.

While transparency is crucial to the exercise of democracy and the performance of government, and may help in some circumstances to advance peacebuilding operations, it is not sufficient by itself and comprises only one component of peaceful governance. As we have emphasized throughout this volume, multiple interlocking conditions are required to reduce the likelihood of armed conflict. Inclusive and participatory forms of

---

[71] Dan Lindley, *Promoting Peace with Information: Transparency as a Tool of Security Regimes* (Princeton University Press, 2007).

[72] Kristin M. Lord, *The Perils and Promise of Global Transparency: Why the Information Revolution May Not Lead to Security, Democracy, or Peace* (SUNY Press, 2012).

[73] Bernard I. Finel and Kristin M. Lord, "The Surprising Logic of Transparency," *International Studies Quarterly* 43 (1999): 315–339.

decision making and the delivery of the full range of public goods are necessary foundations for sustainable peace. Accountability is an essential part of this equation, and can be aided by transparency and the free flow of information, but the prevention of corruption and violence ultimately depends on the power of an engaged citizenry.

ANTICORRUPTION AGENCIES

Many countries have established formal governmental institutions for taming corruption. Some of these have prosecutorial authority with ties to law enforcement institutions that can impose sanctions, a process Jonathan Fox terms "hard accountability."[74] Research shows that in the right circumstances such institutional arrangements can be effective.[75] Particularly useful are judicial mechanisms for addressing specific corruption-related crimes.

In countries with well-developed systems for the rule of law, investigators, prosecutors, judges and police officers are on the front line of the battle against corruption. The problem is that law enforcement agencies themselves can be corrupted and in some countries are predators rather than protectors. In many developing countries the institutional capabilities and resources needed for enforcing the law are not available. As noted above, highly developed countries tend to experience lower levels of perceived corruption, partly because they have stronger and more mature legal and judicial institutions.

An approach taken in some countries is formalizing the review system in a specific institution separate from other forms of law enforcement. In the United States the nearly 100-year-old Government Accountability Office (GAO) reports to Congress and provides investigative reports and audits on US government agencies and activities. The GAO serves as an effective source of independent information, but it has no enforcement powers of its own, other than to issue legal decisions and opinions in rulings on contract bids and agency rule making. The agency has a direct connection to Congress, however, which gives it considerable influence in holding agencies accountable and shaping corrective legislation. Over the decades the GAO has effectively exposed and helped to end many cases of waste, fraud and

---

[74] Jonathan Fox, "The Uncertain Relationship between Transparency and Accountability," *Development in Practice* 17 (2007): 663–671.
[75] Fidelma White and Kathryn Hollingsworth, *Audit, Accountability and Government* (Oxford: Clarendon Press, 1999).

abuse. The agency reports that it recovered or saved more than $54 billion in government funds in fiscal year 2014.[76]

Notwithstanding its benefits, the GAO is not designed to address deeper structures of corruption that enable powerful elites to dominate government decision making. Research suggests that government-created anticorruption agencies are rarely effective. A large-scale literature review of 150 studies on the subject by the Norwegian Agency for Development Cooperation shows that very few top-down anticorruption programs are successful.[77] A Transparency International study confirms that these agencies are limited by the governmental systems in which they are embedded. They are "hampered by structural factors linked to the political economy of government auditing, in particular the dysfunctional linkages between government auditing, legislative oversight and judicial control."[78] Anticorruption agencies generally have little impact in addressing the larger drivers of corruption or improving fiscal performance.[79]

A major problem with top-down accountability initiatives, writes Beyerle, is that they are often established with no citizen involvement or ownership.[80] In the absence of public involvement and fully developed institutional frameworks, anticorruption agencies are often merely window dressing – intended to create the impression of action without actually addressing the root causes of the problem. In some cases elites hijack anticorruption efforts and steer them toward innocuous activities that do not jeopardize their interests.

THE ROLE OF CIVIL SOCIETY

Political accountability comes not only through the structures of state but from the demands of society. Citizens in many countries serve as watchdogs and use the tools of advocacy, research, digital media and protest

---

[76] GAO, U.S. Government Accountability Office, "GAO at a Glance," www.gao.gov/about/gglance.html (November 18, 2015).

[77] Norwegian Agency for Development Cooperation, *Anti-Corruption Approaches: A Literature Review* (Oslo, January 2009), www.norad.no/globalassets/import-2162015-80434-am/www.norad.no-ny/filarkiv/vedlegg-til-publikasjoner/study2_2008.pdf.

[78] Carlos Santiso, "Auditing, Accountability, and Anti-corruption: How Relevant are Autonomous Auditing Agencies?," in Transparency International, *Global Corruption Report 2007: Corruption in Judicial Systems* (Cambridge University Press, 2007), 360, 362.

[79] Patrick Meagher, "Anti-corruption Agencies: Rhetoric Versus Reality," *Journal of Policy Reform* 8 (2005): 69–103.

[80] Beyerle, *Curtailing Corruption*, 269.

when necessary to hold public institutions accountable and prevent or halt wrongdoing. Civil society has a solid record of investigating and disclosing abuse and pressuring governments to reform.[81] Social movements and citizen campaigns build confidence and mutual trust among those who participate and help to strengthen the anticorruption constituency within society.

Perhaps the leading nongovernmental organization against corruption is Transparency International (TI). Since its founding in 1993, TI has developed into a major institution and worldwide network, tracking corruption in every country with its widely cited annual ratings. The influence of the organization goes beyond the publication of reports that expose corruption. TI also performs an agenda-setting function, strengthening the social norm against fraud and abuse of power. The organization has made a significant contribution in identifying and asserting the role of civil society as a previously missing factor in efforts to contain corruption.[82]

The movement against corruption has gained ground in many parts of the world, in some cases sparking dramatic change. In September 2015 Guatemalan President Otto Pérez Molina and dozens of other senior Guatemalan officials were forced to resign after weeks of mass nonviolent protest. The president and vice president were stripped of legal immunity by the Guatemalan Congress and were promptly arrested on criminal charges. The unprecedented mass movement that made this possible, mobilizing under the demand "Resign Already," emerged quickly and unexpectedly following the release of a scathing report of government criminality by the International Commission Against Impunity in Guatemala, a United Nations-sponsored agency established in 2007.[83] The agency's report documented a violent criminal network, referred to as "The Line," operating in the Molina administration with direct links to the president and vice president.[84] In the election following the ouster

---

[81] Alina Mungiu, "Corruption: Diagnosis and Treatment," *Journal of Democracy* 17 (2006): 86–99; Budi Setiyono and Ross H. McLeod, "Civil Society Organisations' Contribution to the Anti-Corruption Movement in Indonesia," *Bulletin of Indonesian Economic Studies* 46 (2010): 347–70.

[82] Fredrik Galtung and Jeremy Pope, "The Global Coalition Against Corruption: Evaluating Transparency International," in *The Self-Restraining State: Power and Accountability in New Democracies*, edited by Andreas Schedler (Boulder: Lynne Rienner Publishers, 1999), 257–282.

[83] Jeff Abbot, "Popular Movement Takes Down Guatemala's President," *Waging Nonviolence*, September 5, 2015, http://wagingnonviolence.org/feature/popular-movement-takes-guatemalan-president/.

[84] Washington Office on Latin America, "The International Commission against Impunity in Guatemala (CICIG): An Innovative Instrument for Fighting Criminal Organizations and Strengthening the Rule of Law" (Washington, DC: WOLA, July 2015).

of Molina former comedian Jimmy Morales won the presidency as a new "honest face" with a mandate to "fight against corruption."[85] The Guatemalan movement is a striking illustration of the power of protest to overthrow corrupt leaders.

A similar example emerged in South Korea in late 2016 as massive protests demanded the ouster of President Park Geun-hye for her involvement in a government influence-peddling scheme. Huge crowds assembled in Seoul on successive Saturdays in October and November to demand Park's impeachment. The protests included the largest demonstration in the country's history.[86] Shortly afterwards the National Assembly voted overwhelmingly to impeach the president and suspended her from office.

Beyerle examines many other civil society efforts to challenge corruption. In India, the organization '5th Pillar' created and distributed a zero-rupee note for citizens to present to those demanding bribes. The group also assisted citizens in filing petitions under the Right to Information law that was passed at the behest of a previous anticorruption movement. The law helps citizens obtain information about public officials who abuse their office. 5th Pillar derives its name from what the organization considers the four pillars of democracy: legislature, executive branch, judiciary and the media. It argues that a healthy democracy needs a fifth pillar, an engaged, active citizenry fighting to rid the country of corruption.[87] Movements in many other countries have similar philosophies and are actively mobilizing the power of civil resistance to fight against corruption.

One of the lessons of these citizen efforts, according to Beyerle, is the need to combine top-down and bottom-up approaches. Official government anticorruption agencies work best when they are supported or pressured by active social movements. Civic initiatives gain legitimacy and effectiveness when they utilize information from official reports and hold wrongdoers accountable to the rule of law. Movements that educate and mobilize citizens help to make top-down mechanisms more accountable. Civil society movements give voice to those who are most often victimized by corruption. They create 'islands of honesty' that can spread

[85] Fernando del Rincón, Rafel Romo and Catherine E. Shoichet, "Guatemalan Election: Comedian Jimmy Morales Poised to become President," *CNN.com*, October 26, 2015, www.cnn.com/2015/10/25/americas/guatemala-election/.

[86] Choe Sang-Hun, "Protest Against South Korean President Estimated to the Largest Yet," *New York Times*, November 26, 2016, www.nytimes.com/2016/11/26/world/asia/korea-park-geun-hye-protests.html.

[87] Beyerle, *Curtailing Corruption*, 140.

within society and give credibility and strength to official institutions.[88] They help to alter the balance of power between corrupt elites and ordinary citizens and create political will for good governance.[89]

CONCLUSION

The struggle to contain corruption is inextricably linked to the challenge of enhancing accountability and the quality of governance. It is especially important to expose official wrongdoing and mobilize citizen involvement. As we have seen, top-down anti-corruption programs can be helpful, but by themselves they are often insufficient to overcome entrenched venality. Civil society is also needed, often motivated by the 'disinfectant' of transparency. Revelations of public abuse by official agencies can spark citizen outrage and force the 'thieves of state' from office, as occurred in Guatemala. The combination of citizen mobilization and multilateral monitoring can be potent, a form of synergy that illustrates the 'new' hybrid forms of governance that are addressing public policy abuses.

Corruption is the antithesis of good governance. Some may benefit, but the common good suffers. The softer corruption of patronage may provide public goods to particular social groups, and serve as a rudimentary form of political representation to 'buy off' aggrieved communities, but by their nature patronage systems cannot overcome the broader conditions of exclusion that can lead to conflict. Greater equity of access across the board is the best approach.

The long-term solution to corruption is the development of fully mature democracies and effective governmental institutions that give voice to all communities and provide public goods to meet the needs of society. The literature shows a significant connection between well-established systems of democracy and honest government. As we examine in the next chapter, democracy is an essential element of good governance and at a high threshold is the foundation of more peaceful governance.

---

[88] Taub, "How 'Islands of Honesty' Can Crush Corruption."
[89] Beyerle, *Curtailing Corruption*, 245–246.

PART III

DIMENSIONS

7

Democracy

In the first part of the book we examined the capacities of governance – the provision of security and the delivery of necessary social services – as requirements for peace. This was followed by a section on the qualities of governance – inclusion, participation and accountability – and their relation to the prevention of ethnic and territorial disputes, the empowerment of women, and the containment of corruption. In this third section of the book we consider the dimensions of governance that relate to the distribution of political power and the management of economic activity. The type of political regime and the degree of economic development in a society are among the most significant determinants of the prospects for peace. We begin in this chapter with an exploration of the complex relationship between democracy and peace. This is followed by two chapters that review the implications for peace of different approaches to economic development and the role of market forces. In each of these chapters we focus on the capacities and qualities of governance that are most likely to reduce the risk of armed conflict and create the conditions for peace.

No aspect of governance is more frequently associated with peace than democracy, and for good reason. The linkages between democracy and peace are significant, although the relationship between the two is more complex than commonly assumed. Governance and democracy are often considered synonymous, but the two terms refer to distinct and separate phenomena. Governance is a broader and more encompassing term. It incorporates regime type, which may or may not be democratic, but it also encompasses regime capacity. Governance is 'good' when the regime is inclusive and participatory, when citizens can voice their grievances and hold leaders accountable, and when governing institutions have the capacity to deliver public goods and services equitably to all major social groups. As Norris emphasizes, all of these dimensions are necessary for democratic governance to foster peace.[1] Democracy is an essential quality for peace when it is fully developed institutionally and linked to effective governance capacity.

Democracy is the ability of people to have a voice in public decision making, and the presence of political constraints that hold leaders and institutions accountable. Robert Dahl defines democracy as "an orderly and peaceful process by means of which a majority of citizens can induce the government to do what they most want it to do and to avoid doing what they most want it not to do."[2] Democracy is a system, writes Lipset, that supplies regular constitutional opportunities for changing governing officials, provides social mechanisms for resolving problems of decision-making among conflicting interest groups, and allows the largest possible part of the population to influence these decisions through their ability to choose among alternative contenders for political office.[3]

These definitions distill democracy to essential functions of voice and veto, as noted in Chapter Six. Voice refers to the degree and form of citizen participation in selecting and holding leaders accountable, while veto includes institutional and political checks on the authority of decision makers. Undergirding these functions are equitable guarantees of freedom, participation, inclusion, openness, and representativeness. Also necessary are systems of accountability and constraint to hold political leaders broadly responsible to the public interest. As the analysis below indicates, all are crucial to the prevention of war and armed conflict.

When we refer to democracy here we are not suggesting a narrow focus on Western-style democracy, or implying that the United States or other democratic states are inherently peaceful. Democracy encompasses much more than holding an election or having a parliament. It includes civilian control of the military, as discussed in Chapter Two, and the right of citizens to speak, assemble and worship freely without state interference. It encompasses economic and social freedoms, as we examine in Chapter Eight, and gender equality, as we emphasize in Chapter Five. Democracy is most likely to foster peace when it is embodied in fully developed and mature institutions that meet the standards of inclusiveness, participation and accountability.

[1] Norris, *Making Democratic Governance Work*.
[2] Robert Dahl, *Democracy and its Critics* (New Haven: Yale University Press, 1989), 95.
[3] Lipset, "Some Social Requisites of Democracy," 71.

Mature democracy makes armed conflict less likely, as the studies below indicate, but it is not a panacea or guarantee of peace. Democratic institutions allow people to voice their opinions and influence policy, but public opinion at times may be intolerant and chauvinist, favoring policies that marginalize other communities. In sharply polarized societies, political candidates may appeal to narrow communal interests to win public office. In Cyprus the Greek and Turkish populations each have democratic freedoms, but they use these rights to elect officials who speak for their respective communities rather than the common good. In Bosnia and Herzegovina, Serbian, Croat and Bosnian voters and political representatives pursue the interests of their respective communities rather than the building of a unified state. History teaches that democratic systems can be susceptible to demagogic appeals of intolerance that exacerbate the risk of armed violence. The countries of democratic Europe have seen this recently with the rise of nativist political forces and greater hostility toward minorities and immigrants.

The democratic peace effect has several components. The first and most familiar is that mature democracies rarely wage war on one another. While there are limits and qualifications to this statement, the democratic peace effect between states stands as one of the most well documented findings in social science. When considering the problem of intrastate conflict, however, the influence of democracy is more uncertain. Fully developed democracies have fewer civil conflicts and are less likely to use violence against their own citizens. In this sense institutionally mature democracy helps to sustain peace. In partial democracies and countries making the transition to democracy, however, the impacts of democratization are often destabilizing and may increase the risk of armed conflict and civil war. The democratic peace effect within states only kicks in when democracy reaches a high threshold, as measured in the Polity scale and other indicators of democracy.

The peaceful influence of democracy within states is strongly correlated with gender equality and high levels of economic development. The evidence suggests that democracy contributes to peace only in the context of institutionally consistent and inclusive governance systems that provide the full range of public goods to all major communities. For researchers this creates dilemmas of reverse causality and makes it difficult to reach firm conclusions about the relationship between democracy and internal peace. We explore these relationships below and attempt to unpack the causal connections. We identify the distinctive elements of democratic governance that are most likely to reduce the risk of armed conflict within states. We also explore the linkage between political rights and democracy and the worrisome trend in recent years of greater challenges to democracy and increasing threats to peace.

THE DEMOCRATIC PEACE BETWEEN STATES

The idea of a direct relationship between democracy and interstate peace was famously articulated by Immanuel Kant more than 200 years ago. Kant based his approach on three fundamental principles, which he called "definitive articles": (1) democratic governance, (2) a federation of nations, and (3) the "cosmopolitan law" of mutual respect through trade and interdependence. He argued that the combination of mutual democracy, international cooperation and economic interdependence would help to prevent war (see Figure 7.1). All three dimensions are necessary for peace, Kant believed. No single factor alone would be sufficient – it is the unique combination of all three that creates the essential foundations for more peaceful relationships among nations. In recent decades these principles have been tested in rigorous empirical studies and have stood up well. Many scholars have found support for the mutually reinforcing impact of democracy, economic integration and international organization on the prospects for peace – what Nils Petter Gleditsch terms the "liberal tripod."[4] The evidence shows that Kant was remarkably prescient in identifying the fundamental political and economic conditions of peace.

Many researchers have confirmed the democratic peace phenomenon.[5] Especially significant has been the work of Bruce Russett and John Oneal, presented in the important 2001 book, *Triangulating Peace: Democracy, Interdependence, and International Organizations*. Russett and Oneal examine every incident of armed conflict between nations from 1886 to 1992, drawing from the Correlates of War database and other widely accepted sources of empirical evidence. They find that the relationship between democracy and peace is statistically significant throughout the entire period and becomes stronger after 1945 as the number of democratic states increases.[6]

---

[4] Nils Petter Gleditsch, "The Liberal Moment Fifteen Years On," *International Studies Quarterly* 52 (2008): 698.

[5] Bruce Russett, *Grasping the Democratic Peace: Principles for a Post-Cold War World* (Princeton University Press, 1993), 4.

[6] Bruce Russett and John R. Oneal, *Triangulating Peace: Democracy, Interdependence, and International Organizations* (New York: W.W. Norton & Company, 2001), 113.

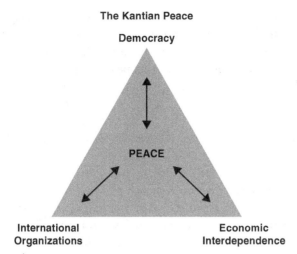

FIGURE 7.1. The Kantian peace
Source: Bruce Russett, "Peace in the Twenty-First Century," *Current History*, January 2010, 11–16

Over the years Russett and Oneal have refined the analytic dimensions of their model and given it precise quantitative definition. The theory provides a statement of statistical probability, not an assertion of certainty. The proposition is not that democracies are always peaceful, but rather that, all else being equal, two mature democratic states are significantly less likely to go to war with each other than non-democratic states.[7] Democracy is best at preventing conflict when it is comprehensive. "The higher the level of democracy a state achieves," the authors conclude, "the more peaceful that state is likely to be."[8] These findings are highly robust and hold constant across a wide range of data sets and different independent variables. The relationship between mutual democracy and peaceful political relations is one of the most consistently valid propositions in international relations.

AN INTERNAL PEACE EFFECT?

The classic statement of Kantian peace theory applies to inter-state conflict and focuses on dyadic relations between states. This neglects the most common form of armed violence in the world today – civil conflicts and one-sided violence within states. Here the relationship between

[7] Russett, *Grasping the Democratic Peace*, 86.
[8] Russett and Oneal, *Triangulating Peace*, 122.

democracy and peace is less certain and more subject to qualification. Researchers have searched for evidence of a democratic peace effect within states, but the results have been inconclusive. Some studies show a link between democracy and internal peace, but this effect could be the result of higher levels of economic development rather than democracy per se. The peace effect is also linked to gender equality and the state's capacity to deliver public goods.

Hegre et al. find that mature "institutionally consistent" democratic regimes are unlikely to experience the onset of civil war.[9] They find firm evidence for what they term a "democratic civil peace" effect.[10] Walter looks at the problem of war recurrence and observes a similar relationship between levels of democracy and the likelihood of internal armed conflict, although she links this peace effect to levels of economic development. Countries characterized by open political systems and economic well-being – i.e., developed democracies – have a much lower probability of renewed civil war than autocratic countries with low levels of economic development.[11] She notes that major civil wars do not occur in mature democratic states. She concludes:

> It may be that liberal democracies are really the only types of regimes that can truly insulate themselves from violent internal challenges. This suggests that citizens who are able to express their preferences about alternative policies and leaders, who are guaranteed civil liberties in their daily lives and in acts of political participation, are less likely to become soldiers. Offering citizens a real outlet for their concerns and having a government that is open to democratic change considerably reduces the likelihood of a civil war.[12]

Gleditsch and his colleagues reach a similar conclusion in their 2009 study for the *Handbook of War Studies*. Their research shows that democratic governance is beneficial for the reduction of civil war. They find that democracy is negatively related to the onset and severity of civil war.[13] Mature democracies experience fewer and less intense armed conflicts, although once a conflict begins it tends to persist.

[9] Håvard Hegre, Tanja Ellingsen, Scott Gates and Nils Petter Gleditsch, "Toward a Democratic Civil Peace? Democracy, Political Change, and Civil War, 1816–1992," *American Political Science Review* 95, no. 1 (2001): 38.

[10] Ibid., 44.

[11] Barbara Walter, "Does Conflict Beget Conflict? Explaining Recurring Civil War," *Journal of Peace Research* 41, no. 3 (2004): 372.

[12] Ibid., 384–385.

[13] Nils Petter Gleditsch, Håvard Hegre and Håvard Strand, "Democracy and Civil War," in Manus I. Midlarsky, *Handbook of War Studies III: The Intrastate Dimension* (Ann Arbor: University of Michigan Press, 2009), 155–156.

While debate continues whether democracy reduces the risk of conflict onset, there is no doubt that civil conflicts within democratic states are less lethal than in authoritarian settings. Bethany Lacina assesses the severity of civil conflicts by measuring casualty levels according to several variables: regime type, state capacity, ethnic and religious diversity, and the impact of foreign military intervention. She finds that the political characteristics of a regime are the strongest predictor of conflict severity. Democratic governments experience much lower casualty levels during civil conflict than autocratic states. Civil wars occurring within democratic states have less than half the battle deaths of conflicts in non-democracies.[14] Gleditsch et al. come to similar conclusions. They find that fatalities from armed conflicts in non-democracies exceed those in democracies by three to one.[15]

State-sponsored violence against civilians is also less likely to occur in democracies. In his book, *Death by Government*, Rudolph Rummel assembles a vast amount of data and numerous examples demonstrating the myriad ways by which governments kill their own citizens – directly through genocide and mass terror and indirectly through starvation and repression. He finds a stark contrast between the behavior of autocracies and democracies. Autocratic governments readily "slaughter their people by the tens of millions; in contrast, many democracies can barely bring themselves to execute even serial murderers."[16] Genocidal killing by governments is directly associated with the absence of democracy.[17] As Rummel documents the appalling litany of governments murdering their people, he is unequivocal about what he considers the necessary remedy: "The solution is democracy. The course of action is to foster freedom."[18] Other studies confirm that one-sided violence by the state against its citizens is significantly more likely in autocracies than democracies.[19]

Barbara Harff's research on genocidal violence comes to similar conclusions. Her examination of 126 cases of internal war and regime collapse finds that autocratic regimes are much more likely to experience genocidal

---

[14] Bethany Lacina, "Explaining the Severity of Civil Wars," *Journal of Conflict Resolution* 50, no. 2 (2006): 287.

[15] Gleditsch et al., "Democracy and Civil War," 175.

[16] Rudolph J. Rummel, *Death by Government* (Piscataway: Transaction Books, 1994), 2.

[17] Rudolph J. Rummel, *Statistics of Democide* (Piscataway: Transaction Books, 1997), 6–10.

[18] Rummel, *Death by Government*, xxi.

[19] Kristine Eck and Lisa Hultman, "One-Sided Violence Against Civilians in War: Insights from New Fatality Data," *Journal of Peace Research* 44, no. 2 (2007): 244.

violence in these circumstances.[20] The lowest levels of mass killing occur in states with a high degree of economic interdependence, which is characteristic of mature democratic regimes with high levels of GDP per capita.[21] Her conclusion is that states are less likely to employ genocidal violence when they have inclusive democratic systems and trade extensively with other countries.

Notwithstanding these results, significant doubts remain about the impact of democracy on civil conflict. Observations of a link between democracy and internal peace may be due to other influences, particularly economic development and higher levels of per capita income. Economic and social development may be the primary causal factor, with democracy as the dependent variable. Higher levels of economic development and GDP per capita make both democracy and peace more likely. This supports the argument of those who contend that the development of democracy depends upon the rise and expansion of the middle class, which is associated with economic development and rising incomes.

This possibility of reverse causality explains why some scholars find little or no evidence of a link between democracy and internal peace. When controlling for development and related factors, researchers often find democracy exerting little or no direct effect on the risk of conflict onset. In their 2004 study Collier and Hoeffler dismiss the influence of democracy and argue that economic development is the most significant factor in determining civil peace.[22] Hegre argues that the peace effect within states depends on the degree of development and the depth of the democratic system in question. Institutionally mature and consolidated democracies have less conflict than semi-democracies.[23] Most regimes that fit this description are in high-income countries with stable institutions.

It's clear that the presence of democratic institutions alone is not sufficient to guarantee peace. Several states that are credited with having competitive elections and functioning democratic institutions – Turkey, Israel, India, Sri Lanka and the Philippines – have experienced outbreaks of armed conflict in recent years. Norris shows in her empirical analyses that "by itself *the strength of liberal democracy is not significantly related*

---

[20] Barbara Harff, "No Lessons Learned from the Holocaust? Assessing the Risks of Genocide and Political Mass Murder since 1955," *American Political Science Review* 97, no. 1 (February 2003): 66

[21] Ibid., 70.

[22] Collier and Hoeffler, "Greed and Grievance in Civil War."

[23] Håvard Hegre, "Democracy and Armed Conflict," *Journal of Peace Research* 51, no. 2 (2014): 1–2.

to the degree of internal armed conflict within a society" [emphasis in original].[24] It is the combination of democracy with high per capita income and effective governance and institutional capacity that accounts for the internal peace effect. For governments to maintain civil peace they must be capable of not only raising living standards but of delivering public goods in an equitable manner and preventing abuses of one group by another.[25]

A DEMOCRATIC THRESHOLD

The democratic peace effect is linked to economic and institutional development. The capacity of governments to deliver public goods is tied to mechanisms of political accountability and opportunities for citizens and communities to voice their grievances and concerns. Higher levels of per capita income are strongly associated with lower conflict risk, but as Hegre observes, economic development presupposes a certain degree of social freedom and political openness, along with legal guarantees of property rights and contractual agreements. Economic development tends to be most effective as an influence for peace when it is embedded in formalized democratic institutions and procedures.[26]

The democratic peace effect within states depends upon the strength and maturity of democratic institutions. Studies of political repression and state violence confirm this analysis and show that domestic peace depends upon the degree of democratic representativeness and inclusivity. Christian Davenport and other scholars show that the severity of repression and human rights abuse is directly related to a state's level of democracy. The higher and more mature the level of democracy within a state, the lower the probability of violent state repression.[27] Institutionally developed democratic political systems are less likely to engage in violent practices such as torture, disappearances and mass killing. This is one of the most consistent results in empirical research on violence within states.[28]

---

[24] Norris, *Making Democratic Governance Work*, 181.
[25] Hegre, "Democracy and Armed Conflict," 9–10.
[26] Ibid., 9.
[27] Christian Davenport, *State Repression and the Domestic Democratic Peace* (Cambridge University Press, 2007), 11, 176.
[28] Christian Davenport and David A. Armstrong, "Democracy and the Violation of Human Rights: A Statistical Analysis from 1976 to 1996," *American Journal of Political Science* 48, no. 3 (2004): 538–539.

The pacifying effect of democracy occurs only in states where political freedom and democratic accountability are fully institutionalized. Davenport and David Armstrong posit the existence of a democratic threshold above which repression is less likely. Below that level, where democracy is only partial, they find no discernible difference in the scale of human rights abuse. Democracy decreases repression only after a state has attained a certain threshold level of maturity, which can be measured on the Polity scale. They argue: "our empirical findings lead us to conclude that only those regimes with fully developed institutional practices and mass political behavior consistent with democratic principles will yield any pacifying effect on state repression."[29]

Governance systems that are inclusive and participatory are less likely to experience repressive violence. The greatest influence in limiting state repression is associated with the highest levels of political opportunity and participation. According to Davenport, "across types of conflict and repressive strategies, voice (specifically competition/participation) is ... the most powerful mechanism of pacification, outpacing the influence of veto (specifically general executive constraints)."[30] Voice is most significant, Davenport argues, because citizens who can influence political decision making through mechanisms of representation are less likely to use violence to be heard.

Bruce Bueno de Mesquita and his colleagues reach similar conclusions. States with high levels of democracy have superior human rights records and protect their citizens from violent abuse and genocide. Political participation at the level of multiparty competition appears to be the most significant factor in generating this effect.[31] Improvements in a state's level of democracy short of full democracy are not enough. Only fully accountable and participatory democracies are able to guarantee full human rights and freedom from state repression.

As democracies become more mature, their risk of violent repression and armed conflict diminishes. Discriminatory policies increase the risk of civil war, while guarantees of political freedom reduce that risk.[32] The more participatory and open the political governance system the lower the chances of armed conflict and political violence. Peace is more likely

---

[29] Ibid., 539, 552.

[30] Davenport, *State Repression*, 31, 62.

[31] Bruce Bueno de Mesquita, Feryal Cherif, George Downs and Alastair Smith, "A Closer Look at Democracy and Human Rights," Thinking Inside the Box, New York University Department of Politics, http://politics.as.nyu.edu/object/politics.facultyData.insidethebox.

[32] Dixon, "What Causes Civil Wars?" 718–719.

when people are free to participate actively in choosing political decision makers and when diverse interests have effective political representation. Programs that foster citizen participation, inclusive institutions, accountability mechanisms and greater public oversight bolster the conditions for peace.

PARTICIPATION AND POWER SHARING

Democracy comes in many different forms. Multiple structures are possible, ranging from systems that concentrate power in a centralized executive to proportional parliamentary systems that distribute power among representatives from local districts. Many permutations and combinations are possible among democratic systems, but three broad categories can be distinguished: majoritarian, presidential and proportional representation. Each offers different ways for addressing issues related to group interest, executive accountability and public participation. Majoritarian parliamentary systems reflect pluralist interests, presidential systems have strong executive authority, and proportional representation systems are highly inclusive and participatory. As noted in Chapter 4, proportional representation systems are most conducive to peace, especially in societies characterized by deep ethnic cleavages. They offer the greatest opportunities for participation and inclusion and reduce the conflict risk associated with the exclusion and marginalization of significant communities.

All models of democracy offer some degree of power sharing, but parliamentary systems based on proportional representation have the most elaborate structures for sharing and dispersing decision-making authority. As Lijphart demonstrates, consensus-based democracies tend to have social policies such as lower incarceration rates and higher welfare spending that are associated with lower rates of state repression and civil conflict.[33] Participatory systems of representation are able to resolve political and social differences in ways that reduce the risk of armed conflict.

For the purpose of preventing armed violence in divided societies, proportional representation systems are better than majoritarian or presidential systems. Larry Diamond argues that majoritarian systems are ill-advised for countries with deep ethnic, regional, religious or other polarizing divisions. The imperative in these settings is to "avoid

---

[33] Lijphart, *Patterns of Democracy*.

broad and indefinite exclusion from power of any significant group."[34] Presidential systems are also problematic. They create zero-sum dynamics, Juan Linz observes, fostering a 'winner-takes-all' mentality that can increase the risk of conflict.[35] When the presidency is the only or preponderant form of political power, electoral losers may be tempted to employ non-democratic means for gaining power. This is the problem in a number of states, where elected leaders from predominant political parties exercise sweeping powers and build vast patronage networks to help them become 'president for life.' Parliamentary systems avoid these problems by dispersing power, constraining executive authority, providing opportunities for minority representation, and treating all constituencies and identity groups in an even-handed manner.[36] This is not to suggest that parliamentary systems are superior in every respect, but for the purpose of reducing conflict risk, they have advantages over other systems.

Empirical evidence confirms the benefits for peace of proportional representation forms of democracy. A study of cases from 1960 to 1994 finds that countries with proportional representation systems have the lowest probability of experiencing a civil war.[37] Among countries in the sample with a majoritarian system, the probability of civil war occurrence was 8.3 percent; for presidential systems it was 7 percent. Among democratic countries with proportional parliamentary representation the percentage was zero. None of the countries in the sample with an inclusive and participatory form of parliamentary democracy experienced civil war.[38]

Analysis of civil war termination provides similar results and confirms the importance of inclusive and representational forms of democracy. Madhav Joshi examines post-war transitions to democracy, which are often fragile and can revert to armed conflict. Drawing from data on post-war transitions during the years 1946 to 2005, Joshi finds that proportional representation parliamentary systems are more likely than majoritarian or presidential systems to sustain a peaceful transition to

---

[34] Larry Diamond, *Developing Democracy: Toward Consolidation* (Baltimore: Johns Hopkins University Press, 1999), 104.

[35] Juan J. Linz, "The Perils of Presidentialism," *Journal of Democracy* 1 (Winter 1990); see the discussion of Linz's theory in Scott Mainwaring and Matthew S. Shugart, "Juan Linz, Presidentialism and Democracy: A Critical Appraisal," *Comparative Politics* 29, no. 4 (1997): 449–471.

[36] Lijphart, "Constitutional Design for Divided Societies," 100.

[37] Marta Reynal-Querol, "Political Systems, Stability and Civil Wars," *Defence and Peace Economics* 13, no. 6 (2002): 466, 481.

[38] Ibid., 477.

democracy. Proportional representation systems have almost double the transition survival rate of majoritarian systems and also have a higher survival rate than presidential systems.[39] Governance systems that provide greater opportunities for political participation are less likely to experience democratic failure and civil war recurrence.

More fine-grained analysis shows that particular forms of proportional representation are better than others. Sustainable peace after armed conflict is most likely in systems with multimember districts of limited size in which representatives are selected through a party list process. Research suggests that the closed list model is especially effective in sustaining strong and representative political parties, which can provide checks on executive power. They also facilitate coalition building and reduce incentives for personalistic voting. Closed list systems are not without flaws, and have been criticized for conferring too much power on political party leaders, but they have the best record for being associated with the prevention of armed conflict.[40]

THE RISKS OF PARTIAL DEMOCRACY

The internal democratic peace effect is limited to specific conditions and subject to significant qualification. It exists only when states have reached a high threshold of democracy. It does not apply to partial or incomplete democracies, referred to as anocracies. These are states that have characteristics of both democracy and authoritarianism or are in the process of transitioning from dictatorship to democracy. Anocracies have weak political institutions and inadequate systems of representative governance.[41] They tend to experience high levels of political instability and state failure and face a greater probability of armed conflict. They are also more likely to repress their own citizens, which can lead to civil war. Hegre et al. observe that regimes scoring in the middle range on the democracy–autocracy index "have a significantly higher probability of civil war than either democracies or autocracies."[42]

When regimes are transitioning from autocracy to democracy, they often lack fully developed institutional means for accommodating

---

[39] Madhav Joshi, "Inclusive Institutions and Stability of Transition toward Democracy in Post-civil War States," *Democratization* (2012): 18–19.

[40] Cammett and Malesky, "Power Sharing in Post Conflict Societies," 982–1016.

[41] Edward D. Mansfield and Jack Snyder, "Pathways to War in Democratic Transitions," *International Organization* 63, no. 3 (2009): 384.

[42] Hegre et al., "Toward a Democratic Civil Peace?" 42.

political differences. The initial stages of democratization lead to greater human rights and political freedom without an accompanying increase in the state's capacity to deliver public goods and maintain order. Political leaders begin to introduce mechanisms of representative democracy, which facilitates social and political mobilization, but the transitioning regime lacks basic governance capacity.[43] Political and ethnic communities have new opportunities to express political or territorial grievances, but political leaders are unable or unwilling to satisfy their demands. This gap between social expectations and state capabilities is a fundamental cause of armed conflict. It is a recipe for frustration and disillusionment, which can lead to instability and a greater risk of armed violence.

Jack Goldstone and his colleagues differentiate more precisely the states categorized as semi-democracies and divide them into three subcategories: partial autocracies, which hold competitive elections for national office but tightly control participation (such as Singapore); partial democracies, which choose chief executives in competitive elections that are not fully free and fair and have limited participation (such as Albania); and partial democracies that have a high degree of political factionalism (such as Thailand before the 2006 coup).[44] The greatest risk of instability and armed violence occurs in the context of polarized politics based on exclusivist identities or ideologies, in conjunction with weak and only partially democratic governance institutions. Semi-democracies are prone to armed conflict because they have weak systems of political accountability and representation, minimal checks and balances, and biased information flows – in short poor governance.[45]

As Figure 7.2 indicates, the number of authoritarian regimes has declined in recent decades, with a concomitant rise in the number of democracies, but also a parallel increase in anocracies. The democratic wave has ebbed in the last few years, however, prompting some scholars to ask "Is authoritarianism staging a comeback?"[46] Because the democratic transition has been partial and incomplete in many states, the post-1970s process of global democratization has not been accompanied by a parallel wave of global peace. Immature democracies and states attempting

---

[43] Norris, *Making Democratic Governance Work*, 38.
[44] Goldstone et al., "A Global Model for Forecasting Instability," 195–197.
[45] Matthijs Bogaards, "Measures of Democratization: From Degree to Type to War," *Political Research Quarterly* 63, no. 2 (2010): 478.
[46] Mathew Burrows and Maria J. Stephan, eds., *Is Authoritarianism Staging a Comeback?* (Washington, DC: Atlantic Council, 2015).

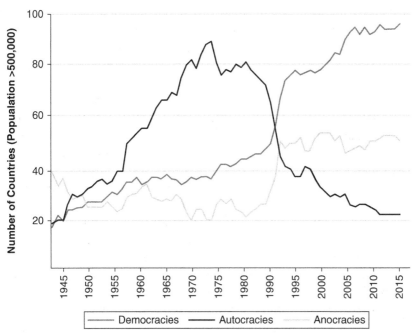

FIGURE 7.2. Global trends in governance, 1945–2015
Source: Center for Sustainable Peace

to transition away from dictatorship are conflict-prone and account for nearly all the armed conflicts and civil wars in the world today.

U-SHAPE OR J-CURVE?

When depicting the effect of regime type on the prospects for internal armed conflict, researchers identify an inverted U-shaped relationship with mature democracies and autocracies at lower risk of civil war and partially democratic states at a higher conflict risk. Fearon and Laitin observe this pattern and find that anocracies have a substantially higher risk of civil war.[47] Gledistch et al. confirm the U-shaped pattern of partial democracies being more prone to war than fully mature democracies or autocracies.[48] The problem with this U-shaped image is that it makes autocracies and mature democracies appear to be equivalent in experiencing less armed conflict. Autocracies have fewer armed conflicts than anocracies, but they are less peaceful than fully democratic

[47] Fearon and Laitin, "Ethnicity, Insurgency, and Civil War," 85.
[48] Gleditsch et al., "Democracy and Civil War," 171

regimes. Authoritarian governments may maintain a domestic peace of sorts, which Hegre et al. characterize as "the peace of a zoo," but this is hardly a durable civil peace.[49] Authoritarian regimes often maintain order through political control and repressive means, which can spark resistance and armed conflict.

Research confirms that authoritarian regimes are more prone to civil war and mass repression than democracies. Hanna Fjelde disputes the notion of an 'authoritarian peace.' She unpacks the authoritarian regime category to include not only military regimes and one-party dictatorships but also some multiparty regimes that are highly authoritarian. She identifies a category of states that have elections and opposition parties but maintain autocratic rule of a single leader (Uganda and Zimbabwe, for example). Countries broadly defined as authoritarian in this manner have higher levels of armed conflict than democracies. Of the 157 armed conflicts she examines during the period 1973 to 2004, more than 80 percent (a total of 130 conflicts) occurred in authoritarian regimes.[50] Among the various types of authoritarian regimes, military dictatorships have the highest level of armed conflict, along with multiparty autocracies.[51]

Other researchers report similar evidence. A study of 68 civil wars observed during the period 1960 to 1994 finds a strong association with high levels of autocracy. Among states with authoritarian governments, 11 percent experienced internal armed conflict, compared to only 4 percent among states rated free.[52] A related study examines data through 2007 and finds that autocracies have higher rates of civil war, with no evidence of civil war in any fully mature institutionally developed democratic state.[53] These studies confirm that autocracies have higher rates of armed conflict than democracies, although the risk among anocracies is even higher. If there is a U-shaped relationship, it is one in which autocracies and partial democracies have higher rates of armed conflict, while developed democracies have almost none.

We prefer to use the image of a J-curve pattern to depict the relationship between regime type and conflict risk. In his book *The J Curve*, Ian

[49] Hegre et al., "Toward a Democratic Civil Peace?" 44.

[50] Hanne Fjelde, "Generals, Dictators, and Kings: Authoritarian Regimes and Civil Conflict, 1973–2004," *Conflict Management and Peace Science* 27, no. 3 (2010): 206.

[51] Ibid., 213.

[52] Reynal-Querol, "Political Systems, Stability and Civil Wars," 477.

[53] Daniel Stockemer, "Regime Type and Civil War: A Re-evaluation of the Inverted U-relationship," *Global Change, Peace & Security*: formerly *Pacifica Review: Peace, Security & Global Change* 22, no. 3 (2010): 261–274.

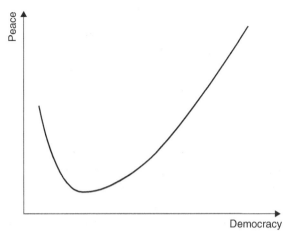

FIGURE 7.3. The J-curve to democracy and peace
Source: Ian Bremmer, "The J Curve: A New Way to Understand Why Nations Rise and Fall." Copyright © 2006 by Ian Bremmer. Reprinted with the permission of Simon & Schuster, Inc. All rights reserved

Bremmer evaluates states according to their stability (on the vertical axis) and openness (on the horizontal axis; see Figure 7.3). Stability is defined as the capacity to maintain state security, the presence of mature government institutions and the ability to withstand and avoid causing political shocks. Openness is characterized by the degree of political and economic freedom and the extent of global integration.[54] The most open societies are generally also the most stable, but dictatorships can maintain a degree of political stability through repression or by buying off potential adversaries. States in the middle ground between closed and open societies have the lowest levels of stability.

We adapt Bremmer's pattern but substitute peacefulness for stability on the vertical axis and democracy for openness on the horizontal axis. The resulting image depicts fully mature democracy as the most peaceful and stable regime type. Autocracies can enforce a degree of peace but they have higher rates of armed conflict than mature democracies. Partial democracies in the middle ground between dictatorship and a free society are the least peaceful and most unstable and violence-prone. Bremmer's analysis is not scholarly or quantitative, but his conclusions about stability and openness are similar to those of empirically based studies on peacefulness

[54] Ian Bremmer, *The J Curve: A New Way to Understand Why Nations Rise and Fall* (New York: Simon & Schuster, 2006), 6–13.

and democracy. The J-curve as an image is more accurate than the U-shape in depicting the relationships between regime type and peace. Rather than implying equivalence between dictatorship and democracy it portrays mature democracy as more stable and peaceful than either anocracy or authoritarianism. We believe the evidence supports this interpretation.

SUPPORTING DEMOCRACY

The evidence of high conflict risk for states transitioning to democracy might suggest that it would be better for dictatorships to remain authoritarian, rather than beginning the dangerous trek toward political openness. Some commentators argue that because of the difficulties in creating democratic governance and the instability that often accompanies the transition, it may be preferable to accommodate autocracy than support democratization. In response to the Egyptian military's bloody suppression of the country's first freely elected government in 2013, Charles Kupchin argued that the United States should "downsize" its support for the spread of democracy in the region and work with transitional governments that are "responsible, even if not democratic."[55]

This recalls Jeanne Kirkpatrick's 1979 critique of the Carter administration's policy of promoting democracy in which she called for a more gradual process of liberalizing autocracies rather than pressing for rapid democratization. Kirkpatrick famously differentiated between totalitarianism and authoritarianism. The former must be resisted, she argued, but the latter could be tolerated because it does not "disturb the habitual rhythms" of work and life and ordinary people can "learn to cope."[56]

People living under dictatorial regimes often refuse to 'cope' with oppression, however. The desire for democracy and greater equality has been growing inexorably over the centuries and seems to be a universal human aspiration.[57] People make demands for freedom regardless of what experts and policy makers in other countries think. When governments reject these demands and resort to repression, violence often results.

Policy makers in most countries continue to support democratization, even as they recognize the risks involved and the need for a long-term perspective. Democracy promotion is widely supported in international

[55] Charles A. Kupchin, "Democracy in Egypt Can Wait," *New York Times*, August 17, 2013, A 19.
[56] Jeanne J. Kirkpatrick, "Dictatorships and Double Standards," *Commentary*, November 1979, www.commentarymagazine.com/article/dictatorships-double-standards/.
[57] Fukuyama, *Political Order and Political Decay*, 542.

policy as necessary for improving social well-being and enhancing the prospects for peace. As we have noted, the assumptions underlying this commitment to democracy are well grounded empirically. Hegre et al. observe that the direction of most transitions is toward democracy and eventual peace, although setbacks often occur and have become more frequent recently. If the process of democratization can continue and mature, the likelihood of regime failure and armed conflict will decrease. In this sense the long-term prospects for states transitioning toward democracy are positive:

if we focus on countries that are at least half-way toward complete democracy, the prospects for domestic peace are promising. There *is* a democratic civil peace, and it may be achieved in the short run in some countries. In the long run most states, possibly all, may reach this condition, especially if we take into account the higher survival rate of open societies, which are less likely to move once again through the doubly dangerous zone of intermediate democracy and political change.[58]

Democracy promotion is a worthy goal of foreign policy, but there is much debate about how to achieve that goal. The invasion of Iraq was justified in part as a mission to expand democracy. The NATO mission in Libya was also described as a means of supporting a peaceful transition to democracy.[59] At times armed intervention can end armed conflict or create a more stable and democratic regime, but foreign-imposed regime change is often ineffective and costly.[60] During the debate about NATO intervention in Libya, Stephen Walt produced a summary of political science studies on attempts to promote democracy through military force. His analysis showed that armed intervention rarely produces democracy and often sparks insurgency and civil war in the affected countries.[61] States with no previous experience of democracy are unlikely to become so after external intervention.[62] Andrew Mack and his colleagues also found that military interventions result in higher levels of casualties in the

[58] Hegre et al., "Toward a Democratic Civil Peace?" 44.

[59] Anders Fogh Rasmussen, Remarks, Carnegie Endowment for International Peace, Forum for New Diplomacy, "NATO and the Arab Spring," Brussels, June 1, 2011, http://carnegieeurope.eu/events/?fa=3260.

[60] Jeffrey Pickering and Mark Penecy, "Forging Democracy at Gunpoint," *International Studies Quarterly* 50, no. 3 (2006): 541.

[61] Stephen W. Walt, "Social Science and the Libyan Adventure," blog, A realist in an ideological age, March 24, 2011, http://walt.foreignpolicy.com/posts/2011/03/24/social_science_and_the_libyan_adventure.

[62] Bruce Russett, "Bushwacking the Democratic Peace," *International Studies Perspectives* 6, no. 4 (2005): 400, 405.

affected countries and on average are twice as deadly as conflicts without such intervention.[63]

Less costly and more effective civilian means are available for helping to build democracy. Examples include the projects of the US National Endowment for Democracy, the democracy support efforts of the European Union and other mature democratic states, and the work of the International Institute for Democracy and Electoral Assistance. Even these peaceful international democratization programs have a mixed record of success, however. Deeply rooted structural impediments often stand in the way of creating democracy. The progress of democracy requires institutions of genuine political competition, a culture of accountability and participation, and the empowerment and initiative of citizens and communities. Democracy depends upon both top-down and bottom-up reforms. It can be nurtured from abroad but must also grow and mature from within.

While it is important to support democracy and help transitioning societies create more representative and accountable institutions of decision making, parallel efforts are needed to build governance capacity. Norris and others argue for a unified approach that fosters both democratic institutions and effective state capacity. Expanding one dimension without the other is not sufficient. Both factors are necessary and must work in tandem to create conditions that are conducive to prosperity, welfare and peace.[64] This requires greater integration of democratic assistance efforts and economic development programs. The multidimensional nature of good governance means that an integrated approach, while presenting its own challenges, is necessary to create the conditions for peace.

POLITICAL FREEDOM

Democracy and human rights are closely intertwined. They are separate subjects of study, but they overlap significantly in practice. Some of the indices that are used to measure democracy include categories for political rights such as free speech and equal protection of the law. Mature democracy depends upon freedoms of assembly, association and expression. For a system to be fully democratic, Dahl notes, citizens must enjoy an extensive array of freedoms, including the right to participate and

---

[63] Human Security Project, *Human Security Report 2012*, 157.
[64] Norris, *Making Democratic Governance Work*, 38.

voice their views, to hear what others are saying, and to discuss issues freely and openly.[65] Guarantees of political freedom and civil rights are at the core of democratic governance. They are essential to the democratic peace effect.

Václav Havel wrote that peace and human rights are inseparable. Lasting peace and disarmament can only be "the work of free people," he wrote.[66] He believed that "respect for human rights is the fundamental condition and the sole, genuine guarantee of true peace."[67] The end of the Cold War confirmed the linkages among human rights, political freedom and international peace. The third wave of democratization was partly a human rights revolution. When the Berlin Wall fell, respect for human rights and democracy spread rapidly through Central and Eastern Europe. International tensions and nuclear dangers ebbed dramatically. In Latin America as well, the end of military dictatorships during the 1980s was accompanied by the spread of democracy, greater guarantees of political and civil rights, and reduced military tensions among the states of the region.

In recent years, global progress toward political freedom has stalled and in some countries has been reversed. The violent repression of popular uprisings in the Arab world, the consolidation of authoritarianism in Russia and other countries, and the rise of restrictive counter-terrorism measures that increase police powers and state surveillance have contributed to a global erosion of civil liberties and human rights. In its annual reports, Freedom House has observed a steady decline in political freedom over the past decade. The most notable reversals have been in the areas of freedom of expression, civil society and the rule of law. The 2015 edition of *Freedom in the World* describes the latest trends as "exceptionally grim," the longest continuous period of decline for global freedom in the organization's more than 40 years of reporting.[68]

The decline in political freedom has been accompanied by a flattening of the trend toward greater democracy and less autocracy. Scholars

---

[65] Dahl, *Democracy and its Critics*, 48–49.
[66] Václav Havel, "Peace: The View from Prague," *New York Review of Books* 32, no. 18 (November 21, 1985): 30.
[67] Václav Havel, "Anatomy of a Reticence," in *Open Letters: Selected Writings, 1965–90*, edited by Paul Wilson (New York: Vintage Books, 1992), 314–315.
[68] Freedom House, *Freedom in the World 2015, Discarding Democracy: A Return to the Iron Fist* (New York: Freedom House, 2015); Arch Puddington, Director Research, https://freedomhouse.org/report/freedom-world-2015/discarding-democracy-return-iron-fist.

debate whether democracy remains resilient or is in retreat, but the evidence of democratic stagnation and instability in many countries is unmistakable.[69] Figure 7.2 depicts the long-term pattern of increasing democracy and declining autocracy, but since 2010 the trend lines have leveled. The growth in the number of democracies has halted, and autocracies are no longer in decline. This pattern is very recent and may be temporary, but it is worrisome and could be related to a broader decline in the prospects for peace.

As trends toward greater freedom and democracy have reversed or halted in recent years, the level of armed conflict in the world has increased. As noted in the Introduction, the last few years have witnessed a reversal of the previous trend toward greater peace in the world. The annual global assessments produced by the Uppsala Conflict Data Program show rising levels of armed conflict and war since 2011. Some of this increase is attributable to the Syrian Civil War and the struggle against the so-called Islamic State in Iraq, but armed conflicts continue in Afghanistan and Pakistan and have emerged in other Arab countries and Ukraine. The causes of these conflicts vary and cannot be attributed to the decline of global freedom or any single cause, but all these conflicts have occurred in settings where democracy and political freedom are weak or non-existent.

The denial of political freedom increases the risk of armed violence. Research shows a direct relationship between the violation of political rights and the likelihood of militancy and armed conflict. As noted earlier, high levels of government repression, especially extrajudicial killings and political arrests, increase the risk of civil war. Countries with poor human rights performance are very likely to experience major civil conflict or may be in the midst of one already.[70] They are also more likely to spawn terrorism and civil war.[71] The presence of democracy may not be a guarantee of peace, but its absence and attempts to suppress it are significant risk factors of war.

---

[69] Steven Levitsky and Lucan Way, "The Myth of Democratic Recession," and Larry Diamond, "Facing Up to the Democratic Recession," in *Democracy in Decline?*, edited by Larry Diamond and Marc F. Plattner (Baltimore: Johns Hopkins University Press, 2015), 58–76 and 98–118.

[70] Fearon, "Governance and Civil War Onset," 22–24.

[71] Alan B. Krueger and Jitka Malesckova, "Seeking the Roots of Terrorism," *Chronicle of Higher Education* 49, no. 39 (2003): b10; Andreas Feldman and Maftu Peraelae, "Reassessing the Causes of Non-governmental Terrorism in Latin America," *American Politics and Society* 42, no. 2 (Summer 2004): 120.

CONCLUSION

The role of democratic governance in advancing peace remains contested. At the inter-state level the Kantian theory of democratic peace is well grounded, but within states the influence of democracy is uncertain. The Kantian triad seems less certain now than it did when Russett and others wrote of its triumph. As Norris, Hegre and others emphasize, the peaceful impact of democracy is linked to other socioeconomic conditions, especially high per capita income, and to the presence of strong institutions of state capacity. Only when democracy reaches a high threshold and is fully mature does it have a direct significant effect in preventing intrastate violence and civil war.

People in almost every society nonetheless value and yearn for democracy. They consider freedom an inherent right and are often willing to fight for it. In that sense the struggle for democracy can be a cause of conflict. Many of the civil wars for autonomy that Gurr and his colleagues examine are fights for political self-determination, often in the name of democracy. Disputes over the nature of governance and the exercise of political power are at the heart of many armed conflicts. The public desire for democracy and political freedom is universal, and when governing authorities impede or attempt to suppress democratic aspirations conflict often emerges.

Democracy is often considered an intrinsic good regardless of its impact on peace and development. The exercise of democratic accountability "is a good thing in itself," Fukuyama writes, "apart from any effects it may have on the quality of government or economic growth."[72] The right to participate politically grants recognition to the dignity and moral value of the person. Amartya Sen makes a similar point: "The freedom to participate in critical evaluation and in the process of value formation is among the most crucial freedoms of social existence."[73] Genuine freedom enables people to live the lives they have reason to value. It is part of one's quality of life and enhances human flourishing. Democracy has emerged as the dominant form of political organization in most parts of the world, however limited it may be in practice in many countries.

Democracy and political freedom are not just normative principles. They are necessary conditions for the stable organization of politics.[74] Free political agency is a driver of good governance and helps to sustain

---

[72] Fukuyama, *Political Order and Political Decay*, 211.
[73] Sen, *Development as Freedom*, 287.
[74] Fukuyama, *Political Order and Political Decay*, 542.

democracy and institutional capacity once they are achieved. It can make governance systems more responsive to social needs and the public interest. The specific institutional forms of democracy vary widely, and debates continue over which forms of democracy are most advantageous. But it is clear that democracy can contribute to peace, and that its positive impact increases as it becomes more mature and institutionally developed.

Norris and others find that the beneficial effects of democracy are greatest in conditions of prosperity and economic growth. This adds to the significance of economic development as an essential dimension of good governance for peace. We turn to this topic in the next two chapters, looking first at the nature of development and how it reduces the risk of armed conflict, and in the following chapter at the role of governance in managing the forces of the market.

8

Development

Political leaders have long recognized that economic development is inextricably linked to the prevention of armed conflict. This understanding is enshrined in Article 1 of the United Nations Charter, which ties the goal of achieving global peace and security to "solving international problems of an economic, social, cultural, or humanitarian character." Article 55 makes these connections explicit:

With a view to the creation of conditions of stability and well-being which are necessary for peaceful and friendly relations among nations based on respect for the principle of equal rights and the self-determination of peoples, the United Nations shall promote: a) higher standards of living, full employment, and conditions of economic and social progress and development; b) solutions of international economic, social, health, and related problems; and international cultural and educational cooperation.

At the founding conference of the United Nations in 1945 US Secretary of State Edwin Stettinius eloquently connected peace and development. His remarks were inspired by Roosevelt's Four Freedoms: "The battle for peace has to be fought on two fronts," he said. "The first front is the security front, where victory spells freedom from fear. The second is the economic and social front, where victory means freedom from want. Only victory on both fronts can assure the world of an enduring peace." Sustainable economic development "is an effective counter to conflict and insecurity."[1]

---

[1] Quoted in Duncan Brack, "Introduction, Trade, Aid and Security: An Agenda for Peace and Development," in *Trade, Aid and Security: An Agenda for Peace and Development*, edited by Oli Brown, Mark Halle, Sonia Pena Moreno and Sebastian Winkler (London: Earthscan 2007), 4.

Many writers over the centuries have emphasized the economic foundations of peace. Kant, Schumpeter and many others have argued that the growth of commerce promotes peace by creating wealth and fostering cooperation and understanding. Contemporary studies provide empirical evidence in support of this linkage. All the standard indicators of economic development, including per capita income, economic growth rates, levels of trade and investment, and the degree of market openness, are significantly correlated with peace. The higher the level of development and trade, the lower the risk of armed conflict.

The conditions conducive for development, we argue, are directly related to the qualities and capacity of governance. The essential political goods of Rotberg include the provision of economic opportunity and support for social development. As we have noted, programs for education, health care and other social services improve economic development outcomes. These policies are more effective when they are inclusive and accountable. They fail if they reinforce the domination of one social group over another, lack mechanisms of broad social participation, or are unaccountable to the needs of significant sectors of society.

In this chapter, we examine the many connections between development and peace. We review the evidence linking poverty, inequality and armed conflict. We highlight the importance of horizontal social equality for peace, and the role of inclusion and social participation in generating trust and economic growth. We probe the relationship between democracy and development and Sen's philosophy of development as freedom. Throughout the chapter we attempt to identify the institutional capacities and qualities of governance that are most likely to advance peaceful economic development.

POVERTY AND WAR

Virtually every study on the causes of war finds a strong correlation between low per capita income and the likelihood of armed conflict. The link between income and conflict risk has been described as "one of the most robust empirical relationships in the economic literature."[2] The finding holds constant across a wide range of countries and diverse social settings in studies conducted by hundreds of scholars. Regardless of the indicators used to measure development levels, the results are "almost entirely consistent in direction – growth, prosperity and development

---

[2] Miguel, "Economic Shocks, Weather and Civil War," 1.

reduce the risk of civil war."[3] Countries scoring low on measurements of per capita income and economic development are significantly more likely to experience armed violence.[4]

As Collier and his associates at the World Bank and Oxford University have shown, civil conflict is heavily concentrated in the poorest countries. The risk of civil war is strongly associated with joblessness, poverty and a general lack of development. Their seminal study, *Breaking the Conflict Trap*, famously concludes, "The key root cause of conflict is the failure of economic development."[5]

Empirical analyses by many other scholars come to similar conclusions. A study of armed rebellion shows that household economic status significantly influences the likelihood of support for rebel groups. The poorer the household is at the start of a conflict, the greater the probability of the household participating in and supporting an armed group.[6] Leading scholars agree that "outbreaks of major collective political violence are strongly associated with various measures of poverty, under-development, and maldistribution of resources."[7]

The likelihood of armed violence is greatest in societies where large numbers of young men have little education and meager employment prospects. Most of those who join armed rebel movements are uneducated young males.[8] Research shows that the overwhelming majority of child soldiers in countries such as Sierra Leone, Cote d'Ivoire, Colombia and Nepal "are drawn from the poorest, least educated and most marginalized sections of society."[9] When large numbers of young people lack economic and educational opportunity, the resulting frustration can intensify political grievances and increase the likelihood of armed conflict. Surveys of young insurgents and militia fighters confirm that many are driven by poverty, unemployment and a lack of education.[10]

---

[3] Dixon, "What Causes Civil Wars?" 714.

[4] Walter, "Conflict Relapse and the Sustainability of Post-conflict Peace," 5, 15.

[5] Collier et al., *Breaking the Conflict Trap*, 53.

[6] Patricia Justino, "Poverty and Armed Conflict: A Micro-level Perspective on the Causes and Duration of Warfare," *Journal of Peace Research* 46, no. 3 (2009): 315.

[7] Monty G. Marshall, "Global Terrorism: An Overview and Analysis," in *Peace and Conflict 2005: A Global Survey of Armed Conflict, Self-Determination Movements, and Development*, edited by Monty G. Marshall and Ted Robert Gurr (College Park: University of Maryland Center for International development and Conflict Management, 2005), 68.

[8] Collier et al., *Breaking the Conflict Trap*, 68.

[9] Peter Singer, *Children at War* (New York: Pantheon Books, 2005), 44.

[10] Cited in Henrik Urdal, "The Demographics of Political Violence: Youth Bulges, Insecurity, and Conflict," in *Too Poor for Peace? Global Poverty, Conflict, and Security*

Low levels of economic development also prolong conflict duration. Collier and his colleagues find that armed conflicts last longer in very poor countries. Income per capita is inversely related to the duration of war. Low income countries face greater difficulty breaking out of the trap of persistent conflict.[11] As we note in the next chapter, the presence of lootable resources such as diamonds or drugs in low income countries also tends to prolong war.[12] Armed conflict lasts longer because the ability to earn money from contraband is greater than the costs of fighting, especially for those with less to lose.[13] Military conflicts often stimulate and become intertwined with organized criminal networks that engage in smuggling and illegal trafficking and benefit economically from continued war. Armed mafia-style gangs operate in many armed conflicts. This self-perpetuating economy of violence is especially pronounced in settings of poverty, where alternative means of livelihood are few.[14]

Poverty is measured not only by joblessness and low income but also by poor health and inadequate nutrition. A direct relationship exists between poor health and the risk of armed conflict. Countries with the worst ratings for access to health care and proper nutrition are most likely to experience armed violence.[15] Development programs that improve health and nutrition in poor countries thus not only help to relieve poverty but may also help to reduce the risk of armed conflict.

The relationship between poverty and conflict risk is subject to qualifications, as we examine below, but the core linkage is undeniable. A Brookings Institution report noted in 2006 that the academic debate on this point "has been resolved." The data "demonstrates compellingly that countries with low income per capita are at increased risk of civil conflict." Irrespective of all other variables and indicators, "poverty as

---

in the 21st Century, edited by Laeal Brainard and Derek Chollet (Washington, DC: The Brookings Institution, 2007), 92.

[11] Paul Collier, Anke Hoeffler and Måns Söderbom, "On the Duration of Civil War," *Journal of Peace Research* 41, no. 3 (2004): 253.

[12] Ballentine, "Beyond Greed and Grievance," 267.

[13] James D. Fearon, "Why Do Some Civil Wars Last So Much Longer than Others?" *Journal of Peace Research* 41, no. 3 (May 2004): 275, 284, 297.

[14] Macartan Humphreys, "Economics and Violent Conflict," Harvard University, February 2003, 18.

[15] Per Pinstrup-Andersen and Satoru Shimokawa, "Do Poverty and Poor Health and Nutrition Increase the Risk of Armed Conflict Onset?" *Food Policy* 33, no. 6 (2008): 513, 519.

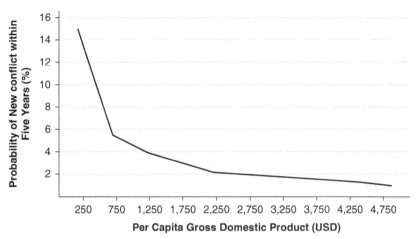

FIGURE 8.1. GDP per capita and the risk of armed conflict
Source: Human Security Research Project, 2011, Human Security Report 2009/2010: The Causes of Peace and the Shrinking Costs of War. By permission of Oxford University Press, USA

measured by low national income per capita bears a strong and statistically significant relationship to increased risk of civil conflict."[16]

The relationship between low income and the probability of armed conflict is graphically illustrated in Figure 8.1.

The link between poverty and conflict risk is real, but this does not mean that poverty causes war. Studies that document a relationship between the two are careful to emphasize that no direct causal link exists between poverty and armed violence. Some very poor countries, such as Zambia or Bangladesh, have not experienced recent armed conflict. Other mid-level developed countries, such as Croatia and Serbia, have fought bitter wars. Impoverished and starving populations often lack the energy and resources to organize violent uprisings.[17] Countries that are partially developed may descend into instability and violence when they experience political or economic shocks and a sharp drop in income levels, as we examine below.

The relationship between poverty and terrorism is also complex.[18] Many of those who lead insurgent movements and organize violent

---

[16] Susan E. Rice, Corinne Graff and Janet Lewis, "Poverty and Civil War: What Policymakers Need to Know," Global Economy and Development Working Paper (Washington, DC: The Brookings Institution, December 2006), 5–6.

[17] Seyom Brown, *The Causes and Prevention of War*, 2nd edition (New York: St. Martin's Press, 1994), 34.

[18] Steven Radelet, "Prosperity Rising: The Success of Global Development—and How to Keep It Going," *Foreign Affairs* 95, no. 1 (January/February 2016): 89.

attacks are not poor. Empirical studies show that militant leaders tend to come from more advantaged socioeconomic backgrounds and have higher educational levels than the people they claim to represent. A 2005 study on democracy and terrorism concluded that "the leaders of militant movements are better educated and of higher status than most of the population from which they come."[19] An analysis of Hezbollah militants found that the socioeconomic and educational status of Hezbollah fighters was higher than that of the average Palestinian. They were less likely to be poor than the Palestinian population as a whole, and had higher educational levels than the general population.[20]

Studies of militant groups in different historical and geographic settings have reached similar conclusions. The leaders of armed rebellion are usually responding to general conditions of underdevelopment and oppression, not to the personal experience of poverty and illiteracy. They see themselves as a vanguard, speaking for and seeking to liberate the oppressed masses. They use their relative social privilege and the skills and perspectives acquired through education to become leaders for what they believe to be a struggle for social justice.[21] As one expert observed, "the more educated segments of the public are generally less accepting of an inferior position in politics and society and are also more aware of their capacity to effect change."[22]

It is not poverty per se but a general lack of economic development that seems to be most strongly associated with armed conflict and violent extremism. Poverty and a lack of opportunity are likely to be most disruptive when communities experience a decline in social and economic status, when they perceive a discrepancy between what they have and what they expect or feel they deserve. This is Gurr's theory of relative deprivation. Social groups are most susceptible to being mobilized for armed rebellion when they perceive that an established regime is unjustly depriving them of benefits enjoyed by other groups, when they feel disadvantaged relative to the resources and status of others.[23] This is consistent

---

[19] Ted Robert Gurr, "Economic Factors," in *Addressing the Causes of Terrorism: The Club de Madrid Series on Democracy and Terrorism* (proceedings of the International Summit on Democracy, Terrorism and Security, Club de Madrid, Madrid, Spain, March 8–11, 2005), vol. 1, 19.

[20] Krueger and Malesckova, "Education, Poverty and Terrorism," 131–132.

[21] Lewis Kriesberg, *Constructive Conflicts: From Escalation to Resolution*, 2nd edition (Lanham: Rowman & Littlefield, 2003), 70.

[22] Shibley Telhami, *The Stakes: America in the Middle East: The Consequences of Power and the Choice of Peace* (Boulder: Westview Press, 2004), 29.

[23] Gurr, *Why Men Rebel*. A similar case is advanced in Amy Chua, *World on Fire: How Exporting Free Market Democracy Breeds Ethnic Hatred and Global Instability* (New York: Random House, 2003).

with research in psychology, which shows that humans are less concerned with their absolute level of resources than what they have in comparison to others.[24] Relative deprivation has been identified as a predictor of militant attitudes in conflicts in Niger and Senegal[25] and in overview analyses examining multiple conflicts.[26]

INEQUALITY MATTERS

Economic inequality is also a risk factor for war, but again the relationship is complex and the empirical results depend on the form of inequality being examined. Major studies by Collier and others find no direct link between conflict risk and income inequality among individuals.[27] Income differences between social groups, on the other hand, have significant impacts. As we note in earlier chapters, horizontal inequalities between social groups generate grievances that can lead to armed conflict. Researchers sometimes fail to find a relationship between inequality and armed conflict because they examine individual-level data rather than the economic differences between social groups.[28] Estimates of inequality based on national-level differences in personal income can mask unequal horizontal patterns among social groups. Frances Stewart and her colleagues at Oxford differentiate between vertical inequality between individuals and horizontal inequalities between groups. They find that conflict more often arises from horizontal than vertical inequalities.[29]

An earlier study of insurgencies found a direct relationship between social inequality and political violence. Using data on shares of personal income accruing to differing groups within society, the study confirmed that the degree of income inequality is directly related to the level of political violence.[30] A high level of income inequality significantly raises the

---

[24] See, for example, Faye Crosby, "A Model of Egotistical Relative Deprivation," *Psychological Review* 83, no. 2 (1976): 85–113

[25] Pyt Douma, "Poverty, Relative Deprivation and Political Exclusion as Drivers of Violent Conflict in Sub-Saharan Africa," *ISYP Journal on Science and World Affairs* 2, no. 2 (2006): 59–69.

[26] Besançon, "Relative Resources," 393–415.

[27] Collier et al., "On the Duration of Civil War," 253; Fearon and Laitin, "Ethnicity, Insurgency, and Civil War," 75–90.

[28] Gudrun Østby, "Polarization, Horizontal Inequalities and Violent Civil Conflict," *Journal of Peace Research* 45, no. 2 (2008): 145.

[29] Stewart, *Horizontal Inequalities and Conflict*.

[30] Edward N. Muller and Mitchell A. Seligson, "Inequality and Insurgency," *American Political Science Review* 81, no. 2 (June 1987): 442.

probability that dissident groups will engage in violent action. The effect of income inequality on levels of violence was observed in 60 out of 62 cases studied. The authors conclude that the "redistribution of income must be ranked as one of the more meaningful reforms that a modernizing government can undertake in the interest of achieving political stability."[31] This confirms what many other studies have found. Equitable economic growth enhances the prospects for peace.

Inequalities among different social groups can affect conflict dynamics within states or across borders when common ethnic communities span national boundaries. If inequality is coupled with identity-based polarization and competition for resources, the potential for conflict-supporting attitudes of anger and prejudice increases.[32] Research on inequalities between regions within a state shows a strong relationship between social inequality and indicators of armed violence. As interregional inequality increases, the likelihood of armed conflict grows.[33]

Horizontal inequality is often determined by government policies and spending priorities. It is a function of governance. It results from decisions and structures that determine access to economic opportunity and the distribution of available resources. States that favor one group over another increase the risk that deprived groups will experience conflict-inducing grievances. By contrast, states with inclusive and representative governance systems are more likely to distribute resources in an equitable manner to major social and geographic communities, thereby reducing the risk of armed conflict.

WAR AS REVERSE DEVELOPMENT

The relationship between conflict risk and economic development also works in reverse. "Poverty is both a cause of insecurity and a consequence of it," write the editors of the Brookings Institution report.[34] War is more likely where income is low, and once unleashed it tends to push

[31] Ibid., 444.
[32] Peter Grant and Rupert Brown, "From Ethnocentrism to Collective Protest: Responses to Relative Deprivation and Threats to Social Identity," *Social Psychology Quarterly* 58, no. 3 (1995): 195–211; D. Conor Seyle and Matthew Newman, "A House Divided? The Psychology of Red and Blue America," *American Psychologist* 61, no. 6 (2006): 571.
[33] Lindsay Heger and Melissa Ziegler Rogers, "Bringing Regions Back In: Territorial Inequality and Civil Conflict," Paper prepared for the 2013 PSS-ISA Joint International Conference, Budapest, Hungary, 12.
[34] Lael Brainard, Derek Chollet and Nica LaFluer, "The Tangled Web: The Poverty-Insecurity Nexus," in *Too Poor for Peace? Global Poverty, Conflict, and Security in*

development levels even lower. Economists agree that armed conflict undermines economic well-being and reduces per capita income levels.[35] From an economic development perspective, war is dysfunctional. It may bring short-term benefits for a few, but it retards development and creates economic misery for many. The high levels of military spending that are associated with war reduce economic growth.[36] They divert resources from education, health services and other social priorities and reduce public well-being. Violent conflicts inhibit foreign investment and disrupt the relationships that are essential for trade and commercial development.

Many studies confirm the harmful effects of war on human development, particularly in regions that experience the most intense fighting. Wars reduce life expectancy and may slow the general decline in infant mortality rates.[37] Many of these impacts result from the indirect effects of warfare: the inability or unwillingness of states in crisis to provide health services, and the spread of malnourishment and disease in refugee camps and communities under siege.[38] The World Development Report 2011 calculates the cost of a major civil war as equivalent to more than 30 years of typical GDP growth for a medium-sized developing country. Trade levels take 20 years to recover.[39] Collier and his colleagues find that average annual economic growth falls 1.6 percent for each year that civil war continues in a poor country.[40] Economic impacts are especially severe in the immediate aftermath of war, with economic output declining 6 percent on average following conflict onset.[41]

The negative impact of conflict on economic growth and per capita income helps to explain why countries that experience civil war face a higher risk of renewed war and are caught in a deadly conflict trap. As Collier et al. observe, countries experiencing internal war are in "far greater danger of further conflict: commonly, the chief legacy of a civil war is another war."[42] A country reaching the end of an internal war has

---

the 21st Century, edited by Laeal Brainard and Derek Chollet (Washington, DC: The Brookings Institution, 2007), 2.

[35] Miguel, "Economic Shocks, Weather and Civil War," 2.

[36] Collier et al., *Breaking the Conflict Trap*, 86–87.

[37] Scott Gates, Håvard Hegre, Håvard Mokleiv Nygard and Håvard Strand, "Development Consequences of Armed Conflict," *World Development* 40, no. 9 (2012): 1717–1718.

[38] Ibid., 1721.

[39] World Bank, *World Development Report 2011*, 5–6.

[40] Cited in Rice et al., "Poverty and Civil War," 8–9.

[41] Valerie Cerra and Sweta Chaman Saxena, "Growth Dynamics," *American Economic Review* 98, no. 1 (2008): 442.

[42] Collier et al., *Breaking the Conflict Trap*, x.

a 44 percent risk of returning to conflict within five years.[43] Solving the dilemma of persistent civil war has become a major priority of the United Nations and led to the creation of the Peacebuilding Commission. A primary purpose of the Commission is to help countries recovering from internal conflict avoid falling back into armed violence. The Commission shows promise but to date its potential has been constrained by a lack of resources.[44] Providing support for peacebuilding and economic development is a major priority in these settings and is an essential means of preventing the recurrence of war.

DEVELOPMENT AND DEMOCRACY

Economic development clearly has a direct impact in helping to make societies more peaceful. It may also have an indirect effect on peace by advancing the prospects for democracy, although this linkage is contested. As observed in Chapter 7, Norris, Collier and other analysts find that high levels of economic development are the most important factor in explaining the impact of democracy in promoting peace.[45] When controlling for the influence of development, scholars find that democracy has only a limited effect in reducing the risk of armed conflict between states.[46] Economic development is the independent variable, they argue, with democracy and peace dependent factors. Does the same pattern hold within states? Is economic development the dominant factor in explaining the influence of democracy as a factor for peace?

The relationship between economic well-being and democracy is well known and has been observed by political thinkers from the time of Aristotle. Many studies show a strong association between the two, but is one subordinate to the other, or are they mutually interdependent? Lipset described economic development as a prerequisite for democracy. His analysis showed a robust correlation between levels of democracy and measures of economic development, urbanization and education. "In each case," Lipset observed, "the average wealth, degree of industrialization and urbanization, and level of education

---

[43] Ibid., 83.

[44] Wallensteen, *Quality Peace*, 200–201.

[45] Norris, *Making Democratic Governance Work*; Collier and Hoeffler, "Greed and Grievance in Civil War."

[46] Azar Gat, *Victorious and Vulnerable: Why Democracy Won in the 20th Century and How It Is Still Imperiled* (Lanham: Rowman & Littlefield, 2010), 92; Erik Gartzke, "The Capitalist Peace," *American Journal of Political Science* 51, no. 1 (2007): 180.

is much higher for the more democratic countries."[47] The indices for these social conditions "are so closely interrelated as to form one common factor." All can be subsumed under the heading of economic development and are correlated with political democracy.[48] Countries with the highest levels of average annual per capita income are more democratic, he argued, while those with the lowest per capita income are less democratic.

Lipset's work on development and democracy "has generated the largest body of research on any topic in comparative politics," according to Adam Przeworski and Fernando Limongi.[49] It has also sparked controversy among critics who contest the implication that development always leads to democracy, and who emphasize the role of social agency in building democracy in all countries, rich and poor alike.[50] Lipset was right in identifying a relationship between development and democracy, but this does not mean that development is a necessary cause or the only path toward democracy. It is obvious from a cursory view of differing nations that high levels of income per capita are not automatically associated with democracy. Some authoritarian states have become quite wealthy but remain firmly autocratic. Prime examples include Saudi Arabia and the other Gulf petro-states. China and Vietnam have experienced rapid economic growth but remain one-party states. The belief that development undermines dictatorships and fosters democracy is not based on consistent evidence. As Przeworski and Limongi wryly note, "Whatever the threshold at which development is supposed to dig the grave for authoritarian regimes, it is clear that many dictatorships passed it in good health."[51]

The spread of democracy is not dependent on high levels of per capita income. Many developing states have made or are in the process of making a transition to democracy. In an increasing number of cases these transitions are powered by nonviolent social movements, as exemplified in recent decades by unarmed revolutions in Tunisia, Nepal, Serbia and other countries. The number of democratic states

---

[47] Lipset, "Some Social Requisites of Democracy," 75.

[48] Ibid., 80.

[49] Adam Przeworski and Fernando Limongi, "Modernization: Theories and Facts," *World Politics* 49 (1997): 156.

[50] See Guilermo O'Donnell, *Modernization and Bureaucratic Authoritarianism: Studies in South American Politics*, 2nd edition (Berkeley: Institute of International Studies, University of California, 1979).

[51] Przeworski and Limongi, "Modernization," 160.

has expanded over the decades, often in less developed countries, as social resistance to dictatorship has spread in Latin America, Eastern Europe, Asia and Africa. These emerging democracies are often fragile, as expected from the J-curve analysis, and there have been major setbacks, notably in Egypt, but in general states shaped by nonviolent resistance movements tend to become more democratic and representative. Nonviolent transformations are based on voluntary social action and are by their nature highly participatory and democratic.[52] They are more likely than armed revolutions to produce political regimes that protect political freedoms and provide opportunities for democratic participation.[53]

High levels of economic development do not automatically lead to democracy, but they help to preserve democratic regimes once they are established. In this sense Lipset was right. Przeworski and Limongi find that democratic governments in countries with low per capita income have poor survival rates. By contrast, there is no example of a democracy reverting to dictatorship in a country with annual GDP per capita above $9,000.[54] While democracy is fragile in poor countries, they note, "It is impregnable in the rich ones." The probability that democracy will die in a rich country "is practically zero."[55] High levels of development have a strong impact on sustaining democratic governance.

It is obvious that development and democracy are interconnected. Whether one is more significant than the other is probably not provable and in any case is not necessary for the purposes of our argument. It is enough to know, as many studies have determined, that both are strongly associated with the prospects for peace. Some scholars find that levels of trade and democracy are comparable in their pacifying effect.[56] Russett and Oneal emphasize that "both democracy and economically important trade are strong and statistically significant constraints" on the use of armed force.[57] Development, democracy and peace go together. This is the classic Kantian liberal peace theory, which is confirmed in contemporary empirical research.

---

[52] Chenoweth and Stephan, *Why Civil Resistance Works*, 201–219.

[53] Karatnycky and Ackerman, "How Freedom Is Won."

[54] The level was $6,000 in the original 1997 study, but it is now $9,000 in inflation adjusted dollars.

[55] Przeworski and Limongi, "Modernization," 166.

[56] Han Dorussen and Hugh Ward, "Trade Networks and the Kantian Peace," *Journal of Peace Research* 47, no. 1 (2010): 41.

[57] Russett and Oneal, *Triangulating Peace*, 145–146.

DEVELOPMENT AS EMPOWERMENT

The evidence shows that promoting economic development is a necessary and vitally important strategy for peace. Raising economic growth rates and levels of income per capita may be the single most important step that can be taken to reduce the likelihood of armed conflict.[58] How to achieve economic development, however, remains a matter of debate. Overseas Development Assistance (ODA) clearly plays an important role in generating human capital and has produced many positive outcomes over the decades in combating disease, improving public health, reducing hunger and promoting public education. On its own, however, development aid cannot eliminate poverty.[59] As we examine in Chapter 9, market reforms and increased trade and investment are also necessary and have generated significant economic growth in recent decades. Aid and markets each have a role to play in advancing development and increasing the prospects for peace, but their effectiveness depends upon the governance context and policy framework in which they are applied.

One scholar has written of "the myth of apolitical development."[60] Development is fundamentally related to governance and cannot be separated from issues of political decision making and the policies and structures that determine access to wealth and resources. Development is not merely a technical or bureaucratic exercise. It requires an understanding of the economic conditions that cause poverty and the patterns of political and economic exclusion that prevent communities from improving their well-being.[61] Poverty is a function of marginalization and the inability of people in affected communities to influence the political and economic decisions that affect their lives. It is not a top-down mechanism but a self-generative process of creativity, entrepreneurship and capacity building. It is not about handouts for the needy but the empowerment of the previously marginalized, the process through which people gain access to the capabilities and assets they need to improve their well-being. As President Benjamin W. Mkapa of Tanzania said, "Development cannot

---

[58] Collier et al., *Breaking the Conflict Trap*, 66.
[59] Brack, "Introduction, Trade, Aid and Security," 2. As William Easterly observes, massive levels of foreign assistance to countries in Africa have not reduced the number of poor people on the continent. See William Easterly, "Tone Deaf on Africa," *New York Times*, July 3, 2005.
[60] Paul J. Nelson, *The World Bank and Nongovernmental Organizations: The Limits of Apolitical Development* (New York: St. Martin's Press, 1995).
[61] Coralie Bryant and Christina Kappaz, *Reducing Poverty, Building Peace* (Bloomfield: Kumarian Press, 2005), 21.

be imposed. It can only be facilitated. It requires ownership, participation and empowerment, not harangues and dictates."[62] Ultimately development is about good governance and the presence of inclusive institutions that enable impoverished communities to strive for self-improvement.

No one has written more cogently about these issues than Amartya Sen. His groundbreaking *Development as Freedom* redefines poverty as capacity deprivation and shifts the focus of attention from the delivery of aid to the expansion of freedom. People are poor, Sen argues, because they lack the capacities needed to achieve development and improve their well-being. "Poverty must be seen as the deprivation of basic capabilities rather than merely as lowness of incomes."[63] Policy debates "have overemphasized income poverty and income inequality, to the neglect of deprivations that relate to other variables, such as unemployment, ill health, lack of education, and social exclusion."[64] Development means removing obstacles to freedom so that individuals and communities can realize their potential. With adequate social opportunities, people will be able to shape their own destiny and develop their economic potential. This can only occur when they acquire necessary assets and have equitable access to resources.

Freedom is fundamentally important not only as the desired goal of life, but also as the means of obtaining the capabilities and opportunities needed to achieve that freedom. The expansion of freedom is both the primary end of development and the principal means of achieving it, Sen argues, the standard by which we assess human happiness and the means of acquiring it. Freedom "enhances the ability of people to help themselves." It includes the right to participate in public life and actively shape and influence the policies that determine development opportunities. Poor people should be seen not as passive and docile recipients of dispensed assistance but as active participants in social change. Assuring inclusive development depends on "free and sustainable agency – and even constructive impatience" by poor people themselves.[65] This can only happen when people are able to act as agents of social and political change.

---

[62] Quoted in H. Benn, "Partnerships for Poverty Reduction: Rethinking Conditionality," Department of Foreign Investment and Development, London, March 2005; cited in Oli Brown, "Promoting 'Good' Governance through Trade and Aid: Instruments of Coercion or Vehicles of Communication," in *Trade, Aid and Security: An Agenda for Peace and Development*, edited by Oli Brown, Mark Halle, Sonia Pena Moreno and Sebastian Winkler (London: Earthscan, 2007), 81.

[63] Sen, *Development as Freedom*, 87.

[64] Ibid., 108.

[65] Ibid., 11, 18.

The ability to participate in economic and political life is greatly influenced by governance systems and their social arrangements. "Individual freedom is quintessentially a social product," Sen writes.[66] This means that freedom of opportunity, while partially a product of individual initiative, is also linked to the structures of governance and public policy. The capabilities of a person "depend on the nature of social arrangements" and the degree to which governments provide the public goods that are necessary for freedom and development. "With adequate social opportunities, individuals can effectively shape their own destiny and help each other," Sen writes.[67] Public investments in education and healthcare are especially important in raising productivity and enabling people to achieve economic development. Quality education for all, affordable and decent health care, adequate housing, water and sanitation, credit and financial services, access to appropriate technology – all are necessary to facilitate balanced economic development.[68] All depend upon good governance.

As we observe in the next chapter, the achievements of the market are also contingent on political and social arrangements. Free markets are essential for effective development, but they depend upon public policies that enable the economic system to function effectively and equitably.[69] To temper the inherent tendency toward inequality of wealth within capitalism, governments have established policies of redistribution and progressive taxation.[70] Cross-country studies find that more equitable patterns of income distribution are associated with greater progress in reducing the number of people in poverty.[71] Markets flourish best in governance systems that promote equality of access, provide social safety nets, enhance human capital, respond effectively to market failures and guard against exploitation and abuse.

PARTICIPATORY DEVELOPMENT

As we have emphasized in other chapters, citizen participation and social capital are essential features of democracy. They are also related

---

[66] Ibid., 31.

[67] Ibid., 11, 288.

[68] Jane Nelson, "Operating in Insecure Environments," in *Too Poor for Peace? Global Poverty, Conflict, and Security in the 21st Century*, edited by Lael Brainard and Derek Chollet (Washington, DC: The Brookings Institution Press, 2007), 143.

[69] Sen, *Development as Freedom*, 142.

[70] Piketty, *Capital in the Twenty-First Century*.

[71] Bryant and Kappaz, *Reducing Poverty, Building Peace*, 88.

to the success of development and the capacity of governance systems to improve the economic and social well-being of communities in need. Aid programs can help communities acquire the capabilities and assets they need to improve their lives, especially when they engage and empower marginalized communities and encourage local initiatives. Empirical studies show that the prospects for development and a state's ability to deliver public services improve with the active participation of people in the affected communities. Just as development helps to sustain democracy, participatory democracy helps to advance development.

This principle is related to the concept of coproduction, which Elinor Ostrom describes as the involvement of citizens in efforts to provide public services. It is the process through which agencies responsible for delivering goods or services receive inputs from individuals at the community level who are not part of the government. Development agencies often refer to the people they serve as clients. This is a passive term indicating that people are to be acted upon. Coproduction is a more engaged and active concept in which citizens participate in developing and delivering the public services that are of consequence to them.

Ostrom examined two contrasting examples of public service delivery: the provision of water and sanitation in urban communities in Brazil, and attempts to increase primary education in villages in Nigeria. When public officials in Brazil actively encouraged a high level of citizen input, the results were positive. By contrast, where public officials in Nigeria discouraged parent and teacher contributions, school enrollment and educational achievement suffered.[72]

In the Brazil case planners engaged local residents from the very start. They organized meetings in every city block and facilitated citizen efforts to make decisions for constructing and maintaining the water lines. They also encouraged citizens to participate in the implementation of these decisions. The overall performance of these systems was mixed. The extensive involvement of local citizens required time and effort on the part of public officials. Some neighborhood groups were more effective and cohesive than others. Monitoring the performance of local groups was a challenge. On balance, however, many of these systems were successful and "dramatically increased the availability of lower-cost, essential urban services to the poorest neighborhoods of Brazilian cities."[73]

---

[72] Elinor Ostrom, "Crossing the Great Divide: Coproduction, Synergy, and Development," *World Development* 24, no. 6 (1996): 1073.

[73] Ibid., 1075.

The participation of residents in project design and implementation fostered an active, vocal constituency that served as an accountability mechanism to improve agency performance.[74]

In Nigeria, by contrast, local efforts by parents and teachers to improve education were impeded by governmental inefficiency and chaotic policies: constant changes in educational policy, and unreliable and fluctuating levels of financing. Coproduction was discouraged by government agencies taking over schools that villagers perceived to be theirs, by constant changes in educational funding and administration, and by top-down command approaches in decision making. In the few villages where parents and teachers were able to actively contribute to school development, children were able to obtain primary education and pass school examinations, with some children going on to secondary school. By contrast, in the villages where parents and teachers contributed little, children received minimal education and few were able to pass examinations.[75]

The beneficial results of coproduction are of particular relevance in developing country contexts where poor neighborhoods and villages are characterized by a severe underutilization of the knowledge, skills and time of local residents. Ostrom argues that governments are more efficient and equitable when they receive the input of citizens.[76] Harnessing the energy of affected communities fosters a form of entrepreneurship that encourages creativity and innovation and allows for a wider array of options in the provision of public services.

The possibilities for citizen participation and coproduction systems are linked to regime type. Centralized political systems tend to be more restrictive and are less conducive to participatory approaches. A polycentric regime, by contrast, offers citizens greater opportunities to participate and facilitates engagement. Coproduction also enhances social capital. The evidence shows that experiences in local participatory development encourage citizens to develop horizontal relationships in other areas of activity.[77]

A survey of more than a dozen empirical studies finds that high levels of social capital generate benefits for economic development. Social

---

[74] Gabriel Watson, *Good Sewers Cheap? Agency-Customer Interactions in Low-Cost Urban Sanitation in Brazil* (Washington, DC: World Bank, Water and Sanitation Division, 1995), 49.
[75] Ostrom, "Crossing the Great Divide," 1078.
[76] Ibid., 1080–1083.
[77] Ibid., 1082–1083.

participation "affects the provision of services in both urban and rural areas; transforms the prospects for agricultural development; influences the expansion of private enterprises; improves the management of common resources; helps improve education; can prevent conflict; and can compensate for a deficient state."[78] Communities with strong associational linkages are better able to band together in locally designed development solutions to provide services for the common good. Social capital also facilitates information and knowledge transfer, which can improve economic efficiency and reduce transaction costs.[79]

Social capital can generate higher levels of public trust, and is also related to development success and effective service delivery. A study measuring the impact of trust on economic performance in 37 countries provides "strong support for the hypothesis that social capital ... is associated with improved economic welfare of societies, as measured by growth, investment, and poverty indicators."[80] The trust generated through social capital also contributes to income growth and improves access to services. High levels of social capital reduce income inequality and help to "alleviate poverty for individuals and for countries as a whole."[81]

These studies indicate that communities with a strong associational life are likely to be more stable, with higher rates of economic development and social equity. When people participate actively in public life they have more trust in one other and are more likely to work together in assuring the delivery of public services upon which all depend. They will seek and acquire greater access to the resources and assets needed to improve their economic well-being. All of these social features improve the prospects for development and peace.

The implications of these findings are significant for the nature of governance and the relationship between state and society. They place a premium on structures and policies that promote personal freedom and social participation. They highlight the importance of civil society and provide further evidence that effective governance depends upon bottom-up participation in addition to effective institutional structures. They show the benefit of inclusive approaches that build bridges across ethnic and communal divides. Governance systems facilitate economic development

---

[78] Grootaert and van Bastelaer, "Understanding and Measuring Social Capital," 14, 21.

[79] Ibid., 6.

[80] Stephen Knack, "Social Capital, Growth and Poverty: A Survey of Cross-country Evidence," World Bank MPRA Paper No. 24893, September 11, 2010, 3.

[81] Grootaert and van Bastelaer, "Understanding and Measuring Social Capital," 11, 14, 21.

when they guarantee personal and social freedoms, and when they assure that access and opportunities are equally available to all.

CONCLUSION

Development involves more than sending money to poor countries. It is about sharing knowledge and technical skills and facilitating more inclusive access to power and resources. It involves support for governance programs that strengthen the rule of law, protect property rights, provide protections against impunity, guarantee political and economic freedom, and foster independent judicial and legislative institutions.[82] Aid programs facilitate development when they enhance human capital and help to overcome structural impediments to growth. Examples include providing access to education and technical training for women and girls, and assisting states to establish tax systems that reduce government dependence on natural resource rents. Especially important are efforts to reduce corruption and increase transparency among governments and private companies. Aid programs are most effective when they help countries build more efficient, inclusive, representative and accountable political and economic institutions.

Sustainable economic development as a condition for peace is directly related to the nature and quality of governance. As Sen and others emphasize, the success of development depends on governance systems and public policies that enable communities to obtain necessary capabilities and assets. Also needed are high levels of social participation and public trust, which in turn require government policies that protect essential freedoms and provide space for active civil society involvement. Economic growth is dependent upon policies that protect and support free markets, but that also balance private sector interests with the needs of society. We turn to these issues in the next chapter.

---

[82] Bryant and Kappaz, *Reducing Poverty, Building Peace*, 79.

9

Markets, Development and Peace

In September 2015 world leaders gathered at the United Nations in New York to launch the Sustainable Development Goals. The assembled leaders expressed pride and satisfaction at the progress achieved by the international community in fulfilling many of the Millennium Development Goals, which UN Secretary-General Ban Ki-moon called the "most successful anti-poverty movement in history."[1] While many leaders emphasized the enormous development challenges that remain, and Pope Francis notably called for greater efforts to help the poor and address the problem of climate change,[2] the overall tone of the gathering was hopeful.

No one doubts that tremendous development advances have been achieved in recent decades. According to the UN *Report on Millennium Development Goals*, aid policies since 2000 have helped to lift more than one billion people out of extreme poverty. The share of people in the world living in extreme poverty has fallen by half over the past 15 years.[3] Overseas Development Assistance (ODA) has reduced hunger and undernourishment, advanced gender equality, lowered child and maternal mortality, reduced infectious disease rates, and enhanced

---

[1] Ban Ki-moon, "Forward," United Nations, *The Millennium Development Goals Report 2015* (United Nations: New York, 2015), 3, www.un.org/millenniumgoals/2015_MDG_Report/pdf/MDG%202015%20rev%20(July%201).pdf.

[2] "Address of the Holy Father," Meeting with the Members of the General Assembly of the United Nations Organization, New York, September 25, 2015, http://w2.vatican.va/content/francesco/en/speeches/2015/september/documents/papa-francesco_20150925_onu-visita.html.

[3] Radelet, "Prosperity Rising," 85.

environmental sustainability.[4] Hundreds of millions of people are living longer, healthier and more productive lives today because of global development efforts. Problems of the 'bottom billion' and pervasive preventable death and disease persist, but development trends overall have been positive. The portrait of global progress depicted in the UN Report is impressive indeed.

If we look closely at the global pattern of poverty reduction, however, an anomaly appears. Regions that received relatively high levels of ODA per capita (the Middle East and North Africa and sub-Saharan Africa) experienced lower levels of poverty reduction, while areas of Asia that received less ODA per capita achieved the greatest progress in poverty reduction.[5] Between 1990 and 2015, according to the UN Report, rates of extreme poverty dropped in Eastern Asia by 94 percent, in South Asia by 73 percent, and in Southeast Asia by 84 percent. By contrast, in sub-Saharan Africa, which received a higher share of development assistance per capita, the reduction in severe poverty levels was 28 percent.[6] These differing regional results confirm what many analysts have observed. The global reduction in poverty over the past 15 years is primarily the result of economic development in China, India and other parts of East Asia, in countries that have benefitted from market-driven economic growth. The most significant factor in lifting people out of extreme poverty has been market reform and the unleashing of private sector development.

This does not mean that development assistance has been ineffective. On the contrary, ODA funding has propelled significant global progress in reducing hunger, improving health, enhancing literacy and numeracy, and promoting gender equality, including in Africa and the Middle East. As Collier observes, aid has had a positive net effect on economic growth, adding about 1 percent on average to the annual growth rate of bottom billion nations. Aid is critically important in addressing the challenge of development, but it is not sufficient by itself to generate the economic growth needed to lift the poorest communities out of poverty.[7] That job belongs to the private sector and the productive power of the market.

[4] United Nations, *The Millennium Development Goals Report 2015* (United Nations: New York, 2015), 4–7, www.un.org/millenniumgoals/2015_MDG_Report/pdf/MDG%202015%20rev%20(July%201).pdf.

[5] Figures for ODA per capita are available at World Bank, Aid Effectiveness Data, 2015, http://data.worldbank.org/topic/aid-effectiveness.

[6] United Nations, *The Millennium Development Goals Report 2015*, 14.

[7] Collier, *The Bottom Billion*, 100, 123.

This is not to suggest that capitalism is a 'hidden hand' for peace, as some have suggested,[8] or that market forces naturally generate positive social outcomes. Markets and their social impacts are shaped by the governance systems and institutional structures in which they are embedded. The political and social context determines whether the private sector enhances or harms the prospects for peace.

In the idealized theory of capitalism markets function freely without governmental constraint, but in the real world they cannot escape the influence of governance and public authority. Indeed the regulation of trade is one of the core functions of government. States establish rules of commercial exchange and define the rights of entrepreneurs. They set regulatory frameworks that extend or limit markets in the interest of perceived public benefits or powerful interests. The functioning of markets is inextricably linked to the structures of governance.

In this chapter, we explore the interrelationship of capitalism, economic development, governance and the prevention of armed conflict. We review the literature on the effects of trade and investment in generating economic growth and rising incomes, thereby reducing the risk of conflict within states. We examine the role of governance in regulating market conditions and providing necessary public goods that boost productivity and growth and mitigate the risks of unfettered capitalism. We review the extraordinary economic success of the Asian tigers and the accompanying phenomenon of the 'East Asian peace.' We discuss China as a potential exception to the theory of peace through good governance. We interpret the well-known phenomenon of the 'resource curse' as a consequence of poor governance rather than resource development per se. Throughout the chapter we highlight the productive potential of market-based development but also the importance of balancing private sector interests with social needs and the requirements of accountable governance.

TRADE, MARKETS AND PEACE

Over the centuries many philosophers, economists and political leaders have extolled the pacific impacts of commerce and free trade. Adam Smith considered free commerce the surest means of achieving human prosperity and securing cooperation among nations. Montesquieu wrote,

---

[8] Patrick J. McDonald, *The Invisible Hand of Peace: Capitalism, the War Machine, and International Relations Theory* (Cambridge University Press, 2009).

"Peace is the natural effect of trade."[9] Thomas Paine declared, "If commerce were permitted to act to the universal extent it is capable it would extirpate the system of war."[10] Contemporary writers echo these views. Richard Rosecrance argues in *The Rise of the Trading State* that trade and commercial interaction reinforce preferences for peace and make war less likely.[11] Of the ten benefits listed by the World Trade Organization for the global system of free trade, the first is that it helps to promote peace.

Empirical analyses confirm these assertions and consistently show a direct relationship between levels of trade and per capita income growth within a state.[12] As noted in Chapter 8, economic growth is strongly associated with a reduced risk of armed conflict.[13] Through its beneficial impacts on economic growth, trade has the effect of helping to foster peace. Research confirms that states which are open to international trade and foreign investment are less likely to experience civil war.[14] Countries with higher levels of trade and per capita income tend to be more peaceful. By contrast, states that attempt to restrict trade usually have lower growth rates and a greater risk of civil conflict.

Trade and commercial development help to reduce the risk of ethnoterritorial disputes, which as noted in Chapter 4 are a frequent cause of civil conflict. Over time industrial, economic and technological advances have diminished the importance of controlling territory. The primary sources of wealth generation have shifted from agriculture and land-based resources to the development of industry, trade, finance and most recently information technology and communications. These trends have severed the link between land and power, Rosecrance argues.[15] Commerce and industrial innovation make it possible to create wealth without the need to control or conquer new lands.

---

[9] Quoted in Dorussen and Ward, "Trade Networks and the Kantian Peace," 31.

[10] Quoted in Michael W. Doyle, *Ways of War and Peace: Realism, Liberalism, and Socialism* (New York: W.W. Norton, 1997), 231.

[11] Richard Rosecrance, *The Rise of the Trading State: Commerce and Conquest in the Modern World* (New York: Basic Books, 1986), ix.

[12] Jeffrey Frankel and David Romer, "Does Trade Cause Growth?" *American Economic Review* 89, no. 3 (1999): 379–399; Douglas Irwin and Marko Terviö, "Does Trade Raise Income? Evidence from the Twentieth Century," *Journal of International Economics* 58, no. 1 (2002): 1–18.

[13] Christopher Blattman and Edward Miguel, "Civil War," *Journal of Economic Literature* 48, no. 1 (2010): 24–25.

[14] Katherine Barbieri and Rafael Reuveny, "Globalization and Civil War," *Journal of Politics* 67, no. 4 (2005): 1229.

[15] Rosecrance, *The Rise of the Trading State*, 139.

The importance of territory also diminishes with the increasing mobility of capital and the rise of economic interdependence. Corporations and investors are no longer bound to a particular country or location and are able to move financial assets quickly to safer havens if their assets are threatened by instability. As Carlos Boix observes, "In economies where wealth is either mobile or hard to tax or confiscate, sustained political violence to grab those assets does not pay off."[16] In a globalized marketplace of diverse producers and consumers in multiple cultures, territorial location and ethnic origin have less significance than in the past.

In regions with diversified economies and high levels of per capita income – Europe, East Asia and North America – the pacifying benefits of trade and development are most pronounced. These trends are far less evident in regions such as sub-Saharan Africa where agriculture remains a primary means of economic activity, and land-based resource extraction, especially oil production, is a significant source of wealth. In these settings economic development is more firmly linked to specific territories, and aggrieved ethnic communities have an incentive to fight for control of land-based resources. This frequent source of civil conflict diminishes with economic diversification and the spread of commerce.

Empirical studies show a similar relationship between increased trade and a reduced risk of war between states, although the results on this question are mixed.[17] Studies yield differing results depending upon the variables measured and the influence of other factors such as the degree of democracy, but the preponderance of evidence points to a positive relationship between peace and commerce.[18] Louis Kriesberg notes that "the level of international trade is inversely related to the incidence of wars … That relationship is quantitatively large and statistically significant."[19] Bruce Russett concurs: "the evidence that trade reduces conflict forms

---

[16] Carlos Boix, "Economic Roots of Civil Wars and Revolutions in the Contemporary World," *World Politics* 60, no. 3 (2008): 432.

[17] Solomon William Polachek, "Conflict and Trade," *Journal of Conflict Resolution* 24, no. 1 (1980): 67; Edward D. Mansfield and Brian M. Pollins, "Interdependence and Conflict: An Introduction," in *Economic Interdependence and International Conflict: New Perspectives on an Enduring Debate*, edited by Edward D. Mansfield and Brian M. Pollins (Ann Arbor: University of Michigan Press, 2003), 1–28.

[18] Gerald Schneider, Katherine Barbieri and Nils Petter Gleditsch, "Does Globalization Contribute to Peace? A Critical Survey of the Literature," in *Globalization and Armed Conflict*, edited by Gerald Schneider, Katherine Barbieri and Nils Petter Gleditsch (Lanham: Rowman & Littlefield, 2003), 19.

[19] Kriesberg, *Constructive Conflicts*, 141, 144, 152.

a strong and robust generalization."[20] The greater the degree of trade and economic interdependence between nations, the lower the probability that they will fight each other. The evidence suggests that trade fosters peace between and within states.

The degree of market freedom is often used as indicator of private sector influence within a society. Market freedom is defined as the ability of economic actors to engage in commerce, set prices and make investment decisions freely without government interference or the risk of confiscation.[21] Researchers have found a strong and statistically significant relationship between commercial openness and the prospects for intrastate peace. States that encourage international trade and investment generally have lower levels of political violence and instability.[22] Policies and conditions that are favorable to free enterprise are associated with a reduced risk of civil war onset.[23] This finding holds even when controlling for related variables such as GDP per capita. The data suggests that greater market openness in a country can reduce the risk of civil conflict. Market freedom also has the effect of boosting per capita income and economic growth rates, thereby contributing indirectly to peace. Countries with a vibrant and well developed market economy are less likely to experience civil unrest and armed conflict.[24]

Investment is essential to economic growth and a core dimension of trade and economic development. We should therefore expect to see a positive relationship between measures of foreign direct investment (FDI) and lower levels of intrastate armed conflict. Statistical studies confirm this connection and provide strong evidence of a direct relationship

[20] Bruce Russett, "Violence and Disease: Trade as a Suppressor of Conflict when Suppressors Matter," in *Economic Interdependence and International Conflict: New Perspectives on an Enduring Debate*, edited by Edward D. Mansfield and Brian M. Pollins (Ann Arbor: University of Michigan Press, 2003), 159.

[21] One of the most widely used measures of market openness is the Economic Freedom of the World index maintained by the Fraser Institute. The index rates the quality of economic institutions and policies within states based on 42 indicators, including such factors as guarantees of property rights, a stable currency and minimal government interference. See the website of Economic Freedom of the World project, at www .freetheworld.com/papers.html.

[22] Margit Bussmann and Gerald Schneider, "When Globalization Discontent Turns Violent: Foreign Economic Liberalization and Internal War," *International Studies Quarterly* 51, no. 1 (2007): 88.

[23] Indra de Soysa and Hanne Fjelde, "Is the Hidden Hand an Iron Fist? Capitalism and Civil Peace, 1970–2005," *Journal of Peace Research* 47, no. 3 (2010): 287.

[24] Art Carden and Joshua Hall, "Why Are Some Places Rich While Others Are Poor? The Institutional Necessity of Economic Freedom," *Economic Affairs* 30, no. 1 (2010): 50.

between high levels of FDI and reduced risk of intrastate armed conflict.[25] The relationship also works in reverse. Armed conflict and political instability reduce development rates and scare off investors. Legitimate entrepreneurs are usually wary of committing financial resources in settings of armed violence. By contrast, countries that avoid conflict and maintain political stability create an environment favorable to foreign investment and economic growth and thus to sustainable peace. The evidence shows that FDI rates usually increase in the aftermath of peace agreements.[26]

The evidence in support of a link between FDI and reduced conflict risk adds further weight to the argument that global economic integration helps to promote peace. Governments that adopt restrictive policies toward international trade and investment are more likely to engage in military conflict, while those that embrace free-trade policies tend to be peaceful internally and in their relations with other states.[27] Countries open to investment and trade are embedded in multiple trading networks that enhance understanding and cooperation with others. They develop a self-interest in maintaining political stability and avoiding armed conflict so that investment flows and trading relationships continue. These multiple overlapping economic dynamics are an important force for peace.

Trade fosters peace not only through its beneficial economic impacts but also through its networking effects. The flow of goods and services within and between countries generates connections between people and facilitates communication and mutual understanding. It creates patterns of cooperation and interdependence that extend to third parties who gain a stake in sustaining the free flow of goods and communication. Studies that measure these network effects show significant pacifying impacts.[28] When regions and states are economically integrated, business and political leaders unavoidably share a great deal of information with each other. In these circumstances, transparency increases, while uncertainty

---

[25] Margit Bussmann, "Foreign Direct Investment and Militarized International Conflict," *Journal of Peace Research* 47, no. 2 (2010): 148.

[26] Madhav Joshi and Jason Michael Quinn, "Implementing the Peace: The Aggregate Implementation of Comprehensive Peace Agreements and Peace Duration After Intrastate Armed Conflict," *British Journal of Political Affairs*, published online, 16 November 2015, www.cambridge.org/core/journals/british-journal-of-political-science/article/implementing-the-peace-the-aggregate-implementation-of-comprehensive-peace-agreements-and-peace-duration-after-intrastate-armed-conflict/E5CCABC853015434FDAEACA40266C393.

[27] McDonald, *The Invisible Hand of Peace*, 90–91, 101–103.

[28] Dorussen and Ward, "Trade Networks and the Kantian Peace," 29–37.

and the risks of miscalculation diminish.[29] The patterns of interaction created through trade enable political leaders to anticipate and resolve disputes before they degenerate into potential violence. Trade also creates mechanisms for resolving disputes through bargaining and adjudication. These systemic features of commerce combine with specific economic benefits in generating the commercial peace effect.

THE GOVERNANCE CONTEXT

The peaceful effects of trade and market-based systems depend upon their governance context. Private enterprise has the greatest beneficial benefit when it is regulated and supported by effective public policies and quality institutions. Economic growth depends on the capacity of government to deliver public goods, including the maintenance of infrastructure, access to health care, and educational and training services. It also depends on the ability to guarantee property rights and the rule of law. Effective governance systems play a decisive role in advancing economic development. Unstable governments with weak institutions lack the ability to guarantee the legal and regulatory framework and the social capacities needed for development. Countries are better able to facilitate economic growth and minimize the resulting disruptions when they have strong infrastructures of social well-being and stable governing institutions.

To measure the legitimacy and impact of economic institutions researchers have developed an indicator of 'contract intensive money.' This is the share of the money supply held in savings deposits and legal commercial contracts relative to the total supply. It provides a rough measure of the degree to which people trust and use banks and financial institutions. High scores on this indicator are strongly associated with peace. States with trustworthy and well regulated financial institutions that protect investments are less likely to experience the onset of armed violence.[30] This finding buttresses the case for the legitimacy–stability link noted in earlier chapters. It underscores the importance of governance capacity and broadly based participatory development for stability and peace.

---

[29] Bussmann, "Foreign Direct Investment and Militarized International Conflict," 144.

[30] Hanne Fjelde and Indra de Soysa, "Conflict, Co-optation, or Cooperation: State Capacity and the Risk of Civil War, 1961–2001," *Conflict Management and Peace Science* 26, no. 5 (2009): 19.

Scholars describe the models of economic governance as "embedded autonomy" and "governed interdependence."[31] These are distinct types of institutionalized partnerships between government and the private sector in which the state shares power with economic actors but does not attempt to dominate. In these models governments and business interests function independently, but their initiatives occur within a negotiated relationship in which the state retains a guiding role, exercising leadership in consultation with industry and society. In Japan, France, Germany, the United Kingdom and other highly developed states, the government plays an active role in the economy and ensures that markets remain relatively open and competitive.

In Japan the Ministry of International Trade and Industry (MITI) emerged after World War II to facilitate the country's economic growth by spearheading investment in heavy metal and shipbuilding industries.[32] The Japanese model was followed by South Korea and other Asian tigers. While MITI's direct role in the economy has diminished over the years and is less relevant in an age of communications and information technology, the general model of active state involvement remains. The system is characterized by close institutionalized linkages between government bureaucrats and private business leaders in a context of constant consultation and cooperation. The relationship between government and business is predominantly one of partnership.

For the effective management of these partnership relationships with business, the capacity of government may be more important than regime type. As noted in Chapter 8, democracy is not necessarily a requirement for economic development. Some states that have achieved successful economic development are democracies – South Korea, Taiwan, India – but others such as China, Singapore and Vietnam are not. All of these states have substantial governance capacity, however, and they use it to provide the public goods necessary for economic growth.

One advantage of democratic states traditionally has been their more certain guarantee of property rights, but in recent decades nominally communist states have also assured the protection of private property.[33] States with effective development policies defend economic freedom whether they are democratic or not. China and other one-party states have capable security forces and systems of stability that enforce the rule

---

[31] Kjaer, *Governance*, 136.

[32] See Chalmers Johnson's classic work *MITI and the Japanese Miracle: The Growth of Industrial Policy, 1925–1975* (Stanford University Press, 1982).

[33] Carl Henrik Knutsen, "Democracy and Economic Growth: A Summary of Arguments and Results," *International Area Studies Review* 15, no. 4 (2012): 393–415.

of law and provide a degree of political legitimacy even without electoral accountability. The China model shows that the capacity to provide a productive workforce and protect market access can be a successful foundation for economic growth.

Democracy may not be necessary for economic growth, but it is helpful for promoting balanced development. Some of the core characteristics of democratic governance – coalition building and compromise, accountability to diverse constituencies, guarantees of political and economic opportunity, limits on the power of landed elites and the military – are also beneficial to economic development. This is evident in the experiences of Botswana and Mauritius, states with relatively high rates of economic growth. The two countries are consolidated democracies with regular elections and representative institutions.[34] Their political systems provide representation for diverse constituencies and ethnic groups. They have enforceable protections for property rights and political and economic freedom. They have provided incentives for export-oriented manufacturing companies to help diversify their economies. These and other institutional capabilities, intimately tied to democratic governance, have been important to their economic development.

Democracy promotes development by providing greater opportunities for the involvement of civil society and the creative contributions of private entrepreneurs.[35] Open societies nurture both political and economic freedom and provide fertile ground for innovation and investment. Because democratic states rely more on dialogue and consensus-seeking rather than coercion, they are better able to provide opportunities for a broader range of social forces. Democratic states are often characterized by the dispersion and decentralization of political authority, which can create greater space for cooperation between state and social actors. In open societies it is easier for social coalitions to emerge and influence government policy in support of development. These and other forms of state–society synergy within democratic systems help to advance the development process.

EAST ASIA: A TALE OF SUCCESS

The rapid economic growth of countries in East Asia shows that capitalism can reduce poverty rates and advance development, but it also shows

---

[34] Kjaer, *Governance*, 143–144.
[35] Ibid., 145–147.

that good governance and public goods provision are necessary for the success of market-driven development. High rates of economic growth in South Korea, China, India and other developing countries are indeed impressive and as noted have lifted hundreds of millions of people out of poverty. These gains followed government decisions to guarantee property rights, privatize markets and liberalize previously restrictive trade and investment policies, opening the door to huge volumes of trade and infusions of capital investment. These policy changes and the resulting economic growth have been the principal factor in reducing global poverty rates. The results have brought difficult dislocations for some communities and huge environmental challenges, but they have raised living standards and improved the quality of life for many people.

These changes did not follow the strict laissez-faire script of the Washington Consensus. Governments in China and other developing countries adopted an activist approach to development in which the state helped to guide economic policy and provided necessary social supports to make development possible. As they opened their markets to global competition, the Asian tigers also adopted national industrial policies and provided incentives for the development of specific sectors.[36] They liberalized some markets but protected others. They acted as investors when private actors found the risks too high. They supported critical research and development in new industries and through tariffs insulated emerging firms from competition until they were considered capable of holding their own in global markets.[37]

The economic success of East Asia resulted not simply from market liberalization but from a synergistic interaction between public policy and private economic initiative. State policies played an important role in creating markets and promoting exports. In South Korea, Taiwan and other countries, governments established public incentive systems to complement normal profit-oriented motives.[38] They offered state subsidies and protections to industries but linked these to specific performance standards. The Asian states funded public programs to increase social capacity, providing substantial government investments in education, workforce training and health care. They also adopted land reform and redistribution policies. These programs were designed to create the

---

[36] Mark Curtis, "Designing Conflict-sensitive Trade Policy," in *Trade, Aid and Security: An Agenda for Peace and Development*, edited by Oli Brown, Mark Halle, Sonia Pena Moreno and Sebastian Winkler (London: Earthscan, 2007), 28–29.

[37] Kjaer, *Governance*, 178.

[38] Ibid., 134.

social capacity and infrastructure needed to achieve progress in economic development.

The promotion of social and economic equity was also a driving factor in the East Asian miracle, according to a World Bank report.[39] The policies that led to this economic growth were described in the 1994 World Bank World Development Report:

Very explicit mechanisms were used to demonstrate the intent that all would have a share of future wealth. Korea and Taiwan carried out comprehensive land reform programs; Indonesia used rice and fertilizer price policies to raise rural incomes; Malaysia introduced explicit wealth sharing programs to improve the lot of ethnic Malays vis-à-vis the better off ethnic Chinese; Hong Kong and Singapore undertook massive public housing programs; in several economies, governments assisted workers' cooperatives and established programs to encourage small and medium-sized enterprises.[40]

Sen credits progressive social policies and capacity building programs with helping to power the Asian tigers. "What we are looking at here is not so much the social consequences of economic reforms, but the economic consequences of social reforms. The market economy nourishes on the foundations of such social development."[41] A report by the UN Research Institute for Social Development concurs: "there is now considerable evidence that high growth in East Asia was due to successful and appropriate developmental public policy interventions rather than economic liberalization."[42] While the opening of markets clearly was important, public interventions played a crucial role in development success.

The East Asian economic miracle has been accompanied by a significant reduction of armed conflict in a region that previously experienced high levels of violence. In the first three decades after World War II, East and Southeast Asia witnessed the world's deadliest wars and severe incidents of mass repression. Beginning in the 1980s, however, the region experienced a dramatic turnaround. East and Southeast Asia went from being the world's bloodiest battleground to one of its most peaceful regions. In 2010, levels of conflict-related fatalities in the region reached an all-time low.[43]

---

[39] World Bank, *The East Asian Miracle* (Oxford University Press, 1993).
[40] Quoted in Wilkinson and Pickett, *The Spirit Level*, 241.
[41] Sen, *Development as Freedom*, 259.
[42] Quoted in Curtis, "Designing Conflict-sensitive Trade Policy," 29.
[43] Stein Tønnesson, Erik Melander, Elin Bjarnegård, Isak Svensson and Susanne Schaftenaar, "The Fragile Peace in East and Southeast Asia," in *SIPRI Yearbook 2013: Armaments, Disarmament and International Security* (Oxford University Press, 2013), 28–40.

The East Asia peace is fragile, however, and lacks institutional ground-ing. Interstate tensions have increased in the last couple of years, with China, Vietnam, the Philippines and Japan vying over control of islands in the South China Sea, and the United States 'tilting' toward military containment of China. Geopolitical rivalries among Japan, the Koreas, China and Vietnam are deeply rooted. Intrastate conflicts continue in Myanmar, the Philippines and Thailand. Nonetheless the region remains relatively peaceful, with the rise of per capita income and economic pros-perity matched by a decline in the incidence of armed conflict.

THE CHINA EXCEPTION

The experience of China seems to contradict our contention that good governance is the key to economic development and peace. China has experienced unprecedented economic growth, and in the last few dec-ades has not engaged in armed conflict internally or with other countries, but it could be considered the poster child of poor governance.[44] It is undemocratic and authoritarian and denies its citizens basic rights of free expression and association. Its communist system is grossly corrupt and lavishes privilege and power on party elites to the detriment of society. Its leadership system remains overwhelmingly male-dominated. How do we explain the apparent success of this corrupt one-party dictatorship that has remained peaceful and achieved dramatic success in economic development?

As we have emphasized, good governance includes both the quality of institutions and their capacity to deliver public goods. Chinese govern-ance has a high degree of capacity for economic growth, but it largely lacks the qualities of inclusion, participation and accountability. China has demonstrated an extraordinary ability to deliver necessary public goods, most importantly the capacity to maintain security and generate economic growth and rising per capita income. It has opened up society to a greater degree of economic participation, and although not allowing national political participation, it has exhibited some level of account-ability to its population. The experience of China illustrates the cardinal importance of state capacity as a core dimension of governance. It sug-gests that even in the absence of political democracy, state capacity to provide security and relative stability can be sufficient to encourage eco-nomic growth and preserve peace – although as we will argue below,

---

[44] The phrase is that of an anonymous reviewer of this manuscript.

China's 'peace' leaves much to be desired, and its internal system of governance is less monolithic than it appears.

As Fukuyama observes, China's communist regime inherited a 2,000-year-old tradition of strong centralized government and administrative control.[45] The traditional model was based on effective, merit-based bureaucracies that were able to register the population, levy taxes and regulate society. As part of the post-1978 economic reform process, China introduced a merit-based civil service examination system, allowing the creation of a more professionalized bureaucracy. In doing so, the communist leaders restored some of the ancient traditions of the Chinese state. They encouraged the creation of effective public institutions with enough bureaucratic autonomy to guide economic development while avoiding the worst forms of predatory behavior.[46]

The Chinese system has demonstrated significant governance capacity. It has the means to assure security, enforce the rule of law (as the communist system defines it), provide education and health care services, and establish a broad social safety net of welfare services. For all of its faults and repressive features, the Chinese governance system has a high degree of institutional capacity. It has delivered the goods for economic growth, lifting hundreds of millions of people out of poverty and creating a large urban middle class.

China's post-1978 shift from a centrally planned economy to a more open market-based system has been accompanied by corresponding changes in the nature of governance. The political system remains under the domination of the Communist Party, but the scope and extent of its influence have diminished since the 1990s, and the nature of Party control has changed. Considerable variation exists between Party rule in market-friendly southern provinces like Guangdong and the more state-dominated Beijing region in the north.[47] To encourage entrepreneurship the state has created opportunities for individuals and local towns and villages to establish enterprises. Economic freedom has increased substantially, even if political freedom has not. While political participation is not an option in China, participation in economic trade has enabled tremendous growth.

One of the most significant triggers of China's dramatic social and economic transformation was the introduction of the "house

---

[45] Fukuyama, *Political Order and Political Decay*, 354–357.
[46] Ibid., 32.
[47] Ibid., 374–375.

responsibility system" in the late 1970s and early 1980s. The new system ended China's disastrous experiment in agricultural collectivization and redistributed land from communist-controlled communes to rural families. This egalitarian process gave land to virtually every rural household and led to an immediate and dramatic improvement in agricultural output and productivity. A USAID briefing paper described China's land reform process as "the greatest poverty alleviation achievement in world history."[48] While farmers still do not have legal title to their land, an increasing percentage of households have long-term leases that enable them to have confidence in making investments in land improvement. Although the state still owns the land, the rural economy in China has become broadly privatized.

Dramatic changes also have emerged in China's booming industrial manufacturing sector. The original "township and village enterprises" that generated industrial growth in the early reform years have given way to private enterprises, many of them foreign-owned.[49] Even some of the companies owned and operated by the People's Liberation Army have been closed or privatized, although the Army still runs a variety of businesses.[50] At the economic level the society is becoming increasingly free. The Communist Party continues to steer the direction of the economy, but agricultural and industrial production is mostly in private hands and responds to market forces more than political direction.

Some steps toward local electoral democracy also occurred in recent decades. Beginning in 1988–1989 the government established the so-called Organic Law of Villagers' Committees. Voters can now elect village committees and leaders with the authority to make locally based decisions. The village electoral system, which was made permanent in 1998, introduces an element of democracy into China's lowest-level political units, although it also provides a mechanism for establishing political control in the villages as privatization proceeds. Whether this process of limited grassroots democratization has improved governance is unclear. In some instances villagers have developed a more rights-based consciousness as they use the process to defend their interests, but in many localities predatory leaders and communist cadres retain dominant

---

[48] USAID, EGAT/NRM/LRM/USAID, "China: Lessons from a Successful Land Rights Reform," Briefing Paper, October 2009, http://pdf.usaid.gov/pdf_docs/PA00J759.pdf.

[49] James Kai-sing Kung and Yi-min Lin, "The Decline of Township-and-Village Enterprises in China's Economic Transition," *World Development* 35, no. 4 (April 2007): 569–584.

[50] Nan Li, ed., *Chinese Civil-Military Relations: The Transformation of the People's Liberation Army* (London and New York: Routledge, 2006).

power.[51] Communist leaders have resisted further democratization and halted experiments in the 1990s that would have introduced open elections at the town and township level.

Limited political changes have also occurred at the national level. Since the time of Deng Xiaoping senior political leaders have adopted a pattern of term limits, serving only ten years in office. This has created a process for political rotation, establishing a pattern of leadership turnover that is traditionally one of the hallmarks of democratic systems. The Standing Committee of the Communist Politburo serves as a kind of collective leadership team that so far has prevented any single leader with extreme views from taking over national policy, although in recent years Xi Jinping has sought to accumulate extraordinary powers as national leader.[52] There are no formal institutional constraints against a leader seizing greater autocratic power.

Over the past decade China has witnessed a growing number of locally based protest actions. These are responses to abuses and disasters caused by corrupt and incompetent officials – anger over arbitrary land seizures, fear over the effects of pervasive air and water pollution, and resentment over the mistreatment and abuse of migrant workers. According to research by the state's official Academy of Governance, the number of protests in China in 2010 rose to 180,000 reported "mass incidents."[53] In 2011 public assemblies for democracy took place in more than a dozen Chinese cities. These were inspired by and named after the Jasmine Revolution in Tunisia.[54] The Chinese government subsequently cracked down on many of these protests.[55]

As we consider whether China is an exception to the rule of peace through governance, it is important not to overstate China's peacefulness. That's not how Tibetans and Uyghurs see it. Many Vietnamese remember China's bloody military incursion into northern Vietnam in 1979. While

---

[51] Bryan Ho, "Village Democracy Shrugs in Rural China," *East Asia Forum: Economic, Politics and Public Policy in East Asia and the Pacific*, July 22, 2014, www.eastasiaforum .org/2014/07/22/village-democracy-shrugs-in-rural-china/.

[52] Daniel A. Bell, "The Limits of Democracy in China," *The Atlantic*, May 29, 2015, www.theatlantic.com/international/archive/2015/05/chinese-democracy-isnt-inevitable/ 394325/.

[53] Alan Taylor, "Rising Protests in China," *The Atlantic*, February 17, 2012, www.theatlantic .com/photo/2012/02/rising-protests-in-china/100247/.

[54] Ho, "Village Democracy Shrugs in Rural China."

[55] Li Xiaorong, "What's Behind the New Chinese Crackdown," *NYR Daily/New York Review of Books*, July 29, 2013, www.nybooks.com/daily/2013/07/29/whats-behind-new-chinese-crackdown/.

China has not used force against another state recently and is not battling internal insurgency, its policies in the border regions have been repressive and militaristic. The invasion and occupation of Tibet prompted armed resistance and led to horrific atrocities. China's actions left many dead and were accompanied by a systematic policy that continues to this day of undermining the region's unique religious and cultural heritage. For years Beijing has waged a relentless campaign of repression against Uyghur Muslims in Xinjiang. Violent clashes in July 2009 left many dead, with official estimates ranging in the hundreds.[56] Nor can we forget the infamous 1989 massacre at Tiananmen Square when the communist regime opened fire on peaceful demonstrators, killing hundreds.[57] China's militarized policies toward the Paracel and Spratly islands in the South China Sea are also worrisome. Recent disputes with Japan and Vietnam have been mostly non-militarized, but naval clashes between China and Vietnam led to dozens of fatalities in 1974 and again in 1988. China's declared control zone covers virtually the entire South China Sea and if pursued actively could spark armed conflict. These and other actions hardly count as pacific policies and should temper any classification of China as peaceful.

Yes, China is an exception, as any massive state of its scale would have to be. China sets patterns; it does not follow them. But its experience confirms one of the essential elements of the governance and peace theory – the importance of state capacity. China has displayed an extraordinary ability to deliver public goods through policies that promote economic growth and raise living standards. By opening the country to greater levels of trade, China has also fostered greater economic participation. On the other hand, China is an outlier on issues of democracy and lacks accountable institutions of public political participation. Yet even here the picture is mixed. China is not democratic at the national or regional level, but it is partially democratic at the local level. Citizens are able to participate in electing local leaders and have engaged in civil protests. These are not the attributes of

[56] Kilic Kanat, "Repression in China and its Consequences in Xinjiang," *Hudson Institute*, July 28, 2014, www.hudson.org/research/10480-repression-in-china-and-its-consequences-in-xinjiang.

[57] A *New York Times* investigation in the aftermath of the massacre put the number of likely fatalities in the range of approximately 400–500. See Nicholas Kristoff, "A Reassessment of How Many People Died in the Military Crackdown in Beijing," *New York Times*, June 21, 1989, www.nytimes.com/1989/06/21/world/a-reassessment-of-how-many-died-in-the-military-crackdown-in-beijing.html.

mature democracy, but neither are they features of rigid autocracy. We are left with a mixed picture of a country that is less peaceful than many assume, that has some limited democratic features at the local level, and that confirms the importance of state capacity for effective governance.

PRIVATE SECTOR, PUBLIC IMPACT

Many of the post-colonial regimes that came to power in Africa and Asia after World War II adopted state socialist practices and nationalized economic resources. They did so in the name of justice and equality, claiming that resources belong to the people and should be used for social benefit. The results were mostly disappointing, as revenues from nationalized companies flowed into the pockets of authoritarian leaders and their domestic and foreign patrons, while people in resource-rich regions were neglected and impoverished. This led to new forms of inequality and exploitation and the outbreak of armed conflict in many countries.

Nigeria is a classic example of this exploitive pattern. The country's rich oil revenues have been diverted to benefit the wealthy, while communities in the oil-producing Niger delta remain in poverty. Many of the developing states that own and control oil and other mineral revenues continue to suffer from poor governance. They have minimal tax structures and weak regulatory frameworks and institutions. In these settings the government is less dependent on society and less subject to political constraint. Regimes are free to use resource windfalls for any purpose, including repression and armed conflict.

Governments are more stable and publicly accountable when they are dependent on a healthy private sector that generates domestic tax revenues. States that draw their financial resources from taxes tend to have more representative governance and greater institutional capacity for providing public goods.[58] A high ratio of tax revenue to GNP reflects the ability of political authorities to extract tax revenues from citizens and companies. It is a measure of economic and social strength and reflects a degree of political legitimacy, an indication of relatively stable bonds between state and society. Taxation in a diversified economy means that governing authorities have sufficient public legitimacy to rely upon citizen and corporate compliance, however grudging that may be in the case

---

[58] Mike Moore, "Revenues, State Formation, and the Quality of Governance in Developing States," *International Political Science Review* 25, no. 3 (2004): 299.

of paying taxes. By contrast, when states lack taxation capacity and a diversified economic foundation, they tend to have weak governance and are more likely to experience internal armed conflict.

State ownership of economic resources in countries without institutional accountability or effective governance is associated with higher levels of poverty and armed conflict. The source of the problem is not the presence of resources per se, but the unaccountable institutional structures that shape the development of those resources. In Norway, where the government maintains extensive public ownership of oil production but has robust mechanisms of democratic accountability, resource development has been beneficial rather than harmful. By contrast, where governments lack institutions of accountability or choose not to develop them, resource wealth often exacerbates conditions of corruption and instability. The paradox, as one study notes, is that "the concentration of wealth impoverishes the state whereas the dispersion of wealth enriches the state."[59]

Private ownership patterns are associated with stronger governance capacity. Private owners have an incentive to establish effective institutions and fiscal regulatory mechanisms in the states where they operate to protect their investments and maintain profitability. Research shows that in developing countries "strong fiscal and regulatory institutions are more likely to emerge under private domestic ownership." Private sector investors have an interest in "establishing formal guarantees to increase fiscal predictability and reduce transaction and monitoring costs."[60] In some instances multinational corporations encourage good governance and stability in the countries where they invest and seek to reduce corruption.[61]

Of course the behavior of private sector firms is not always so benign. Oil and mining companies have been among the worse corporate offenders in exploiting local communities, abusing human rights, despoiling the environment and contributing to corruption.[62] In many development settings companies have taken advantage of weak governments and venal

---

[59] Pauline Jones Luong and Erika Weinthal, "Rethinking the Resource Curse: Ownership Structure, Institutional Capacity, and Domestic Constraints," *Annual Review of Political Science* 9 (2006): 241, 243.

[60] Ibid., 242.

[61] C.C.Y. Kwok and S. Tadesse, "The MNC as an Agent of Change for Host-country Institutions: FDI and Corruption." *Journal of International Business Studies* 37, no. 6 (2006): 767–785.

[62] See the classic critical assessment, Richard J. Barnet and Ronald E. Muller, *Global Reach: The Power of Multinational Corporations* (New York: Simon & Schuster, 1973).

officials to reap large profits and gain market advantage, often disregarding the rule of law and the needs of local populations. Corporations that operate in this manner exacerbate conditions that increase the risk of armed violence. In recent decades multinational corporations have faced increasing pressure to comply with social responsibility and environmental sustainability standards. More than 90 of the world's largest oil, gas and mining companies have joined the Extractive Industries Transparency Initiative, pledging to uphold standards of public accountability.[63] Changes in actual business practice have come slowly, however, or not at all in many instances. Stronger and more effective protections are needed to guard against corporate abuse and harness the power of business for balanced and sustainable economic development.

THE 'RESOURCE CURSE' AS WEAK INSTITUTIONAL CAPACITY

These considerations shed fresh light on the well-known relationship between dependence on primary commodity exports, especially oil, and an increased risk of armed conflict. Research shows that countries in which oil exports are a major source of revenue account for one-third of the total armed conflicts in the world. Two core findings emerge from the empirical evidence: dependence on oil exports is directly linked to an increased risk of civil war onset; and the presence of lootable resources, such as diamonds or drugs, tends to prolong armed conflict once it begins.[64]

Trade in primary commodities such as oil and mineral resources is often highly corrupt and generates negative political and economic effects. States that rely on resource rents for the bulk of their national income are more conflict-prone. Such states tend to have weak governing institutions and less incentive to provide public goods to maintain domestic peace.[65] Some of the wealthy oil-exporting states can buy off potential adversaries, but in other countries resource dependency slows economic growth, increases inequality and exacerbates conflict risk.[66]

---

[63] The Extractive Industries Transparency Initiative, "Stakeholders," (Oslo, 2015), https://eiti.org/supporters/companies.

[64] Michael T. Ross, "What Do We Know About Resources and Civil War?" *Journal of Peace Research* 41, no. 3 (2004).

[65] Halvor Mehlum, Karl Moene and Ragnar Torvik, "Cursed by Resources or Institutions," *The World Economy* 29, no. 8 (2006): 1117.

[66] Hanne Fjelde, "Buying Peace? Oil Wealth, Corruption, and Civil War, 1985–99," *Journal of Peace Research* 46, no. 2 (2009): 200.

The presence of valuable land-based resources tends to increase the motivation for insurgency among local opposition groups. Insurgents seeking greater autonomy or independence in a region often attempt to gain control over the resource riches generated by onshore oil production and mineral development. The presence of oil and other wealth-producing resources makes autonomy or independence more lucrative and desirable for those who seek to dominate such regions. The incentive for armed conflict increases in proportion to the value of controlling natural resource wealth.

The relationship also works in reverse. The presence of armed conflict and instability may inhibit legitimate investment in resource development. In a 2001 survey, mining industry executives were asked why they refrained or withdrew from otherwise sound investment opportunities in some countries; nearly 80 percent cited political instability and conflict risk as the main reason.[67] In Afghanistan reports of lucrative deposits of mineral wealth have created optimism that the country could develop economically,[68] but international mining countries have been reluctant to invest in the absence of an effective governance system and in the midst of armed conflict and instability.

Scholars have debated whether the link between armed conflict and resource dependency is caused by economic or governance-related factors. Collier and his colleagues initially focused on economic conditions, reasoning that the availability of lootable resources such as oil or diamonds provides an economic incentive for the onset of civil war and the means to sustain it.[69] Collier later qualified this analysis in a paper finding that resource-dependent states "with sufficiently good institutions" are less likely to face a high risk of armed conflict.[70] If revenues from oil and mineral production are invested domestically to increase wealth and GDP per capita, the resulting benefits offset any detrimental effects of the resource curse.[71]

---

[67] Cited Brainard et al., "The Tangled Web," 22.

[68] James Risen, "U.S. Identifies Vast Mineral Riches in Afghanistan," *New York Times*, June 13, 2000, www.nytimes.com/2010/06/14/world/asia/14minerals.html.

[69] Paul Collier and Anke Hoeffler, "Greed and Grievance in Civil War," Centre for the Study of African Economies, WPS/2002-01 (University of Oxford, February 13, 2002), 1, www.csae.ox.ac.uk/workingpapers/wps-list.html.

[70] Paul Collier and Benedikt Goderis, "Commodity Prices, Growth, and the Natural Resource Curse: Reconciling a Conundrum," CSAE, WPS/2007–15 (University of Oxford, August 2007).

[71] Michael Ross, "A Closer Look at Oil, Diamonds and Civil War," *Annual Review of Political Science* 9 (2006): 267.

Fearon explained the resource curse on the basis of governance factors rather than economic incentives. He traced commodity dependence to underlying weaknesses in state capacity. "States with high oil revenues have less incentive to develop administrative competence and control throughout their territory."[72] Others have probed this connection and trace it to the failure of states to enforce property rights.[73] In the absence of accountable governance systems that enforce the rule of law, armies or militia groups can simply capture natural resources and use the revenues for their own benefit to the exclusion of others. These conflict-inducing dynamics are less likely to occur in states with effective governance capacity.

Governance and economic factors reinforce each other in accounting for the resource curse. As we have emphasized, states that are dependent on oil earnings rather than taxation from a diversified economy tend to be weaker politically with less developed governance systems. Regimes that rely predominantly on oil revenues tend to lack systems of broad public taxation and as a result do not have the political legitimacy that a taxation system requires.[74] Such regimes tend to spend less on social needs and more on weapons and war. They often disregard the rule of law and are less able to attract sufficient investment and trade to diversify the economy and meet the needs of society. They are vulnerable to the threat of armed violence and are more easily caught in the conflict trap.

BALANCING MARKETS AND SOCIAL NEEDS

The importance of the private sector for advancing economic development is not an argument for diminishing the role of the public sector. The structural adjustment and privatization policies promoted by international financial institutions require low-income countries to privatize state assets and resources, deregulate markets, remove trade and investment controls, and reduce government spending. In instances where the state dominates the economy and is the main source of employment, government downsizing may be necessary and appropriate, but the process should be gradual and combined with measures that cushion the

---

[72] James D. Fearon, "Primary Commodity Exports and Civil War," *Journal of Conflict Resolution* 49, no. 4 (2005): 487.

[73] Leif Wenar, "Property Rights and the Resource Curse," *Philosophy and Public Affairs* 36, no. 1 (2008): 2–32.

[74] Cameron Thies, "Of Rulers, Rebels, and Revenue: State Capacity, Civil War Onset, and Primary Commodities," *Journal of Peace Research* 47, no. 3 (2010): 323.

resulting social hardships. Developing countries need help in building effective institutions, attracting investment and trade, and providing necessary public goods. Privatization mandates in the absence of such help can lead to cuts in government services, rising prices and interest rates, and greater levels of unemployment. As Joseph Stiglitz notes, trade liberalization accompanied by high interest rates is "an almost certain recipe for job destruction" and economic instability.[75] The results in some instances have been disastrous – rampant corruption, weakened local economies, greater inequality and exposure to destabilizing financial shocks. These consequences exacerbate social tensions and increase the risk of conflict.

The impacts of rapid financial market liberalization are of special concern. Trade and productive investment can enhance economic development, but the impacts of unregulated financial liberalization can be harmful for local economies. The structural adjustment loans of the IMF require countries to remove controls on financial investment, which can open the door to large flows of international finance capital. The rapid movement of funds in and out of unregulated currency markets weakens banking systems and undermines national attempts to stabilize the currency. The infusion of financial capital into emerging markets with high interest rates fuels speculation and economic instability.[76]

Many of the states affected by market liberalization do not have sufficient social safety nets. They lack effective governance systems for delivering public goods or controlling financial transactions. Their educational institutions are not fully capable of producing the highly trained technical workers that international firms often require. Opening these countries to unregulated financial speculation makes local citizens and communities vulnerable to the resulting adverse economic and social consequences.

Empirical evidence confirms the potential harmful effects of rapid market liberalization.[77] While economic globalization generally has a pacifying effect, the process of opening a previously protected economy to global competition can have short-term disruptive impacts. The initial steps toward market liberalization are often harmful to vulnerable local communities and may cause instability and conflict. Struggles over

---

[75] Joseph E. Stiglitz, *Globalization and its Discontents* (New York: W.W. Norton & Company, 2002), 84.

[76] Ibid., 65.

[77] Bussmann and Schneider, "When Globalization Discontent Turns Violent," 94.

the redistributive effects of rapid liberalization can turn violent and may increase the risk of armed conflict.

Private enterprise is a powerful engine for development, but it cannot function effectively without public protection and regulation. Many of the policies being imposed in the name of free market orthodoxy hinder employment growth and impede development.[78] Effective institutions are necessary to ameliorate the consequences of economic change and assure more balanced growth. If privatization is deemed necessary it should be part of a comprehensive approach that includes economic adjustment assistance, the provision of social welfare services and alternative job creation programs. The free enterprise system functions best in the context of governance structures that protect its creative powers but also tame its excesses.

CONCLUSION

For decades it has been a cardinal principle on the left that capitalism is a system of injustice and exploitation that creates poverty and inequality. Marx and Lenin argued that capitalism is inherently self-destructive and that unbridled competition for markets breeds imperialism and war. World War I and the subsequent rise of fascism seemed to confirm these judgments, but the dominant trend in capitalist societies over the decades has been toward social democracy. Capitalism proved to be highly dynamic and adaptable, evolving from initial unregulated phases toward an active welfare state and redistributive social programs. As Schumpeter and other economists noted, some private interests may benefit from war and arms production, but the inherent tendency of capitalism is toward trade, innovation and interdependence. History confirms that while capitalist countries are at times bellicose, the majority have evolved toward peaceful cooperation. States that ruled in the name of Marxism meanwhile tended to be highly repressive and militaristic. So much for the theory of capitalism and war.

History did not follow Marx's expectations, but many of the domestic social and economic reforms advocated by labor parties and socialist movements were adopted as policy, especially in Europe. Governments established effective social safety nets and public welfare programs and developed the capacity to deliver necessary public goods and services. These reforms trimmed some of the harsh edges of capitalism and

---

[78] Stiglitz, *Globalization and its Discontents*, 59–60.

ironically helped to save the free enterprise system. In East Asia a new kind of socialist capitalism emerged, directly out of communist rule in China and Vietnam and indirectly from guided capitalism in Japan, South Korea and other states. Among all of the most highly developed capitalist states, per capita income has increased, social well-being has advanced, and the risk of internal armed conflict has diminished.

The findings of social science reviewed in these pages help to explain these trends. Through its ability to generate economic growth and rising per capita income, capitalism creates social conditions that reduce the risk of armed conflict. The guarantees of market access and economic freedom that propel entrepreneurship and investment are also associated with more open societies and a reduced risk of war. Free trade and economic interdependence help to create peaceful relations among and within countries.

These observations do not mean that the impacts of capitalism are uniformly beneficial. Unfettered capitalism obviously has its dark side. Its "creative destruction" not only changes economic conditions but can have disruptive impacts socially and politically.[79] Capitalism is Janus-faced, offering possibilities for prosperity and development to enhance the human condition, but also unleashing forces of avarice and exploitation that can lead to social and environmental degradation.[80] As we have observed, the impacts of market liberalization and privatization can be highly disruptive and may exacerbate the risk of armed conflict. Piketty's finding of an inherent trend toward inequality of wealth within capitalism poses a profound challenge and argues for even greater emphasis on redistributive social programs. As we have argued, the beneficial impacts of capitalism are dependent upon the governance context. Capitalism is most likely to promote peaceful relations when it is embedded in governance systems that assure the equitable delivery of public goods and services and that guarantee economic freedom, market access and the rule of law.

[79] Joseph A. Schumpeter, *Capitalism, Socialism and Democracy* (New York: Harper, 1975), 82–85.
[80] The term Janus-faced comes from Peter Wallensteen, remarks at the Workshop on Governance and Quality Peace, Kroc Institute for International Peace Studies, University of Notre Dame, November 12, 2013; see also Ian Linden, "Idols in Hyperspace: The Janus-Face of Capitalism," Catholic Institute for International Relations, 97/165, no date, www.sedosmission.org/web/en/sedos-bulletin/doc_view/ 1409-idols-in-hyperspace-the-janus-face-of-capitalism.

Transnational trade and investment have great potential to enhance peace within and between states, but the current rules and decision-making structures of the global economy are stacked against the interests of the poor and less developed states and too often contribute to instability. As we observe in the next chapter, the structures of global governance have a significant role to play in advancing the prospects for international peace and development if they promote inclusive, participatory and accountable governance.

PART IV

CONCLUSION

10

Global Governing

More than two hundred years ago Immanuel Kant wrote that peace among nations requires the creation of a "federation of free states." He envisioned a voluntary association of democratic nations joining together to avert war. Kant's idea remains a distant dream, but over the past century political leaders in many countries have recognized the necessity of cooperating to end and prevent wars, address common threats and secure the peace. This was the hope that animated the creation of the League of Nations and United Nations and that has led to the formation of an increasing number of international organizations. While the world lacks anything like a federated government, a rudimentary scaffolding of international cooperation has emerged,[1] a patchwork of mechanisms for resolving disputes and transnational challenges.[2] As noted in Chapter 1, governance and global governance are often considered synonymous – for good reason since the international arena is where effective systems of collective action are most clearly needed to prevent war between and within states.

The purpose of this chapter is to explore the structures and conditions of governance at the global level that reduce the risk of armed conflict. Our focus remains the problem of civil war and intrastate conflict, but we also look at the role of international institutions in addressing disputes between nations. An emphasis on intrastate conflicts is appropriate

[1] Seyom Brown, *Higher Realism: A New Foreign Policy for the United States* (Boulder: Paradigm Publishers, 2009), 21.
[2] Daniel W. Drezner, "'Good Enough' Global Governance and International Finance," Foreign Policy Blogs, January 30, 2013, http://drezner.foreignpolicy.com/posts/2013/01/30/good_enough_global_governance_and_international_finance.

not only because these are most prevalent but also because many international institutions are focused precisely on efforts to resolve and prevent conflicts within states. From Colombia to Syria, Afghanistan and beyond, the United Nations, the European Union and other international institutions are deeply engaged in efforts to end intrastate conflict and build conditions for sustainable peace.

We examine some of these efforts below as we review the rise of multilateralism and the extraordinary expansion of international peacemaking efforts in recent decades. We consider the imperatives that have driven states to work together and the empirical evidence confirming the benefits of such cooperation. We look at the quality and capacity of global institutions in relation to peacemaking, development assistance and the role of civil society. We address the shortcomings of international institutions, including their significant deficits of inclusion and accountability and limitations of capacity, and highlight the importance of good governance principles for enhancing global cooperation.

TOWARD COMMON SECURITY

Multilateralism is the process of international cooperation to perform common tasks and achieve shared objectives. It includes a wide variety of formal institutions and an array of rules and norms, often established in treaties, which reflect agreed-upon rights, obligations and expectations.[3] International institutions have become increasingly dominant in world politics and the global economy and play a substantial role in shaping interactions among peoples and states.[4]

Today's multilateral system, with the United Nations at its center, grew directly out of World War II. It was created to prevent a repeat of the devastating carnage that took tens of millions of lives, "to save succeeding generations from the scourge of war."[5] The UN Security Council was established as the supreme international authority for preventing war and securing peace, although it did not begin to realize its potential in the peacemaking arena until the 1990s and to this day remains hampered by competition among the major powers and their unwillingness to limit their veto power and yield greater authority to the Council. The post-World War II multilateral architecture also includes the Bretton Woods

---

[3] G. John Ikenberry, *Liberal Order and Imperial Ambition* (Cambridge: Polity Press, 2006), 248.
[4] Robert Keohane, "Multilateralism: An Agenda for Research," *International Journal* 45, no. 4 (1990): 731.
[5] United Nations, *Charter of the United Nations*, 1945, 1.

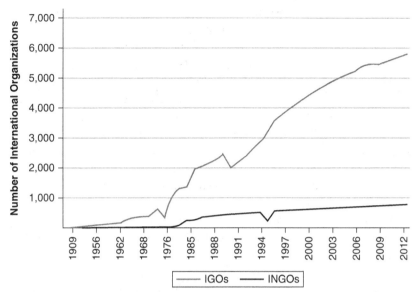

FIGURE 10.1. Increase in the numbers of IGOs and INGOs, 1909–2013
Source: T.G. Weiss, D.C. Seyle, and K. Coolidge, *The Rise of Non-State Actors in Global Governance: Opportunities and Limitations* (Broomfield, CO: One Earth Future Foundation, 2013)

institutions, the World Bank and the International Monetary Fund, which were created to promote economic development. The World Trade Organization emerged in the 1990s to coordinate and support the rapidly rising volume of international trade and investment.

Many other international institutions and regional organizations have evolved over the decades to address a wide range of political, security, economic, social, scientific, environmental and cultural purposes. The number of international governmental and nongovernmental organizations has increased from approximately 70 in 1940 to many thousands today (see Figure 10.1).[6] The number of multilateral legal conventions, treaties and formal agreements has increased apace and also numbers in the thousands.[7] Multilateralism is a process that "has taken on a life of its own," John Ikenberry writes, and is likely to assume an ever greater role in the affairs of states into the future.[8]

---

[6] Robert O. Keohane, "International Institutions: Can Interdependence Work?", *Foreign Policy* 110 (Spring 1998): 84.
[7] Thomas J. Mils and Eric A. Posner, "Which States Enter into Treaties, and Why?", John M. Olin Law & Economics Working Paper No. 420 (2nd series), Public Law and Legal Theory Working Paper No. 225, Law School of the University of Chicago, August 2008, 12.
[8] Ikenberry, *Liberal Order and Imperial Ambition*, 261, 8.

Since the nineteenth century, transnational organizations have been created largely for functional purposes to address humanitarian and commercial issues. One of the first of these was the International Red Cross and Red Crescent and the first Geneva Convention, established in 1864. The International Telegraph Union and the Universal Postal Union were formed in 1865 and 1874 respectively. Since World War II the number of IGOs has multiplied, ranging from organizations such as the Food and Agriculture Organization based in Rome, and the International Atomic Energy Agency (IAEA) headquartered in Vienna, to the creation of the UN Counter Terrorism Committee and its Counter-Terrorism Executive Directorate following the al-Qaida attacks in the United States in September 2001.

Many international institutions perform functional tasks for specific technical purposes. In the process they develop working relationships that facilitate generalized cooperation, leading to the gradual emergence of a de facto "peace system."[9] Functionalism enables states "to acquire benefits for their peoples which were hitherto unavailable," according to Inis Claude, enhancing their capacity to provide security and deliver other public goods.[10] This type of functional cooperation can continue even when states have sharp disagreements on larger policy issues. Many states strongly opposed the US-led invasion of Iraq, but they continued to work with American officials in a range of functional agencies, including in counterterrorism and intelligence cooperation.

Many factors help to explain the rise of multilateralism: the accelerating pace of globalization, the growing economic and political interdependence of states and regions, and the necessity of functional coordination in a growing number of transnational activities from finance to counterterrorism. Multilateral systems have spread because states find it in their interest to work together in addressing mutual needs and challenges. As global economic and political interdependence grows, the opportunity costs of not coordinating policy increase. States benefit by sacrificing a small portion of their sovereignty to participate in partnerships.[11] They willingly give up some autonomy and discretion for themselves, to obtain more predictability and cooperation in the behavior of others.[12]

---

[9] David Mitrany, *A Working Peace System* (Chicago: Quadrangle, 1966).

[10] Inis Claude, *Sword into Plowshares* (New York: Random House, 1964), 352.

[11] Keohane, "Multilateralism," 742.

[12] Ikenberry, *Liberal Order and Imperial Ambition*, 122.

International cooperation is a natural response to the rise of transnational challenges and threats that cannot be resolved by any single state or small group of states acting on their own. The decision to act together often emerges in response to a threat. It could be considered a form of "asocial sociability," to use Kant's phrase, resistance to a common enemy that forges bonds of cooperation among those who are threatened.[13] It is no accident that the United Nations emerged from the horrors of world war. The common global concern for preventing nuclear nonproliferation led to the Nuclear Non-Proliferation Treaty in 1970 and sustains the International Atomic Energy Agency today. The UN Framework Convention on Climate Change emerged in the 1990s to coordinate global responses to the threat of rising temperatures and ocean acidity and the urgent need to reduce greenhouse emissions. The UNFCCC coordinated the important December 2015 Paris Agreement, which could be a landmark for environmental sustainability and global cooperation if states follow through with pledges to implement national plans for reducing emissions.

International institutions provide important security, economic and other benefits for states. They reduce uncertainty, enhance trust and minimize risks of miscalculation.[14] They facilitate political bargaining and provide mechanisms for preventing and managing intrastate and interstate conflicts. They establish the ground rules for multilateral cooperation and help to set the agenda for international action. Mutual participation in international organizations helps to address the problem of political commitment, getting political actors to cooperate. Institutions bind states together in commitments to implement joint decisions. This increases the likelihood of mutual agreement, thus serving the interests of each state individually and of the whole. Security partnerships help dampen the inherent anarchy of the international system and tame strategic rivalries. Each state naturally seeks its own advantage, but the interests of all are advanced when they choose to collaborate. Mutually binding security arrangements are the institutional form of this process. They establish mechanisms of collective action, mutual constraint and enhanced transparency that improve the security of all participating members. This is the essence of common security.

---

[13] Immanuel Kant, "Idea for a Universal History with Cosmopolitan Intent," in Immanuel Kant, *Perpetual Peace, and Other Essays on Politics, History, and Morals*, edited by Ted Humphrey (Indianapolis: Hackett Publishing, 1983).

[14] Keohane, "International Institutions," 13, 86–87.

THE BENEFITS OF INTEGRATION

Empirical studies confirm that multilateral institutions help to build peaceful relations among and within participating states. The pacific benefits of membership in international organizations are greatest when the participating states have high levels of democracy and mutual trade. The democracy effect is particularly strong in these settings.[15] Russett and Oneal find that democracy, commercial interdependence and joint participation in international organizations combine to lower the probability of armed conflict.[16] As noted in previous chapters, mature democracy and mutual trade are associated with a reduced risk of civil conflict. The conflict-reducing effects of democracy are reinforced by membership in multilateral organizations.[17] The combination of a democratic regime and participation in international institutions boosts the prospects for peace.

Other studies identify the specific characteristics of international organizations that seem to be most responsible for reducing the risk of conflict. An examination of 25 regional intergovernmental agreements finds that the pacifying effect is greatest for organizations in which political leaders cooperate on a wide range of economic issues and have regular institutionalized face-to-face meetings among high-level officials. Extensive economic cooperation and regular meetings of high-level officials have significant effects in reducing the probability of militarized disputes.[18]

Some scholars focus on the socializing effects of participation in international organizations. States that interact with each other on a regular basis tend to share a common sense of identity and pursue similar interests in international politics.[19] Mutual membership in regional and international institutions is associated with and helps to build greater compatibility of political interests among the participating states. This has been true, for example, with new member states of the European Union, which adopt a broader European outlook as they cooperate

---

[15] Jon Pevehouse and Bruce Russett, "Democratic International Governmental Organizations Promote Peace," *International Organization* 60 (Fall 2006): 983–984.

[16] Russett and Oneal, *Triangulating Peace*.

[17] Pevehouse and Russett, "Democratic International Governmental Organizations," 994.

[18] Yoram Z. Haftel, "Designing for Peace: Regional Integration Arrangements, Institutional Variation, and Militarized Interstate Disputes," *International Organization* 61, no. 1 (2007): 218–219, 230.

[19] David Bearce and Stacy Bondanella, "Intergovernmental Organizations, Socialization, and Member-State Interest Convergence," *International Organization* 61, no. 4 (2007): 711–713.

on EU policies. EU member states are required to accept human rights standards and respect the rights of national minorities, stipulations which when followed help to reduce the risk of civil conflict. This is both a cause and effect of the reduced likelihood of armed conflict among and within member states.

Data shows that participation in regional organizations is strongly associated with the likelihood of a state transitioning to democracy. A review of political transitions from 1950 to 1992 finds that membership in a regional organization significantly increased the odds of a state making a successful democratic transition.[20] As noted in Chapter 7, states are more likely to be peaceful as they reach higher levels of democracy. A 'supply-side' effect also exists: regional organizations with a greater density of democratic states, such as the European Union, are more likely to be associated with democratic transitions. Participation in international organizations can foster democratization and peace in transitioning states through the inducements of membership, especially the benefits of mutual trade, and the resulting socialization effects among regime elites and influential domestic constituencies.

Heightened international cooperation can lead to greater political, economic and social integration. Peace becomes more likely, Boulding argues, through the enlargement of an 'integrative structure' in which states and regions within countries preserve their identity but no longer view others as enemies.[21] Nations and social groups interact with each other according to rules and regulations rather than the brandishing of coercive power. They agree to standards of mutual accountability and responsibility.[22] Political, economic and social actors are increasingly linked in a globalized world in which all are interdependent, sharing unbroken links of economic exchange, social communication and mobility of persons.[23] Dense networks of social exchange develop and strengthen the integrative process, creating incentives for further interdependence. These tendencies are most prevalent in nations that are democratic, economically interdependent, and legally and institutionally linked. They are the glue that holds communities together in democratic peace.

The European Union is a manifestation of this process. Despite its current travails, the EU has been an outstanding example of the potential

---

[20] Jon Pevehouse, "Democracy from the Outside-In? International Organizations and Democratization," *International Organization* 56, no. 3 (2002): 529, 537.

[21] Boulding, *Three Faces of Power*, 183.

[22] Brown, *Higher Realism*, 11.

[23] Dorussen and Ward, "Trade Networks and the Kantian Peace," 30.

benefits of international cooperation and integration. Its emergence is of historic significance to an understanding of the prospects for multi-lateral cooperation and peace. As Russett and Oneal observe, the economic and political transformation of Western Europe after World War II was based on interlocking "virtuous circles" that directly and indirectly promoted peaceful relations among previously warring states.[24] The EU has also fostered peace and human rights within member states. The development of European cooperation confirms the core insights of the Kantian model: democracy, international cooperation and economic interdependence are the foundations upon which a more peaceful future can be built between and within states. The future of the EU is more in doubt now than in the past, but its record in fostering peace and prosperity in a region that was the cauldron of world war stands as an historic achievement.

REGIONAL CONFLICT AND PREVENTION

No other regional organization has the integrative character or institutional capacity of the European Union, but the role of regional bodies is important and has increased in recent decades. This is in keeping with Chapter VIII of the UN Charter, which specifies that "regional arrangements or agencies" may help in the "pacific settlement of local disputes."[25] In recent decades regional and sub-regional organizations have become significant players in addressing intrastate conflicts. Organizations such as the Association of South East Asian Nations, the Economic Community of West African States and the Intergovernmental Authority on Development in East Africa were created for the purpose of boosting trade and development, but over the decades they have also addressed intrastate conflict issues within member states and in their respective regions.

Regional solutions to peacemaking are necessary given the trans-border dimensions of many of intrastate armed conflicts. Ethnic and sectarian conflicts in particular spill across borders and can lead to political disruption and armed conflict in more than one country.[26] Ethnic communities often reside in contiguous states and share a common sense of identity distinct from that of the nation in which they live. Members of

[24] Russett and Oneal, *Triangulating Peace*, 24.
[25] United Nations, *The Charter of the United Nations*, Articles 52 and 53.
[26] See Beebe and Kaldor, *The Ultimate Weapon is No Weapon*, 105–106.

border-transcending communities may feel similar grievances or at a minimum strongly sympathize with one another. If conditions become severe enough to spark armed conflict in one country, the effects are likely to be felt in neighboring states and may generate similar violence in ethnically related regions. Attempts to resolve these conflicts require responses in multiple jurisdictions at national and regional levels.

The spillover effects of trans-border conflict can generate broad-based problems of conflict and instability in an entire region. They are most severe in settings where the institutions of governance are corrupt and weak. These spillover effects include refugee flows, criminalized networks, arms trafficking and environmental ruin, generating what Kaldor describes as "clusters of war economies" that emerge from and sustain regional armed conflicts.[27] In the Balkan Wars, hundreds of thousands of people fled across borders, legitimate economic activity declined, criminal supply networks thrived (often linked to specific fighting units), and armed groups extracted 'taxation' through plunder and predation. The effects of the Syrian Civil War are worse and have spread to Lebanon, Jordan, Turkey and Iraq, generating economic and humanitarian hardships in the entire region.

The problem of neighborhood effects is compounded by the existence in some regions of artificial borders, usually created by colonial authorities in the nineteenth or early twentieth centuries, which cut through the land of specific ethnic groups. In these settings normal political and social interactions among local ethnically based communities may appear to state officials and international organizations as illegal cross-border activity.[28] Many Pashtun insurgents in Afghanistan and Pakistan do not accept or recognize the Durand Line that separates their two countries. The Pashtuns and the Kurds are examples of significant ethno-national communities that have many of the characteristics of a nation – a substantial population with a common language and cultural heritage residing in contiguous territory – but no state of their own. When such communities lack political representation or economic opportunity in the countries where they reside they may be prompted to resort to violence, often drawing in related ethnic communities beyond their borders.

Support from ethnic kin in neighboring countries and from émigrés in other states also drive this form of armed conflict. In Somalia combatants receive support from neighboring ethnic kin and in some instances

[27] Kaldor, *New and Old Wars*, 10.
[28] Azam, "The Redistributive State and Conflicts in Africa," 431.

from diaspora communities as far away as North America. Indeed émigré or neighboring communities are often more bellicose than their kin in the country of contention.[29] A study of armed conflicts during the 1990s found that three-quarters of these conflicts involved some degree of external support, mostly from neighboring states.[30]

Empirical evidence confirms the importance of clustering and contagion effects in the onset of civil war. Hegre and Sambanis find that the presence of armed conflict in an adjacent country is a major predictor of civil war.[31] States in 'dangerous neighborhoods' are far more likely to experience armed conflict within their borders than countries in more peaceful regions. The major economic and political factors that are associated with the risk of war also cluster geographically in ways that overlap with and reinforce the risk of war. The most significant of these trans-border influences are the presence of strong ethnic linkages, low levels of democracy in the region, and inadequate levels of economic development and commercial interdependence. The likelihood of civil war in these unstable regions is several times higher than in more favorable neighborhoods.[32] Trans-border factors can be as important as the domestic characteristics of individual states in explaining the onset of civil war.

If armed conflict often has a trans-border effect, peacebuilding strategies must be similarly oriented. As Wallensteen emphasizes, the solutions to armed conflict require the involvement not only of affected countries but of relevant regional organizations.[33] Attempting to achieve greater peace and stability in Afghanistan, for example, requires stemming the spread of violent extremism in the northern regions of Pakistan and reducing Pakistani government support for the Taliban. Continued armed violence in Somalia is the result not only of failed governance in Mogadishu but of instability and marginalization in neighboring states and the social mobilization of diaspora communities in other countries. Strategies for resolving these trans-border conditions require peacebuilding approaches

---

[29] Kristian Skrede Gleditsch, "Transnational Dimensions of Civil War," *Journal of Peace Research* 44, no. 3 (2007): 298.

[30] Peter Wallensteen and Margareta Sollenberg, "Armed Conflict and Regional Conflict Complexes, 1989–1997," *Journal of Peace Research* 35 (1998): 593–606.

[31] Sambanis and Hegre, "Sensitivity Analysis of the Empirical Literature on Civil War Onset," 529, 533.

[32] Gleditsch, "Transnational Dimensions of Civil War," 304.

[33] Peter Wallensteen, "Regional Peacebuilding: A New Challenge," *New Routes* (Life and Peace Institute) 4 (2012): 4.

in multiple jurisdictions involving a wide range of civil society, government, regional and international interests. More capable, inclusive, participatory and accountable institutions are needed not only in particular states but throughout affected regions. Integrated multi-stakeholder approaches are essential for overcoming the complex dynamics of cross-border and regionally based armed conflict. Efforts to build the peacemaking capacity of regional organizations are sound investments in international conflict prevention.

MULTILATERAL PEACEMAKING

Multilateral institutions play an important direct role in helping to resolve and prevent armed conflict in global trouble spots. International peacemaking has increased dramatically since the end of the Cold War and has become a major factor in addressing problems of intrastate conflict and creating more peaceful conditions in many parts of the world. The result has been a veritable revolution in international peacemaking, conflict prevention and post-conflict peacebuilding. *Human Security Report 2005* documents this unprecedented surge in peacemaking activism for the years 1987 through 1999:[34]

- a sixfold increase in the number of preventive diplomacy missions;
- a fourfold increase in peacemaking activities designed to stop ongoing conflicts;
- a sevenfold increase in the number of 'Friends of the Secretary-General,' 'Contact Groups' and other government initiatives to support peacemaking and peacebuilding missions;
- an elevenfold increase in the number of Security Council sanctions regimes; and
- a fourfold increase in the number of UN peacekeeping operations.

The United Nations has been at the center of many of these efforts, but it does not act alone. Other international and regional organizations, coalitions of states, and local and international NGOs also play a critical role in helping to prevent and resolve armed conflict. None of these peacemaking programs on its own has a major impact on global security, *Human Security Report 2005* notes, but taken together "their effect has been profound."[35]

---

[34] Human Security Centre, *Human Security Report 2005: War and Peace in the 21st Century* (New York: Oxford University Press, 2005), 9.
[35] Ibid.

A RAND corporation study notes that, despite the many limitations of UN operations, United Nations peacemaking missions are often successful.[36] International activism for conflict prevention and mitigation has made a significant difference in reducing the frequency and intensity of armed conflict within states.

A major study of UN peace operations by Michael Doyle and Nicholas Sambanis shows that the negotiation of a peace agreement and the presence of UN peacekeepers are key factors in achieving a successful end to armed conflict.[37] Especially important are multidimensional peace operations that involve the deployment of peacekeepers in support of comprehensive agreements in post-war settings. In addition to traditional military functions, peacekeepers are often engaged in various police and civilian tasks. The key ingredients in successful peace missions, according to the study, are: (1) fostering economic and social cooperation to build confidence among previously warring parties, (2) developing social, political and economic opportunities, and (3) transforming police, military, judicial, electoral and civil society institutions.[38]

Negotiated settlements double the chances of peacebuilding success. The presence of a comprehensive UN mission has a positive and significant impact. UN peace operations have a very large and significant advantage over situations in which there is no UN involvement. In the absence of a negotiated agreement and a broad UN mission, the chances for sustainable peace are low.[39] In probability models Doyle and Sambanis find that the likelihood of sustainable peace drops from an initial value of about 80 percent for negotiated accords with a comprehensive UN mission to less than 5 percent in the absence of a treaty and UN peacekeeping.[40]

Roland Paris has been highly critical of international peacemaking missions and the pro-Western neo-liberal ideologies and interests they often serve. He analyzes 14 major cases of peacekeeping: Angola, Bosnia, Cambodia, Croatia, East Timor, El Salvador, Guatemala, Kosovo, Liberia, Mozambique, Namibia, Nicaragua and Sierra Leone.[41] In these

---

[36] James Dobbins, Seth G. Jones, Keith Crane, Andrew Rathmell, Brett Steele, Richard Teltschik and Anga Timilsina, *The UN's Role in Nation-Building: From the Congo to Iraq* (Santa Monica: RAND Corporation, 2005), xv–xxxviii.

[37] Michael Doyle and Nicholas Sambanis, *Making War and Building Peace: United Nations Peace Operations* (Princeton University Press, 2006), 72.

[38] Ibid., 14–15.

[39] Ibid., 104, 109–110.

[40] Ibid., 128.

[41] Roland Paris, *At War's End: Building Peace after Civil Conflict* (Cambridge University Press, 2004).

cases international peace missions played an important role in helping to end armed conflict and support negotiated agreements, although substantial problems remained in many of these countries. Rebel group fighting occasionally flared in some, while in other countries high levels of criminalized violence emerged. Paris is especially critical of rushed efforts in many of these cases to organize elections and introduce rapid market liberalization, noting that these policies often create increased social tensions and political instability. As Joshua Goldstein observes, however, Paris's critique does not disprove the impact of UN peace missions in helping to prevent the recurrence of war.[42] In some of the cases examined by Paris the presence of third-party peacekeeping forces was decisive in containing violent incidents and preventing the spread of conflict.

Peacemaking missions cannot guarantee the flowering of positive peace, but they are usually successful in reducing levels of violent conflict and in some settings can help to create conditions for the gradual evolution of more sustainable peace. Wallensteen observes that international missions and negotiated agreements contribute to quality peace and facilitate democratic transitions.[43] Research confirms that the chances of a democratic transition are much higher when UN peacekeeping forces are present than when major powers intervene.[44] UN peace missions and peacekeeping deployments have a measurable impact in helping to spread democracy and prevent conflict recurrence.

THIRD-PARTY PEACEKEEPING

Well-resourced, multi-dimensional peacekeeping forces can play an important role in ending intrastate armed conflict and sustaining peace. The prospects for peace in the wake of a ceasefire increase substantially in the presence of a credible peacekeeping force that is part of a comprehensive UN peace mandate. While peacekeeping missions have many flaws and limitations, some of which we note below, scholarly studies show convincingly that the deployment of multilateral forces to support peacemaking diplomacy is an effective means of preventing war and advancing peace within states.

In her book *Does Peacekeeping Work?* Virginia Page Fortna compares cases of civil war where third-party peacekeepers were deployed following

---

[42] Goldstein, *Winning the War on War*, 106–107.
[43] Wallensteen, *Quality Peace*, 50, 206.
[44] Pickering and Penecy, "Forging Democracy at Gunpoint," 552–553.

a negotiated agreement with those where belligerents were left to their own devices. Her conclusion is unambiguous: "The statistical evidence is overwhelming ... peacekeeping works." To the question, does peacekeeping work, the "answer is a resounding yes."[45] The presence of third-party peacekeepers in post-conflict countries reduces the risk of renewed war by between 55 and 85 percent, according to her calculations.[46] Multi-dimensional peacekeeping missions that incorporate civilian peacebuilding activities have the largest effect on preserving peace in the aftermath of civil conflict, but more limited UN peacekeeping missions also have a stabilizing effect. Both forms of peacekeeping have positive impacts. The beneficial effects continue even after a peacekeeping force is withdrawn. This indicates that third-party peacekeepers contribute to sustaining peace not only while they are present, but also after they depart.[47] Other scholars look at the data from different angles but arrive at very similar findings. UN peacekeeping missions decrease the likelihood of a country returning to war by significant margins.[48]

A peace settlement alone does not guarantee peace. Fighting often resumes in a civil conflict unless a third-party force steps in to verify or enforce a ceasefire and post-conflict agreement. Barbara Walter shows that the presence or absence of a third-party security guarantee is a critical factor in determining whether combatants sign and implement peace settlements. She finds that agreements were implemented in 11 out of 12 cases studied where peace accords included third-party security guarantees. By contrast, only two of 11 settlements that lacked a third-party security guarantee were successful. Without security guarantees and the presence of a third party capable of enforcing an agreement, the chances of combatants signing and implementing a negotiated settlement are low. When third-party security guarantees are combined with power-sharing arrangements, the chances for successful implementation of peace agreements are high.[49]

---

[45] Virginia Page Fortna, *Does Peacekeeping Work? Shaping Belligerents' Choices after Civil War* (Princeton University Press, 2008), 125.

[46] Ibid.; Virginia Page Fortna and Lise Morjé Howard, "Pitfalls and Prospects in the Peacekeeping Literature," *Annual Review of Political Science* 11 (2008): 289.

[47] Fortna, *Does Peacekeeping Work?* 111.

[48] In Michael J. Gilligan and Ernest J. Sergenti, "Do UN Interventions Cause Peace? Using Matching to Improve Causal Inference," *Quarterly Journal of Political Science* 3 (2008): 94.

[49] Barbara Walter, *Committing to Peace: The Successful Settlement of Civil Wars* (Princeton University Press, 2002), 80, 86.

When the Nobel Committee awarded the 1988 Nobel Peace Prize to UN Peacekeeping Forces it cited the "decisive contribution" these forces make to reducing tensions and realizing the fundamental UN mission of achieving peace through negotiations. Peacekeeping missions have continued to be a significant part of multilateral efforts to end and prevent armed conflict. As of July 2016 more than 100,000 peacekeeping troops were deployed in 16 operations around the world.[50]

This does not mean that peacekeeping deployments are always successful. Some UN missions have been disastrous. UN peacekeepers failed tragically in Rwanda in 1994, when they withdrew during the height of the genocide, and in Srebrenica a year later, as UN peacekeepers stood aside while thousands of Bosnian men and boys were massacred. UN interventions in Somalia since the 1990s and in Darfur over the past decades have failed to bring peace. In these cases, the UN entered conflict zones without a peace agreement between the warring parties and attempted to use force to achieve peace. In the recent Malakal incident in South Sudan UN peacekeepers were unable to maintain security in a camp specifically created to provide protection for civilians.[51]

Many efforts have been made over the years to reform and improve UN peace and security operations. The 2000 Panel on United Nations Peace Operations, chaired by former Algerian Foreign Minister Lakhdar Brahimi, recommended the creation of more robust UN peace operations that could, where necessary, use force to protect civilians and enforce a peace settlement. Peacekeepers should not stand on the sidelines when faced with persistent abuses and violations of peace agreements, the report argued. The traditional impartiality of UN operations "is not the same as neutrality or equal treatment of all parties." In some cases, "peacekeepers may not only be operationally justified in using force but morally compelled to do so."[52]

Proposals for stronger efforts to prevent mass atrocities fit within the framework of the Responsibility to Protect (R2P), which was endorsed by the UN World Summit in September 2005 and approved by the UN

---

[50] United Nations, United Nations Peacekeeping, "Peacekeeping Fact Sheet," June 30, 2016, www.un.org/en/peacekeeping/resources/statistics/factsheet.shtml.

[51] Somini Gupta, "What Can the United Nations Do When Its Own Troops Can't, or Won't, Protect Civilians?" *New York Times*, July 13, 2016, www.nytimes.com/2016/07/14/world/africa/un-peacekeepers-south-sudan-massacre.html.

[52] United Nations General Assembly Security Council, *Report of the Panel on United Nations Peace Operations*, A/55/305 S/2000/809, August 21, 2000, ¶ 50, www.un.org/en/ga/search/view_doc.asp?symbol=A/55/305.

Security Council in April 2006. When people face an imminent threat of mass killing that is either caused by or cannot be prevented by their government, the international community has a responsibility to step in and protect innocent life. The R2P principle was developed in the report of the International Commission on Intervention and State Sovereignty, chaired by former Australian Foreign Minister Gareth Evans and former Algerian ambassador Mohamed Sahnoun. The Commission's report called for a broad range of actions, including diplomacy, sanctions and law enforcement, to prevent mass killing. Intervention with police or armed forces may be necessary in some circumstances to protect civilians, according to the report, but only in the most exceptional and extraordinary circumstances and only when strict 'just cause' criteria are met.[53] The report defined two conditions as meeting the just cause threshold for using force: actual or imminent harm involving large-scale loss of life caused by deliberate state action or neglect; and large-scale state repression in the form of killings, forced expulsion, acts of terror and mass rape.[54]

In March 2013, in response to the inability of UN peacekeepers to suppress armed violence in Eastern Congo, the Security Council took the unprecedented step of approving the deployment of a special offensive unit, the Force Intervention Brigade. The mission of the unit was to neutralize rebel forces in Eastern Congo. This was described by the UN Secretariat as a "peace enforcement" mission, a first-ever combat force authorized to conduct military operations against specific militia forces. The Intervention Brigade had some success in its first year of operations, but the challenge of suppressing the complex and constantly changing threats posed by the web of rebel groups in the region has proved difficult and controversial.[55] Some argue that such a combat mission harms peacekeeping operations by jeopardizing the UN's traditional role of impartiality in conflict mediation and by creating greater risks for UN missions.[56] The report of the High-level Independent Panel on Peace Operations

---

[53] International Commission on Intervention and State Sovereignty, *The Responsibility to Protect* (Ottawa: International Development Research Centre, December 2001).

[54] Ibid., xii.

[55] Scott Sheeran and Stephanie Case, "The Intervention Brigade: Legal Issues for the UN in the Democratic Republic of the Congo," International Coalition for the Responsibility to Protect," International Peace Institute, November 2014, www.responsibilitytoprotect .org/index.php/crises/151-the-crisis-in-drc/5651-the-intervention-brigade-legal-issues-for-the-un-in-the-democratic-republic-of-the-congo.

[56] Lars Müller, "The Force Intervention Brigade—United Nations Forces Beyond the Fine Line Between Peacekeeping and Peace Enforcement," *Journal of Conflict & Security Law* 20, no. 3 (2015): 359–380.

in June 2015 argues for "extreme caution" in the approval of offensive enforcement operations, recommending that such missions should be exceptional and time-limited.[57] The UN is best at traditional peacekeeping missions that are deployed after the warring parties have signed an agreement and given consent to third-party intervention. Waging war to force a settlement is not a mission the UN performs well.[58] UN peacekeeping works best when there is an actual 'peace to keep.'

The report of the High-level Independent Panel calls for restoring the search for peaceful political settlements as the central focus of UN missions in conflict settings. The Secretary-General's action plan following up on the Panel's report contains three pillars: a renewed focus on prevention and mediation; stronger regional–global partnerships; and new ways of planning and conducting United Nations peace operations to make them faster, more responsive and more accountable to the needs of countries and people in conflict. A United Nations peace operation "does not pursue military victory," the Secretary-General emphasized.[59] Its fundamental objective is the pursuit of a negotiated political settlement. As the earlier Brahimi report noted, peacekeeping forces are most effective when they are part of broader civilian peacebuilding mission that includes ongoing political efforts to encourage cooperation among previously warring parties, governance reform efforts to build civilian and security sector capacity, and multifaceted economic development and market support programs. All of these dimensions are necessary for the prevention and resolution of armed conflict.

GLOBAL GOVERNANCE GAPS

While the rise of multilateralism has been a positive development for mitigating intrastate conflicts and advancing international peace, many problems remain. The current structures of global governance are jury-rigged and inadequate to the enormity of the challenges facing the world. The multilateral system was created over the decades in a piecemeal fashion

---

[57] United Nations, General Assembly Security Council, *Report of the High-level Independent Panel on Peace Operations on Uniting Our Strengths for Peace: Politics, Partnership and People*, A/70/95 S/2015/446, June 17, 2015, 12, 45–46.

[58] Doyle and Sambanis, *Making War and Building Peace*, 145.

[59] United Nations, General Assembly Security Council, *The Future of United Nations Peace Operations: Implementation of the Recommendations of the High-level Independent Panel on Peace Operations; Report of the Secretary-General*, A/70/357–S/2015/682, September 2, 2015, ¶ 15.

to address specific problems. It lacks strategic vision and sustained capability and is often slow to respond to developing crises and new global challenges. At all levels significant governance gaps exist between the nature of current problems and the feeble policies and structures that are available to address them.[60]

The quest for a framework of governance solutions at the international level can draw lessons from the models of governance we have identified for conflict prevention within states. Good governance for peace results when institutions have sufficient capacity to provide security and deliver public goods and when they have qualities of inclusiveness, participation and accountability. These principles apply within and between states. Global institutions need the capacity to perform their designated tasks. They need sufficient resources to maintain international peace and security through the prevention and resolution of armed conflict. International institutions also need greater qualities of inclusion and accountability to foster equitable participation in international peacemaking and development and to help overcome the problems of exclusion and marginalization that lead to armed violence. Global governance is lacking at multiple levels.

The institutional capacity of the UN system is woefully inadequate. The core budget for UN operations has remained relatively constant in recent years despite the growing number of armed conflicts in the world, the rising threat posed by international terrorist organizations, and the horrific consequences of the Syrian Civil War. The UN peacekeeping budget has increased, but the overall level of deployment remains modest and is far below what is needed to improve security in post-conflict settings – not to speak of the additional capacities that would be needed if peace agreements are negotiated in Syria, Yemen and other conflict zones and are structured to include the deployment of peacekeeping forces. The evidence shows convincingly that peacekeeping forces enhance the prospects for sustainable peace. This means that greater third-party security capacity is needed in support of efforts to end current civil conflicts. In Afghanistan, for example, the presence of a 'Muslim-led' peacekeeping force could spur discussions about possible political settlements that might be more acceptable on both sides.

The UN also lacks capacity for conflict mediation and prevention. Ban Ki-moon has urged additional resources for envoys, regional offices,

---

[60] Thomas G. Weiss, Ramesh Thakur and John Gerard Ruggie, *Global Governance and the UN: An Unfinished Journey* (Bloomington: Indiana University Press, 2010), 8.

standby mediation experts and support to United Nations country teams.[61] Especially important is the need to strengthen the inclusion of women in peace processes.[62] Similar gaps in peacemaking and peacekeeping capacity exist in the African Union and other regional organizations. The lack of institutional capacity for implementing comprehensive peace missions means that the policies and decisions agreed upon at the UN and in other international fora have little meaning and are often not enforced.

The problems of limited institutional capacity are compounded by the lack of accountability and transparency in the decision-making and implementation procedures of the UN and other global bodies. The Security Council is dominated by the interests of the permanent five, who use the Council to advance their own national agendas or impede those of rival states. Other global and regional powers such as Germany, Japan, Brazil, India, Indonesia, Nigeria and South Africa are denied an institutional role commensurate with their influence. The democratic deficit in international policy making marginalizes much of the world community and has long been recognized as a critical fault in the architecture of global governance. Greater inclusion and participation are needed to make international institutions more accountable and effective in preventing armed conflict. As the report of the 1995 Commission on Global Governance argues, governance must be underpinned by democracy at all levels. "As at the national level, so in the global neighborhood: the democratic principle must be ascendant."[63]

The international agencies charged with managing trade and development face similar challenges. The operations of the World Trade Organization, the International Monetary Fund, the World Bank and related agencies often fall short of good governance principles. Many of the inequalities of globalized trade are reflected in the undemocratic and unaccountable nature of international financial institutions, which often neglect the social dimensions of the policies they implement. The decision-making structures of the IMF are the domain of the commercial and financial interests of the richest and most powerful states.[64] Similar

---

[61] United Nations, General Assembly Security Council, *The Future of United Nations Peace Operations.*

[62] Commission on Global Security, Justice & Governance, *Confronting the Crisis of Global Governance: Report of the Commission on Global Security, Justice & Governance* (Hague Institute for Global Justice and Stimson Center, 2015), xvii, 32.

[63] *Our Global Neighborhood*, The Report of the Commission on Global Governance (Oxford University Press, 1995), 48, 66.

[64] Stiglitz, *Globalization and its Discontents*, 18–19.

criticisms have been levied against the World Trade Organization, which is nominally more democratic in its procedures but allows powerful states to exclude other nations and interests from meaningful participation.[65] The ordinary people whose lives are affected by international development policies have little or no voice in determining how decisions are made.

Many developing nations and citizen groups advocate a more participatory, empowerment-based approach to global governance. At the political level they urge a greater emphasis on peacemaking and conflict prevention and increased investments in peacekeeping and mediation support. In development policy they favor a balanced approach that combines support for private enterprise with active government regulation and public investments in human capital and social services. UN development agencies have emphasized the importance of strong institutions that are capable of providing social safety nets and delivering public goods. These ideas are part of the call for greater representation and public participation within global institutions and more responsive and inclusive decision-making procedures. They are necessary elements of good governance at both national and international levels.

THE ROLE OF CIVIL SOCIETY

The search for global governance solutions goes beyond the role of states and government institutions. It also involves greater participation for civil society and nongovernmental organizations and networks. The emergence of globalized civil society creates new possibilities for advancing cosmopolitan principles and norms and can help to build greater international understanding and cooperation. Activist networks have multiplied throughout the world, building consensus and mobilizing support through the Internet, a trend Keohane describes as "voluntary pluralism under conditions of maximum transparency."[66] The worldwide nonprofit sector is huge, with estimated annual expenditures in 2010 of more than $1.3 trillion.[67] People power movements

[65] Aileen Kwa, *Power Politics in the WTO* (Bangkok: Focus on the Global South, 2003), 5; Robert Wade, *What Strategies are Viable for Developing Countries Today? The World Trade Organization and the Shrinking of "Development Space,"* Crisis States Programme Working Paper Series, No. 1 (London: Development Research Centre, 2003).

[66] Keohane, "International Institutions," 93–94.

[67] Emile van der Does de Willebois, "Nonprofit Organizations and the Combatting of Terrorism Financing: A Proportionate Response," World Bank Working Paper No. 208 (Washington, DC: World Bank, 2010), xi, 1, 4.

and citizen networks have become increasingly important actors on the global stage.

Civil society groups have been prime movers of some of the most important innovations for addressing global challenges.[68] They have articulated moral and political standards that in some cases have crystallized into policy. Civil society initiatives and pressures have spurred governments and international organizations to address common social, economic and environmental challenges. In some instances states and NGOs work together on human rights and economic development projects, for example in programs to increase the role of women in peace and security. The cumulative effect of civil society has been to boost the UN and international agenda for development and peacebuilding. Civil society is extraordinarily diverse, of course, and not all groups are progressive. As noted in Chapter 1, an 'uncivil' society also exists. Some groups advocate narrow political/religious agendas and promote intolerance toward others.[69] On balance, however, most civil society movements are nonviolent in practice and philosophy and have contributed positively to global governance.

Studies of peace processes show that civil society participation in negotiations is critical to securing long-term peace. One study of 20 peace negotiations found that high levels of civil society involvement are associated with more sustained peace processes. Peacemaking missions without civil society involvement tend to relapse more often into war or a 'cold peace' of unresolved hostilities. A seat at the negotiation table for civil society "appears to be *an essential contribution* to sustaining peace," according to the study [emphasis in original].[70] Civil society involvement helps to bring broader social and political interests to the negotiating table, making the process more inclusive and participatory. In some cases civil society groups have developed communication channels with insurgent groups and have conducted back-channel discussions to nudge violent groups to the bargaining table.

Another analysis of civil society participation in peace processes reaches similar conclusions. An examination of 83 peace agreements

---

[68] Fernando Henrique Cardoso, "Transmittal letter dated 7 June 2004 from the Chair of the Panel of Eminent Persons on United Nations-Civil Society Relations addressed to the Secretary-General"; United Nations General Assembly, *We the Peoples*, 3.

[69] Thania Paffenholz, Christoph Spurk, Roberto Belloni, Sabine Kurtenbach and Camilla Orjuela, "Enabling and Disenabling Factors in Civil Society Peacebuilding," in *Civil Society and Peacebuilding: A Critical Assessment*, edited by Thania Paffenholz (Boulder: Lynne Rienner, 2010), 414.

[70] Wanis-St. John and Kew, "Civil Society and Peace Negotiations," 27–28, 31.

signed from 1989 to 2004 at the end of intrastate conflict shows that civil society participation in negotiations substantially decreases the risk of signatories reverting to violence. The risk of renewed armed conflict falls by 50 percent when civil society is at the negotiating table. These results hold even when controlling for the effect of peacekeeping missions.[71] The participation of civil society enhances the legitimacy of the peace process, builds social consensus around the terms of the accord, and helps to hold political elites accountable to their pledges. The inclusion of civil society actors in peace processes helps to anchor the peace.[72]

At times civil society groups have played an historic role in placing new ideas on the global agenda. Examples include the Nobel Prize-winning campaign to ban landmines and efforts to advance the role of women in international peacemaking through the implementation of UN Security Council Resolution 1325. The emergence of civil society is an expression of global democracy, an assertion by ordinary citizens of the right to influence decisions that affect their lives. Each nongovernmental group or network, typically small and relatively weak by itself, makes a contribution to global governance – a tiny "patch" in the developing "patchwork quilt" of global governance.[73]

Citizen movements and civil society networks help to narrow the 'democratic deficit' that exists in national governments and international institutions. They create greater public accountability by independently monitoring the performance of governments and international organizations. They are a leavening influence in the distribution of power nationally and globally and help to transcend the limitations of formalized and hierarchical systems of top-down government decision making. They help to balance the centralized power of states, international organizations and multinational corporations.

CONCLUSION

Despite the many gaps and limitations that exist, global governance institutions have proven that they can be effective in addressing problems of armed conflict between and within nations. The UN is but one of many

---

[71] Desirée Nilsson, "Anchoring the Peace: Civil Society Actors in Peace Accords and Durable Peace," *International Interactions: Empirical and Theoretical Research in International Relations* 38, no. 2 (November 2012): 258, 262.

[72] Ibid., 244.

[73] Thomas Weiss, Conor Seyle and Kelsey Coolidge, *Non-State Actors and Global Governance: A Look at the Numbers* (Broomfield: One Earth Future Foundation), 2013.

international and regional organizations that play a role in helping to prevent war and promote economic development. The UN is particularly important in providing political, legal and moral authority for states to cooperate for peace and security, although as noted its operational capacity is limited. UN-led or authorized multidimensional peace processes have been successful at times, especially when they incorporate third-party security assurances and are linked to effective programs for development and democratization. States that participate in international institutions have fewer internal armed conflicts and are more peaceful toward one other.

Kant's utopian vision of a liberal democratic order for peace has not materialized of course, but some of the factors he identified have proven to be significant in helping reduce the risk of armed violence. As we have noted, states that are highly developed economically and have mature democratic institutions tend to have fewer armed conflicts and are less likely to wage war against one another. The characteristics of governance that help to prevent armed conflict at the domestic level are also applicable at the international level. Global governance institutions need the capacity to deliver public goods, which at the international level means the ability to address threats to the peace and take action to prevent or end armed conflicts. This requires resources for peacekeeping and peacebuilding, and for programs that advance sustainable development goals. Global governance mechanisms are also more effective when they have the qualities of inclusiveness, equity and accountability. At the international level as within states, institutions are more effective at fostering peace when they form partnerships with major stakeholders, apply comprehensive and multidimensional approaches, and are accountable to the communities they are intended to serve.

The evidence in support of multilateral solutions is strong and convincing, yet states often bypass the UN and attempt to resolve security threats through unilateral action or by forming ad hoc coalitions. Political leaders still cling to outdated notions of the state as a coherent unitary actor capable of independently controlling social, economic and environmental developments. Military force is still viewed as the dominant factor in international politics, while the many political, economic, social and cultural forces that shape conflict dynamics are often overlooked.[74] This approach to international affairs is called political realism.

---

[74] Robert O. Keohane and Joseph S. Nye, *Power and Interdependence*, 3rd edition (New York: Longman, 2001), 20–21.

In many respects, however, it is unrealistic. It ignores the ways in which security itself has changed, as reflected in the emergent concept of human security examined in Chapter 2. Security is no longer narrowly concerned with the protection of the state but also encompasses the well-being of communities and individuals and includes economic, social and cultural dimensions. The security of any one nation is increasingly linked to the security of others and depends on the development of more effective means of global governance.

A higher form of realism is needed to address the challenges of an interdependent globalized world in which non-military components of power and economic, social and ecological forces are radically re-shaping the international agenda.[75] A genuine realist perspective acknowledges the multiple factors that influence the exercise of political power and the need for multidimensional approaches that incorporate all relevant actors, including the private sector and civil society. In the concluding chapter we examine some of these new approaches and discuss implications of a good governance perspective for international policy making.

---

[75] Brown, *Higher Realism.*

Governance Present and Future

Visitors to our time from the nineteenth century, transported by an imaginary time machine, would be amazed by the complex systems of governance that exist in much of the world today. The Texas Ranger of the old Wild West would see the rule of the gun replaced in most regions by established governments and institutionalized systems for settling disputes and protecting communities from outlaws. Diplomats from Europe's Concert of Powers would see the continent united as never before in relative peace and prosperity, notwithstanding many frictions, attempting to work together collectively rather than divided by war. They would observe many regional and international organizations around the globe seeking to promote development and prevent and resolve conflicts within and between nations. Many of the poor from the former colonies would find themselves in independent states that did not exist previously, earning incomes in vast megacities, increasingly educated and literate, experiencing longer and healthier lives. All the visitors would see the pervasiveness of democratic governance and citizen participation, and the more prominent role of women in public life and the workplace. Our visitors would see a world with many armed conflicts but would also observe, as Steven Pinker notes, that inter-state wars and levels of armed violence in many parts of the world have diminished.

Less visible to our time travelers but increasingly evident and important for today is the accumulation of social science knowledge on the causes of armed conflicts and the pathways to peace. In recent decades scholars and practitioners have forged an evidence-based framework for understanding the conditions that are most likely to foster armed violence and advance peace. That knowledge is incomplete, of course, and many uncertainties exist about the quality of data and methodologies of research, but we now know a great deal about how to avoid war and create a more peaceful future. War is not inevitable or engrained in human nature. It is the result of specific conditions and policies – the presence or absence of particular governance arrangements – that make conflict more likely.

The research surveyed in this volume identifies key dimensions of good governance. Long-term, sustainable peace is most likely when:

1. Governance systems include security institutions that have adequate capacity to defend territory and deter aggression but are accountable to civilian authority and balanced with social priorities and human development needs.

2. Societies invest substantially in education, health care and other public goods and social services that are available for all societal groups equitably.

3. Political institutions have adequate legitimacy and capacity, and effective mechanisms for resolving conflicts and identity-based grievances nonviolently.

4. Societies are democratic, with inclusive and representative political institutions and opportunities for all citizens to participate freely.

5. Women participate fully in political, economic, and social life and leadership and have a seat at the table in decision making.

6. Development programs empower people to gain access to assets and capabilities to improve their economic and social well-being.

7. Open markets enable trade, investment and economic growth and are regulated to maintain equitable access and protect social interests and the environment.

8. Accountable multilateral institutions have the authority and resources to manage regional and global political, economic and security challenges.

We argue throughout this book that the qualities of governance that most consistently predict peace are inclusivity, participation and accountability. When governance systems have these characteristics, they are more stable and able to manage conflict without violence. We also emphasize the importance of governance capacity to meet public needs and establish conditions for more peaceful societies. This concluding chapter addresses some of the policy implications of these findings. We examine the challenges of attempting to implement the principles of good governance and the need to move beyond collective action to coordinated response in the face of crises. We summarize some of the lessons of governance reform efforts and offer the experience of the International Dialogue on Peacebuilding and Statebuilding as a promising model for the integration of development, peacebuilding and governance approaches. We conclude with some reflections on the meaning and possible directions of governance for the future.

HARD CHOICES

Questions related to the capacity and qualities of governance are becoming an important focus of international policy. Many donor governments and private aid agencies have adopted governance as a cross-cutting theme in their work for development and poverty relief.[1] The US Agency for International Development (USAID) is incorporating democracy, human rights and governance concerns into development programming at multiple levels.[2] The same is true for the British Department for International Development (DFID), which provides support for "capable, accountable and responsive states that provide security, enable growth, reduce poverty and improve the delivery of public services."[3] Catholic Relief Services (CRS) applies a peacebuilding, governance and gender lens in its programs for emergency assistance, health services and food security. Mercy Corps and other development agencies have similar programs. Organizations around the world increasingly recognize the importance of governance to the success of development and peacebuilding policy.

Security assistance programs also incorporate governance perspectives.[4] An April 2013 Presidential Policy Directive, *U.S. Security Assistance Policy*, directs the US government to help partner nations build sustainable capacity and "promote universal values such as good governance,

---

[1] Thomas Carothers and Diane de Gramont, "Aiding Governance in Developing Countries: Progress Amid Uncertainties" (Washington, DC: Carnegie Endowment for International Peace, November 2011), 13–14.

[2] USAID, *USAID Strategy on Democracy, Human Rights, and Governance*, USAID Strategy, Washington DC, June 2013, www.usaid.gov/sites/default/files/documents/1866/USAID%20DRG_%20final%20final%206-24%203%20(1).pdf.

[3] Department for International Development, "Governance Portfolio Review Summary," London, July 2011, www.gov.uk/government/system/uploads/attachment_data/file/67458/governance-portfolio.pdf.

[4] Gordon Adams and Richard Sokolsky, "Governance and Security Sector Assistance: The Missing Link—Part II," *Lawfare: Hard National Security Choices*, July 19, 2015, www.lawfareblog.com/governance-and-security-sector-assistance-missing-link%E2%80%94part-ii.

transparent and accountable oversight of security forces, rule of law, transparency, accountability, delivery of fair and effective justice, and respect for human rights."[5] The White House subsequently announced the Security Governance Initiative, a program with six African states that seeks to reinforce democratic security sector governance and build capacity for justice, democracy, rule of law and respect for human rights.[6] These and related initiatives by governments and international agencies represent steps toward the mainstreaming of governance in international policy making.

Translating good governance principles into effective policy making involves difficult trade-offs. The evidence indicates that inclusive political systems are preferable for peace, but does this mean that negotiators should seek power-sharing agreements with terrorists and war lords?[7] Power sharing has worked satisfactorily in some cases, in Northern Ireland for example where former IRA leader Martin McGuinness served as a minister of state, but in Sierra Leone the decision to give a cabinet post to rebel leader Foday Sankoh in the 1999 peace agreement was disastrous. Proportional representation systems are highly participatory and have a low risk of armed conflict, but they can be inefficient at times and may allow extremist groups to enter the political mainstream.[8] The involvement of civil society can make governance structures more accountable and representative, but civil society groups themselves need good governance and are not always democratic or 'civil.'[9]

A major challenge for international policy making is whether to provide direct assistance to corrupt governments. Some of the major recipients of US foreign aid and security assistance are corrupt and repressive

---

[5] The White House, "Fact Sheet: U.S. Security Assistance Policy," Washington DC, April 5, 2013, http://fas.org/irp/offdocs/ppd/ssa.pdf.

[6] The White House, "Fact Sheet: Security Governance Initiative," Washington DC, August 6, 2014, www.whitehouse.gov/the-press-office/2014/08/06/fact-sheet-security-governance-initiative.

[7] Scott Gates and Kaare Strøm, "Power-sharing and Civil Conflict," Centre for the Study of Civil War, CSCW Policy Brief, 1/2008, available at http://file.prio.no/Publication_files/Prio/Theoretical%20Framework%20Policy%20Brief_Power%20sharing.pdf.

[8] UK Engage, "What are the Advantages and Disadvantages of Using a Proportional Representation (PR) Political System?" www.uk-engage.org/2013/08/what-are-the-advantages-and-disadvantages-of-using-a-proportional-representation-pr-electoral-system/.

[9] Thania Paffenholz, "What Civil Society Can Contribute to Peacebuilding," in *Civil Society and Peacebuilding: A Critical Assessment*, edited by Thania Paffenholz (Boulder: Lynne Rienner, 2010), 392; and Paffenholz et al., "Enabling and Disenabling Factors in Civil Society Peacebuilding," 414.

governments, including Afghanistan, Pakistan and Egypt. This funding props up regimes that violate the core principles of good governance, creating conditions that increase the risk of armed conflict. USAID programs generally avoid making direct grants to governments. They channel funds instead through private donor agencies or contractors who disperse funds to partner agencies in recipient countries for local development and humanitarian purposes. If donors bypass the state, however, it becomes more difficult to build capacity and strengthen government institutions. The Organization for Economic Cooperation and Development warns that 'off-budget' foreign assistance may weaken public accountability and state legitimacy.[10] There are no easy answers when trying to help weak states build strong institutions, as the UNDP *Governance for Peace* report acknowledges: "The promotion of governance and the restoration of the social contract between states and societies in fragile and conflict-affected settings is a balancing act. There are no simple recipes for success."[11]

Dilemmas may arise with aid programs that empower women and girls. These have been successful in many countries and are known to advance the prospects for economic development and reduce the risk of armed conflict. But imposing such programs without consideration of local customs and attitudes can lead to social frictions. This was the case in Afghanistan where the agenda of women's empowerment was seen by some as a Western imposition and became associated with external military intervention and a corrupt regime in Kabul. Programs to improve women's access to health care and education in Afghanistan produced some positive results, but the broader project of attempting to elevate women's status in government and society has had less success.[12]

Humility is needed in translating research into practice. Even when the findings are universally accepted, for example that higher per capita income is associated with reduced conflict risk, the policy options for generating that beneficial impact are not always clear, and may be hotly debated. We know that economic development and prosperity result from open markets and high levels of trade and investment, but does this mean that capitalism fosters peace? Many on the left would find that

[10] OECD, *Do No Harm: International Support for Statebuilding, Conflict and Fragility* (OECD Publishing, 2009), 15.

[11] United Nations Development Programme, *Governance for Peace: Securing the Social Contract* (New York: United Nations Development Programme and Bureau for Crisis Prevention and Recovery, 2012), 113.

[12] Cortright and Wall, *Afghan Women Speak*.

hard to swallow. They point to industries that profit from and encourage weapons production, and to corporate abuses and exploitive practices that damage the environment and disrupt local communities – in some instances exacerbating grievances that lead to armed conflict.[13] Piketty's finding of an inherent trend toward inequality of wealth raises profound questions about the nature of capitalism, and strengthens the case for redistributive social policies. Despite the critiques, most progressives recognize that a healthy corporate sector is necessary for economic growth and prosperity, even as they also support the regulation of capital and stronger sustainability and social responsibility standards.

Mary Anderson's classic *Do No Harm* has become an essential guide for many development and security assistance programs, and it applies to international peace operations as well.[14] In all arenas practitioners must be aware that well-intentioned projects can have unintended consequences, inflaming rather than alleviating the conditions that lead to conflict. In situations of intense ethnic grievances and horizontal inequalities, development aid delivered unwittingly to one side of a conflict and not another can exacerbate polarization. Security assistance given to abusive forces can lead to repression and civil violence and in some cases to military violence. Mistakes in one area can cascade into problems in another.

An important way to practice 'do no harm' principles in the international security arena is to avoid unnecessary 'wars of choice' and ill-defined overseas military operations. Armed regime change has proven to be particularly ill-advised. If the use of force is deemed necessary for the responsibility to protect, it should have multilateral authorization, ideally through the UN Security Council. Security assistance programs are most helpful when they are linked to training for democracy and human rights and to institutional reforms for public oversight and accountability to civilian authority. Traditional military 'train and equip' programs without attention to underlying governance reforms can do more harm than good.

If it is true that 'good things go together' in governance, the reverse is also true. Dysfunctional systems can reinforce dysfunction in multiple ways. Interventions that address one element of governance in isolation from others may be undone by challenges outside the area of focus. To

---

[13] See, for example, Naomi Klein, *This Changes Everything: Capitalism vs. The Climate* (New York: Simon & Schuster, 2014), and *The Shock Doctrine: The Rise of Disaster Capitalism* (New York: Macmillan, 2007).

[14] Mary B. Anderson, *Do No Harm: How Aid Can Support Peace—Or War* (Boulder: Lynne Rienner, 1999).

avoid unwanted damage it is necessary to tread cautiously, and to apply approaches that assess and address the multifaceted dimensions of governance, conflict and peacebuilding.[15] Most important is the need for a thorough contextual analysis and nuanced understanding of local conflict dynamics before attempting to engage.

MULTIDIMENSIONAL APPROACHES

Reducing armed conflict and achieving peace in fragile conflict-affected states is a complex endeavor that involves a wide range of interconnected political, economic and social activities. International missions to build good governance and support peace require multidimensional approaches. 'Good things' need to be provided together. Without adequate economic development, opportunities for health care and education will be limited. Purely economic approaches are insufficient without efforts to build inclusive political institutions and mechanisms for resolving social grievances. If women are not included in economic life, countries face lower economic development growth and attendant social strains. Security approaches that neglect the need for effective civilian control often backfire. A narrow focus on any one facet of governance is insufficient. Each element is critical in relation to all the others.

International development agencies increasingly address multiple challenges in their programs. World Bank rules stipulate that indigenous peoples in affected areas are to be incorporated into the planning and approval process of development loans.[16] USAID programming on HIV/AIDS has included capacity building efforts to improve human rights advocacy among local civil society groups, resulting in more inclusive access and better governance and management of HIV/AIDS services.[17] CRS food assistance programs sometimes include services for maternal and child health, water and sanitation, agriculture, microfinance and adult literacy. In post-conflict countries such as Bosnia and Herzegovina USAID-funded projects seek to rebuild trust and encourage reconciliation across ethnic divides by engaging youth of different backgrounds

---

[15] Collaborative for Development Action, "The Do No Harm Handbook (The Framework for Analyzing the Impact of Assistance on Conflict)" (Cambridge, MA: CDA, November 2004).

[16] World Bank "O.P. 4.10 – Indigenous Peoples", in *The World Bank Operations Manual* (World Bank, 2005 (revised April 2013)).

[17] U.S. Agency for International Development, *USAID Strategy on Democracy, Human Rights and Governance*, June 2013, 24.

in peace camps and in cultural and sporting events. In these and other settings multiple goals are served within one program. A study of such approaches in Guinea found that the integration of political reform and service delivery was mutually reinforcing, fostering more transparent and accountable governance as well as greater utilization of services and improved resource mobilization in targeted sectors.[18]

The maintenance of security in post-conflict settings often requires external military support. This is best accomplished through multi-national peacekeeping missions under UN authority. As noted in Chapter 10, negotiated peace settlements backed by third-party security guarantees and supported by the UN are more likely to endure. In return for this external support, Paul Collier suggests, post-conflict governments should be required to downsize their armed forces so that they can focus on meeting the needs of their citizen and building consent-based governance.[19]

Coordination between security forces and civilian agencies in international missions is critically important. In today's complex peace operations military forces often interact with multiple international and national civilian agencies and civil society groups. All are working on the same set of conditions in local settings, aiming generally toward the common purpose of preventing or ending armed conflict, improving governance and promoting economic development. In Europe this is called the "integrated approach," an attempt to find the most effective combination of instruments and actors to promote security and stability. In some missions a military command exists, but in other cases the emphasis is on education and coordination, allowing citizen groups to maintain an independent status. This coordination and communication process is sometimes referred to as the "whole of society" approach, recognizing that no single actor can resolve complex problems, and that all stakeholders should contribute according to their roles and responsibilities.[20]

Attempts to integrate civilian and military operations in Mali, South Sudan and Afghanistan have been difficult. Unintended consequences include duplication of effort, competition among groups, unclear goals,

---

[18] Ibid.

[19] Collier, *The Bottom Billion*, 177.

[20] Lisa Schirch, "Civil Society's Peacebuilding Approach to Civil-Military-Police Coordination in Security Sector Reform," in *Civil Society, Peace, and Power*, edited by David Cortright, Melanie Greenberg and Laurel Stone (Lanham: Rowman & Littelfield, 2016).

institutional tensions, and at times resistance from local populations.[21] Military officers and civilian practitioners have not developed sufficiently effective protocols for interaction in shared spaces. They have different approaches and theories about how to ensure peace and stability in fragile settings. They operate with huge asymmetries of budget and capability, with very different approaches to local populations. The effectiveness of combined operations depends on greater clarity and unanimity of political purpose, more emphasis on addressing the drivers of conflict, greater equality of resources and capabilities, and better coordination of planning and implementation among military and civilian decision makers. Joint training and education of the military and civilian practitioners might help to facilitate such coordination.

LEARNING LESSONS

The components of good governance are highly interconnected and mutually reinforcing. The conditions we have identified – institutional capacity and accountability, greater political and economic inclusion, the participation of all sectors of society – work in concert to create the conditions for more peaceful and prosperous societies. In the case of governance reform, the whole is greater than the sum of the parts. Gains in one area can support progress in other areas.

Governance reform efforts over the decades have generated a growing body of knowledge regarding best practices. A report from the Carnegie Endowment for International Peace summarizes key insights from these efforts. The first is that poor governance is often intentional and serves the political purposes of corrupt and violent elites. Autocratic rulers use exclusivist political and economic arrangements to maintain their power and wealth, diverting state resources for personal benefit and to pay off supporters. Accountability structures threaten such arrangements, and the corrupt leaders who benefit as a result consciously obstruct and repress reform efforts.[22] Attempts to improve governance through narrow technical training programs usually fail because they do not address the underlying incentive structures that determine the allocation of resources and power. As we note in Chapter 1, governance

---

[21] Findings from the workshop "Towards a Comprehensive Approach? Civil Society and Security Sector Engagement in Dutch Missions," Cordaid, the Global Partnership for the Prevention of Armed Conflict, and PAX, The Hague, February 24, 2014.

[22] Carothers and de Gramont, "Aiding Governance in Developing Countries," 7.

is about political power. Unless that reality is faced squarely, reform efforts will falter.

Persuading ruling elites to accept power-sharing arrangements is never easy, but some approaches have been used with relative success. In Eastern Europe and South America guarantees of personal safety or immunity were provided to some former leaders, to protect them against retaliatory repression and politically motivated prosecution. Truth and reconciliation commissions in various settings have allowed for the accounting of past crimes and abuses without recrimination and further violence. Successful transitions require efforts to create social trust and build confidence in political rather than military means of contending for power. Soft power approaches can be effective means of facilitating political transformation, but time and effort are needed to build the social basis for cooperation, especially in conflict-torn societies. In some cases, the United States and other countries have pledged substantial economic assistance and security assurances to transitioning governments.

Effective governance reform efforts in Eastern Europe, Southeast Asia and other regions have focused on engaging with and empowering democratically oriented political forces, especially those that advocate and embody the principles of quality governance. International donors and civil society groups have sought ways to improve accountability and state–society relations, with the goal of enhancing the capacity of citizens to demand better governance and the ability and willingness of governments to respond positively.[23] In some countries aid policies have been targeted to assist community-based groups seeking to build more representative governance systems and expand political and economic freedom. Support provided to such subnational networks can be a step toward gradually transforming state–society relations.

In countries beset by fragility and weak institutions, the most effective governance reforms are those that work with existing institutions rather than attempting to import "best practice" templates from other settings. Universal models for governance have limited utility or feasibility. Institutions are rooted in local conditions and usually evolve gradually over time. Rather than aiming for unrealistic levels of efficiency and quality, "best fit" approaches seek to build institutions that are adapted to local contexts and balance ideals with practicality.[24]

[23] Ibid., 9.
[24] Ibid., 10–11.

In some developing countries armed conflict arises from the clash between local communities and predatory and oppressive state structures that emerged during the colonial and post-colonial eras and continue today. In these settings local communities view state institutions with mistrust and foreboding, while political elites exploit the state and its natural resources for personal enrichment and the benefit of favored clients. As David Roberts notes, instability and conflict result from "the clash between violent and penetrative state institutions, on the one hand, and a deepening of mistrust, disrespect and rejection of the legitimacy of state institutions and elites" on the other.[25] The challenge for modern state-building is to find an approach that can close the gap between state and society by building institutions that are seen as legitimate. The equitable provision of social services is an important means of demonstrating that linkage. Inclusiveness and accountability in the delivery of public goods are crucial for building state legitimacy.

In her influential article "Good Enough Governance" Merilee Grindle suggests that governance reforms prioritize the most useful and feasible interventions. Given the need for humility and the complexity of governance challenges, practitioners with limited resources must focus on those strategies that are most essential and efficient. This means accepting a more nuanced understanding of the evolution of institutions and government capabilities, being explicit about trade-offs, taking the role of government in poverty alleviation seriously, and grounding action in the contextual realities of each country.[26] In her later article "Good Enough Governance Revisited" Grindle emphasizes the need to build upon existing governance capacity. Respect for local political realities and capacity levels are essential for understanding the types of governance reform needed, identifying space for potential change, and analyzing potential support for and resistance to change.[27]

This is not an argument for accommodating corruption and oppression, or turning away from the sweeping transformations that are needed in many societies to overcome the conditions that produce armed violence. Policy changes need to be radical enough to address the root problems of political exclusion and repression, while also ameliorating immediate

[25] Roberts, "Post-conflict Statebuilding and State Legitimacy," 545.

[26] Merilee S. Grindle, "Good Enough Governance: Poverty Reduction and Reform in Developing Countries." *Governance: An International Journal of Policy, Administration, and Institutions* 17, no. 4 (2004): 525.

[27] Merilee S. Grindle, "Good Enough Governance Revisited," *Development Policy Review* 25, no. 5 (2007): 565.

grievances. Movements for nonviolent change need to attract the support of reformers and revolutionaries alike. Effective strategies involve a delicate balancing act between demands for systemic transformation and programs for practical reform, creating short-term momentum toward long-term goals.

A "NEW DEAL" FOR FRAGILE
AND CONFLICT-AFFECTED STATES?

One of the most innovative recent multilateral policy initiatives for governance reform is the International Dialogue for Peacebuilding and Statebuilding (IDPS). The IDPS emerged in 2008 when a group of fragile states – the g7+ – joined with donor states and global civil society organizations to develop a new governance and peacebuilding approach to international development policy.[28] The initiative reflects the widespread understanding that successful development depends upon good governance and is directly linked to the prevention of armed conflict. As the IDPS founding states and agencies stated in one of their early declarations, "Conflict and fragility are major obstacles for achieving the Millennium Development Goals (MDGs)." The same is true for the new international agenda in support of the Sustainable Development Goals. To realize these objectives it is necessary "to address conflict and fragility by supporting country-led peacebuilding and statebuilding processes."[29]

At the Fourth High Level Forum on Aid Effectiveness in Busan, Republic of Korea in 2011, the IDPS members created the New Deal for Fragile and Conflict-Affected States. The New Deal is an historic achievement, the first global agreement that seeks to address conflict and the lack of development in fragile states through promoting good governance. It contains five core principles for reversing fragility:

1. Legitimate politics – Foster inclusive political settlements and conflict resolution.
2. Security – Establish and strengthen people's security.
3. Justice – Address injustices and increase people's access to justice.

---

[28] The g7+ states are Afghanistan, Burundi, Central African Republic, Chad, Comoros, Cote d'Ivoire, DRC, Guinea, Guinea-Bissau, Haiti, Liberia, Papua New Guinea, Sierra Leone, Solomon Islands, Somalia, South Sudan, Timor-Leste and Togo.

[29] International Dialogue on Peacebuilding and Statebuilding, *Dili Declaration – A New Vision for Peacebuilding and Statebuilding* (Dili: IDPS, 2010).

4. Economic foundations – Generate employment and improve livelihoods.
5. Revenues and services – Manage revenue and build capacity for accountable and fair service delivery.

The New Deal promotes the principle of "country-led and country-owned transitions out of fragility."[30] This principle addresses the democratic deficit in many multilateral institutions and processes by recognizing that peacebuilding and statebuilding must be led by affected countries rather than donor states. It also acknowledges that state-led implementation is not enough and that building peaceful societies depends upon the participation of non-state actors.

The IDPS and the New Deal explicitly recognize the central role of civil society in peacebuilding and legitimate governance. The New Deal founding document states that "constructive state-society relations ... are at the heart of successful peacebuilding and statebuilding. They are essential to deliver the 'New Deal.' "[31] Civil society has been integrated into the structural architecture and official decision-making processes of the New Deal. A global Civil Society Secretariat coordinates international NGO oversight efforts with implementation activities of local country-led civil society leaders.

The New Deal principles emphasize that state legitimacy depends on its responsiveness to the needs of local communities. The involvement of civil society is a critical factor in making that possible: "an engaged public and civil society, which constructively monitors decision-making, is important to ensure accountability."[32] Civil society organizations promote the inclusion of marginalized voices. They build feedback loops within society and can help repair damaged trust in post-conflict countries.

In its pilot phase (2012–2015) the New Deal faced many challenges to effective implementation, including resistance from g7+ governments whose own political legitimacy stands to come under greater scrutiny. The initial stages of the process fell short of fully integrating civil society and local community perspectives. Governments in fragile states are often hostile to civil society organizations and see them as opponents rather than legitimate partners. Implementation efforts have not yet addressed the political dimensions of governance or built the political will needed

---

[30] International Dialogue on Peacebuilding and Statebuilding, *A New Deal for Engagement in Fragile States*, 2.
[31] Ibid., 1.
[32] Ibid., 2.

to overcome entrenched governance deficiencies. Awareness of the process among g7+ and donor states is low. It remains to be seen whether the New Deal will be the 'real deal.'

A 2016 independent review of the New Deal by the New York University Center on International Cooperation offered a cautiously optimistic assessment. The authors argued that the g7+ states have "the opportunity to make a unique contribution to the sustainable development agenda as a leading coalition for leaving no-one behind." To realize its potential, however, "the IDPS needs to involve a wider range of regional and international public and private actors." The international agencies and countries that created the process "could do much more to deliver their side of the New Deal bargain."[33]

The concept of the New Deal is important and demonstrates a growing awareness of the links between governance and peace in the international community. It integrates global networks of donors, fragile countries and civil society in a common effort to foster peace and promote development.[34] The New Deal is an alignment of governments and civil society organizations around the principles of good governance through participation, inclusion and accountability. The implementation of this integrated vision is necessarily slow and challenging, but the New Deal offers an innovative model of governance to promote conditions for peace and development. Many of the goals and lessons gleaned from the IDPS process are incorporated in the Sustainable Development Goals that were adopted at the United Nations in September 2015.

GOVERNANCE FUTURES

At the risk of overusing an analogy, we conclude with speculation on the kind of world our time travelers might find if they could venture forward a century or so. Our vision is hopeful, perhaps utopian, which we offer as a way of illustrating the possibilities that could unfold through better governance.

In our imagined future the world is much more highly developed economically and technologically, increasingly populous, urbanized, literate

---

[33] Sarah Hearn, *Independent Review of the New Deal for Engagement in Fragile States* (NYU Centre on International Cooperation, 2016).

[34] Paul Okumu, "State-Society Relations: The Prospects for the New Deal Engagement in Addressing an Enabling Environment in Conflict-Affected and Fragile States," *State of Civil Society 2013* CIVICUS.

and interconnected. Nations have been forced by common security threats and the challenges of climate change to strengthen systems of collaboration. International and regional organizations have greater capacity to prevent and resolve conflicts within nations and regions. Civil society networks and hybrid forms of governance are more prevalent, as vast numbers of political actors crowd the global political stage. Local communities have assumed a greater role in managing their own public affairs. Women and formerly marginalized communities have greater political and economic status. Inequalities based on gender and ethnicity have diminished.

In this future a new cosmopolitan consciousness has emerged, based on Kant's principle of universal hospitality, the "right of a stranger not to be treated with hostility" in another land.[35] People have acquired the ability, evident in many communities even today, to celebrate the diversity of global cultures and identities, even as they remain attached to their own nation.[36] The global norm has become respect for the dignity and worth of every person and for the primacy of reasoned dialogue and free expression.[37]

This vision of the future may seem hopelessly naive in light of the clashes and chaos of the present. The hostility toward immigrants espoused by some political leaders in Europe and the United States is a far cry from cosmopolitan hospitality. The British referendum vote to leave the EU raises fears of reversals in European integration. The election of Donald Trump and the rise of nativist politics in Europe indicate growing intolerance toward immigrants and those with different religious and ethnic backgrounds. Yet in spite of these trends, social realities in many parts of the world reflect growing empathy for others and support for collaboration and inclusiveness. In many arenas of social life patterns of greater collaboration and inclusiveness are evident and have expanded over the decades. Cosmopolitan values are part of today's social consciousness, especially among young people. The World Values Survey shows that people under 25 are more likely to identify as citizens of the world, favor the UN, and support global integration and free trade.[38] Young voters in the UK overwhelmingly favored remaining in the

---

[35] Immanuel Kant, "Perpetual Peace: A Philosophical Sketch," in *Kant: Political Writings*, 2nd edition, edited by Hans Reiss (New York: Cambridge University Press, 1991), 106.

[36] Mary Kaldor, *New and Old Wars: Organized Violence in a Global Era* (Stanford University Press, 2001), 6, 115–116.

[37] Held, "Cosmopolitanism," 309–310.

[38] Pippa Norris, "Global Governance & Cosmopolitan Citizens," in *Governance in a Globalizing World*, edited by Joseph S. Nye Jr. and John Donahue (Washington, DC: Brookings, 2000), 155–177; see also Florian Pichler, "Cosmopolitanism in a Global

EU.[39] People in the most developed countries tend to have greater global consciousness and more socially tolerant values and are less accepting of casualties in war.[40] Cooperative principles are enshrined in many of today's constitutions and international conventions, even if they are often ignored and trampled upon in political practice. Government leaders nonetheless find it necessary to invoke these world values. They are ideals to which many people aspire, and an inspiration for advocates of human rights, development and peace.

Whether cosmopolitan consciousness will grow and shape a better future is unknown, but the need for global cooperation and coordination within and among nations is undeniable and will likely grow in the years ahead – to preserve the progress that has been achieved and respond to the many global threats that exist now and will emerge in the future. Without new and more effective forms of governance these global threats could become flashpoints of armed violence within nations and perhaps between them. The evidence shows that the mechanisms of good governance can address the conditions that give rise to armed conflict and can ameliorate and transform disputes before they degenerate into war. The challenge of preventing war depends upon our ability to utilize and strengthen these mechanisms. If the capacities and qualities of governance can be improved, a better and more peaceful future awaits.

Perspective: An International Comparison of Open-minded Orientations and Identity in Relation to Globalization," *International Sociology* 27, no. 1 (2011): 21–50.

[39] Hortense Goulard, "Britain's Youth Voted Remain," *Politico*, June 24, 2016, www.politico.eu/article/britains-youth-voted-remain-leave-eu-brexit-referendum-stats/.

[40] Ronald F. Inglehart, B. Puranen and C. Welzel, "Declining Willingness to Fight for One's Country: The Individual-level Basis of the Long Peace," *Journal of Peace Research* 52, no. 4 (2015): 418–434.

Select Bibliography

Abbott, Kenneth W. and Duncan Snidal, "Why States Act through Formal International Organizations," *Journal of Conflict Resolution* 42, no. 1 (1998): 3–32.

Aidt, Toke S., "Corruption, Institutions, and Economic Growth," *Oxford Review of Economic Policy* 25, no. 2 (2009): 271–291.

Albertus, Michael and Victor Menaldo, "Coercive Capacity and the Prospects for Democratization," *Comparative Politics* 44, no. 2 (2012): 151–169.

Anderson, Mary B., *Do No Harm: How Aid Can Support Peace – Or War* (Boulder: Lynne Rienner, 1999).

Appiah, Elizabeth N. and Walter W. McMahon, "The Social Outcomes of Education and Feedbacks on Growth in Africa," *Journal of Development Studies* 38 no. 4 (2002): 27–68.

Aspinall, Edward, "Parliament and Patronage," *Journal of Democracy* 25 (2014): 96–110.

Azam, Jean-Paul, "The Redistributive State and Conflicts in Africa," *Journal of Peace Research* 38, no. 4 (2001): 429–444.

Ballentine, Karen, "Beyond Greed and Grievance: Reconsidering the Economic Dynamics of Conflict," in *The Political Economy of Armed Conflict: Beyond Greed and Grievance*, edited by Karen Ballentine and Jake Sherman (Boulder: Lynne Rienner, 2003).

Barbieri, Katherine and Rafael Reuveny, "Globalization and Civil War," *Journal of Politics* 67, no. 4 (2005): 1228–1247.

Barro, Robert J., "Determinants of Democracy," *Journal of Political Economy* 107 no. S6 (December 1999): S158–S183.

Beebe, Shannon D. and Mary Kaldor, *The Ultimate Weapon Is No Weapon: Human Security and the New Rules of War and Peace* (New York: Public Affairs, 2010).

Berman, Sheri, "Civil Society and the Collapse of the Weimar Republic," *World Politics* 49 no. 3 (April 1997): 401–429.

"Populism Is Not Fascism," *Foreign Affairs* 95, no. 6 (2016): 39–44.

Besancon, Marie, "Relative Resources: Inequality in Ethnic Wars, Revolutions and Genocides," *Journal of Peace Research* 42, no. 4 (2005): 393–415.

Bevir, Mark, *Governance: A Very Short Introduction* (Oxford: Oxford University Press, 2012).

Beyerle, Shaazka, *Curtailing Corruption: People Power for Accountability and Justice* (Boulder: Lynne Rienner, 2014).

Blainey, Geoffrey, *The Causes of War*, 3rd edition (London: Macmillan Press, 1988).

Blattman, Christopher and Edward Miguel, "Civil War," *Journal of Economic Literature* 48, no. 1 (2010): 3–57.

Boulding, Kenneth, *Three Faces of Power* (Newbury Park: Sage Publications, 1989).

Brack, Duncan, "Introduction, Trade, Aid and Security: An Agenda for Peace and Development," in *Trade, Aid and Security: An Agenda for Peace and Development*, edited by Oli Brown, Mark Halle, Sonia Peña Moreno, and Sebastian Winkler (London: Earthscan, 2007): 1–17.

Brainard, Lael, Derek Chollet, and Nica LaFluer, "The Tangled Web: The Poverty-Insecurity Nexus," in *Too Poor for Peace? Global Poverty, Conflict, and Security in the 21st Century*, edited by Laeal Brainard and Derek Chollet (Washington, DC: Brookings Institution, 2007): 1–30.

Bremmer, Ian, *The J Curve: A New Way to Understand Why Nations Rise and Fall* (New York: Simon & Schuster, 2006).

Brett, Rachel and Irma Specht, *Young Soldiers: Why They Choose to Fight* (Boulder: Lynne Rienner, 2004).

Breuning, Marijke, "Women's Representation and Development Assistance," *Women & Politics* 23, no. 3 (2001): 35–55.

Brown, Seyom, *The Causes and Prevention of War*, 2nd edition (New York: St. Martin's Press, 1994).

Higher Realism: A New Foreign Policy for the United States (Boulder, CO: Paradigm Publishers, 2009).

Bryant, Coralie and Christina Kappaz, *Reducing Poverty, Building Peace* (Bloomfield: Kumarian Press, 2005).

Buhaug, Halvard, "Relative Capability and Rebel Objective in Civil War," *Journal of Peace Research* 43, no. 6 (2006): 691–708.

Burris, Val, "From Vietnam to Iraq: Continuity and Change in Between-Group Differences in Support for Military Action," *Social Problems* 55, no. 4 (2008): 443–479.

Bussmann, Margit, "Foreign Direct Investment and Militarized International Conflict," *Journal of Peace Research* 47, no. 2 (2010): 143–153.

Bussmann, Margit and Gerald Schneider, "When Globalization Discontent Turns Violent: Foreign Economic Liberalization and Internal War," *International Studies Quarterly* 51, no. 1 (2007): 79–97.

Cammett, Melani and Edmund Malesky, "Power Sharing in Post Conflict Societies: Implications for Peace and Governance," *Journal of Conflict Resolution* 56, no. 6 (2012): 982–1016.

Caprioli, Mary, "Primed for Violence: The Role of Gender Inequality in Predicting Internal Conflict," *International Studies Quarterly* 49, no. 2 (June 2005): 161–178.

Caprioli, Mary and Mark A. Boyer, "Gender, Violence, and International Crisis," *Journal of Conflict Resolution* 45, no. 4 (August 2001): 503–518.

Carden, Art and Joshua Hall, "Why Are Some Places Rich While Others Are Poor? The Institutional Necessity of Economic Freedom," *Economic Affairs* 30, no. 1 (2010): 48–54.

Carothers, Thomas and Diane de Gramont, *Aiding Governance in Developing Countries: Progress amid Uncertainties* (Washington, DC: Carnegie Endowment for International Peace, 2011).

Cederman, Lars-Erik and Luc Girardin, "Beyond Fractionalization: Mapping Ethnicity onto Nationalist Insurgencies," *American Political Science Review* 101, no. 1 (2007): 173–185.

Cederman, Lars-Erik, Kristian Skrede Gleditsch and Halvard Buhaug, *Inequality, Grievances, and Civil War* (Cambridge University Press, 2013).

Cederman, Lars-Erik, Nils B. Weidman and Kristian Skrede Gleditsch, "Horizontal Inequalities and Ethnonationalist Civil War: A Global Comparison," *American Political Science Review* 105, no. 3 (2011): 1260–1288.

Cerra, Valerie and Sweta Chaman Saxena, "Growth Dynamics," *American Economic Review* 98, no. 1 (2008): 439–457.

Chayes, Sarah, *Thieves of State: Why Corruption Threatens Global Security* (New York: W.W. Norton & Company, 2015).

Chenoweth, Erica and Maria J. Stephan, *Why Civil Resistance Works: The Strategic Logic of Nonviolent Conflict* (New York: Columbia University Press, 2011).

Choi, Seung-Whan and Patrick James, "Civil-Military Relations in a Neo-Kantian World, 1886–1992," *Armed Forces & Society* 30, no. 2 (2004): 227–254.

Cincotta, Richard P., Robert Engelman and Daniele Anastasion, *The Security Demographic: Population and Civil Conflict After the Cold War* (Washington, DC: Population Action International, 2003).

Claude, Inis, *Sword into Plowshares* (New York: Random House, 1964).

Cohen, Eliot, Lieutenant Colonel Conrad Crane, U.S. Army Retired; Lieutenant Colonel John Horvath, U.S. Army; and Lieutenant Colonel John Nagl, U.S. Army, "Principles, Imperatives, and Paradoxes of Counterinsurgency," *Military Review* 86, no. 2 (March/April 2006): 49–53.

Coleman, Isobel and Gayle Tzemach Lemmon, *Family Planning and U.S. Foreign Policy: Ensuring U.S. Leadership for Healthy Families and Communities and Prosperous, Stable Societies* (New York: Council on Foreign Relations, April 2011).

Collier, Paul, *The Bottom Billion: Why the Poorest Countries are Failing and What Can Be Done About It* (Oxford University Press, 2007).

Collier, Paul and Anke Hoeffler, "Greed and Grievance in Civil War," *Oxford Economic Papers* 56, no. 4 (2004): 563–595.

Collier, Paul, V.L. Elliot, Håvard Hegre, Anke Hoeffler, Marta Renal-Querol and Nicholas Sambanis, *Breaking the Conflict Trap: Civil War and Development Policy* (Washington, DC: World Bank and Oxford University Press, 2003).

Commission on Global Governance, *Our Global Neighborhood: The Report of the Commission on Global Governance* (Oxford University Press, 1995).

Commission on Global Security, Justice & Governance, *Confronting the Crisis of Global Governance: Report of the Commission on Global Security, Justice & Governance* (Hague Institute for Global Justice and Stimson Center, 2015).

Commission on Human Rights, *Human Security Now: Protecting and Empowering People* (New York: Commission on Human Security, 2003).

Conover, Pamela Johnston and Virginia Sapiro, "Gender, Feminist Consciousness, and War," *American Journal of Political Science* 37 no. 4 (November 1993): 1079–1099.

Cortright, David and Kristen Wall, *Afghan Women Speak: Enhancing Security and Human Rights in Afghanistan* (Kroc Institute for International Peace Studies, University of Notre Dame, 2012).

Curtis, Mark, "Designing Conflict-Sensitive *Trade Policy*," in *Trade, Aid and Security: An Agenda for Peace and Development*, edited by Oli Brown, Mark Halle, Sonia Peña Moreno, and Sebastian Winkler (London: Earthscan, 2007): 19–40.

Dahl, Robert, *Democracy and Its Critics* (New Haven: Yale University Press, 1989).

Dal Bó, Ernesto, Pedro Dal Bó and Rafael Di Tella, "'Plata o Plomo?': Bribe and Punishment in a Theory of Political Influence," *American Political Science Review* 100, no. 1 (2006): 41–53.

Davenport, Christian, "Multi-Dimensional Threat Perception and State Repression: Inquiry into Why States Apply Negative Sanctions," *American Journal of Political Science* 39, no. 3 (1995): 683–713.

State Repression and the Domestic Democratic Peace (Cambridge University Press, 2007).

Davenport, Christian and David A. Armstrong, "Democracy and the Violation of Human Rights: A Statistical Analysis from 1976 to 1996," *American Journal of Political Science* 48, no. 3 (2004): 538–554.

de Soysa, Indra and Hanne Fjelde, "Is the Hidden Hand an Iron Fist? Capitalism and Civil Peace, 1970–2005," *Journal of Peace Research* 47, no. 3 (2010): 287–298.

Desch, Michael C., *Civilian Control of the Military: The Changing Security Environment* (Baltimore: Johns Hopkins University Press, 1999).

Diamond, Larry, *Developing Democracy: Toward Consolidation* (Baltimore: Johns Hopkins University Press, 1999).

Dixon, Jeffrey, "What Causes Civil Wars? Integrating Quantitative Research Findings," *International Studies Review* 11 (2009): 707–735.

Dobbins, James, Seth G. Jones, Keith Crane, Andrew Rathmell, Brett Steele, Richard Teltschik and Anga Timilsina, *The UN's Role in Nation-Building: From the Congo to Iraq* (Santa Monica: RAND Corporation, 2005).

Dorussen, Han and Hugh Ward, "Trade Networks and the Kantian Peace," *Journal of Peace Research* 47, no. 1 (2010): 29–42.

Doyle, Michael and Nicholas Sambanis, *Making War and Building Peace: United Nations Peace Operations* (Princeton University Press, 2006).

Elshtain, Jean Bethke, *Women and War* (University of Chicago Press, 1995 [1987]).

Esteban, Joan and Debraj Ray, "Polarization, Fractionalization and Conflict," *Journal of Peace Research* 45, no. 2 (2008): 143–162.

Fearon, James D., "Governance and Civil War Onset," World Development Report 2011 Background Paper (World Bank, 2010).

"Primary Commodity Exports and Civil War," *Journal of Conflict Resolution* 49, no. 4 (2005): 508–537.

Fearon, James D. and David D. Laitin, "Ethnicity, Insurgency, and Civil War," *American Political Science Review* 97, no. 1 (2003): 75–90.

Finel, Bernard I. and Kristin M. Lord, "The Surprising Logic of Transparency," *International Studies Quarterly* 43 (1999): 315–339.

Finkelstein, Lawrence S., "What Is Global Governance?" *Global Governance* 1, no. 3 (1995): 367–372.

Fjelde, Hanne, "Buying Peace? Oil Wealth, Corruption, and Civil War, 1985–99," *Journal of Peace Research* 46, no. 2 (2009): 199–218.

Florini, Ann M., "Increasing Transparency in Government," *International Journal on World Peace* 19 (2002): 3–37.

Foa, Roberto Stefan and Yascha Mounk, "The Danger of Deconsolidation: The Democratic Disconnect," *Journal of Democracy* 27, no. 3 (2016): 5–17.

Fortna, Virginia Page, *Does Peacekeeping Work? Shaping Belligerents' Choices after Civil War* (Princeton University Press, 2008).

Fox, Jonathan, "The Uncertain Relationship between Transparency and Accountability," *Development in Practice* 17 (2007): 663–671.

Frankel, Jeffrey and David Romer, "Does Trade Cause Growth?" *American Economic Review* 89, no. 3 (1999): 379–399.

Freedom House, *Freedom in the World 2015, Discarding Democracy: A Return to the Iron Fist* (New York: Freedom House, 2015).

Fukuyama, Francis, *Political Order and Political Decay* (New York: Farrar, Straus and Giroux, 2014).

Gartzke, Erik, "The Capitalist Peace," *American Journal of Political Science* 51, no. 1 (2007): 166–191.

Gates, Scott, Håvard Hegre, Håvard Mokleiv Nygard and Håvard Strand, "Development Consequences of Armed Conflict," *World Development* 40, no. 9 (2012): 1713–1722.

Gilley, Bruce, "The Meaning and Measure of State Legitimacy: Results for 72 Countries," *European Journal of Political Research* 45 (2006): 499–525.

Gilligan, James, *Preventing Violence* (New York: Thames & Hudson, 2001).
Violence: Our Deadly Epidemic and its Causes (New York: G.P. Putnam, 1996).

Gleditsch, Kristian Skrede, "Transnational Dimensions of Civil War," *Journal of Peace Research* 44, no. 3 (2007): 293–309.

Gleditsch, Nils Petter, "The Liberal Moment Fifteen Years On," *International Studies Quarterly* 52 (2008): 691–712.

Gleditsch, Nils Petter, Håvard Hegre and Håvard Strand, "Democracy and Civil War," in *Handbook on War Studies III: The Intrastate Dimension* (Ann Arbor: University of Michigan Press, 2009).

Goldstein, Joshua S., *Winning the War on War: The Decline of Armed Conflict Worldwide* (New York: Dutton, 2011).

Goldstone, Jack A., Robert H. Bates, David L. Epstein, Ted Robert Gurr, Michael B. Lustik, Monty G. Marshall, Jay Ulfedler and Mark Woodward, "A Global Model for Forecasting Instability," *American Journal of Political Science* 54, no. 1 (2010): 190–208.

Granovetter, Mark S., "The Strength of Weak Ties," *American Journal of Sociology* 78 (1973): 1360–1380.

Gray, Cheryl and Daniel Kaufman, *Corruption and Development* (Washington, DC: World Bank, 1998).

Grootaert, Christiaan and Thierry van Bastelaer, "Understanding and Measuring Social Capital: A Synthesis of Findings and Recommendations from the

Social Capital Initiative," *Social Capital Initiative Working Paper*, No. 24 (World Bank, April 2001).

Gurr, Ted Robert, *People versus States: Minorities at Risk in the New Century* (Washington, DC: U.S. Institute of Peace, 2000).

Why Men Rebel (Princeton University Press, 1970).

Hanushek, Eric A. and Dennis D. Kimko, "Schooling, Labor-Force Quality, and the Growth of Nations," *American Economic Review* 90, no. 5 (2000): 1184–1208.

Hardin, Garrett, "The Tragedy of the Commons," *Science* 162, no. 3859 (December 1968): 1243–1248.

"The Tragedy of the Unmanaged Commons," in *Evolutionary Perspectives on Environmental Problems*, edited by Dustin J. Penn and Iver Mysterud (New Brunswick: Transaction Publishers, 2007).

Harff, Barbara and Ted Robert Gurr, *Ethnic Conflict in World Politics*, 2nd edition (Boulder: Westview Press, 2004).

Harkness, Kristen A., "The Ethnic Army and the State: Explaining Coup Traps and the Difficulties of Democratization in Africa," *Journal of Conflict Resolution* 60, no. 4 (2016): 587–616.

Harling, L.M., E. Lindner, U. Spalthoff and M. Britton, "Humiliation: A Nuclear Bomb of Emotions?" *Psicología Política* 46 (2013): 55–76.

Hartzell, Caroline and Matthew Hoddie, "Institutionalizing Peace: Power Sharing and Post-Civil War Conflict Management," *American Journal of Political Science* 47, no. 2 (2003): 318–332.

Havel, Václav, "Anatomy of a Reticence," in *Open Letters: Selected Writings, 1965–90*, edited by Paul Wilson (New York: Vintage Books, 1992).

"Peace: The View from Prague," *New York Review of Books* 32, no. 18 (21 November 1985): 28–30.

Hegre, Håvard, "Democracy and Armed Conflict," *Journal of Peace Research* 51, no. 2 (2014): 159–172.

Hegre, Håvard, Tanja Ellingsen, Scott Gates and Nils Petter Gleditsch, "Toward a Democratic Civil Peace? Democracy, Political Change, and Civil War, 1816–1992," *American Political Science Review* 95, no. 1 (2001): 33–48.

Hegtvedt, Karen A. and Cathryn Johnson, "Power and Justice: Toward an Understanding of Legitimacy," *American Behavioral Scientist* 53, no. 3 (2009): 376–399.

Held, David, "Cosmopolitanism: Ideas, Realities and Deficits," in *Governing Globalization: Power, Authority and Global Governance*, edited by David Held and Anthony McGrew (Cambridge: Polity Press, 2002).

Ho, Bryan, "Village Democracy Shrugs in Rural China," *East Asia Forum: Economic, Politics and Public Policy in East Asia and the Pacific* (July 22, 2014), www.eastasiaforum.org/2014/07/22/village-democracy-shrugs-in-rural-china/

Hooghe, Liesbet and Gary Marks. "Unravelling the Central State, but How? Types of Multi-level Governance," *American Political Science Review* 97, no. 2 (2003): 233–243.

Horowitz, Donald L., *Ethnic Groups in Conflict* (Berkeley: University of California Press, 1985).

Howell, Jude, Armine Ishkanian, Ebenezer Obadare, Hakan Seckinelgin and Marlies Glasius, "The Backlash against Civil Society in the Wake of the Long War on Terror," *Development in Practice* 18, no. 1 (February 2008): 82–93.

Human Security Report Project, *The Human Security Report 2013: The Decline in Global Violence: Evidence, Explanation, and Contestation* (Vancouver: Human Security Research Group, Simon Fraser University, 2014).

Human Security Report 2012 (London: Oxford University Press, 2012).

Ikenberry, G. John, *Liberal Order and Imperial Ambition* (Cambridge: Polity Press, 2006).

Johnston, Michael, *Public Officials, Private Interests, and Sustainable Democracy: When Politics and Corruption Meet* (Washington, DC: Institute for International Economics, 1997).

Jones, Seth G. and Martin C. Libicki, *How Terrorist Groups End: Lessons for Countering al Qa'ida* (Santa Monica: RAND Corporation, 2008).

Kaldor, Mary, "Civil Society," in *Encyclopedia of Globalization*, edited by Roland Robertson and Jan Aart Scholte (New York: MTM Publishing, 2007).

Human Security: Reflections on Globalization and Intervention (Cambridge: Polity Press, 2007).

New and Old Wars: Organized Violence in a Global Era, 2nd edition (Stanford University Press, 2007).

Kaldor, Mary, Denisa Kostovicova and Yahia Said, "War and Peace: The Role of Civil Society," in *Global Civil Society 2006/7. Global Civil Society – Yearbooks*, edited by Helmut K. Anheier, Mary Kaldor and Marlies Glasius (London: Sage, 2006).

Karatnycky, Adrian and Peter Ackerman, "How Freedom Is Won: From Civic Resistance to Durable Democracy," *International Journal of Not-for-Profit Law* 7, no. 3 (2005): 47–59.

Kaufmann, Daniel, "Rethinking Governance: Empirical Lessons Challenge Orthodoxy," Brookings Institution Working Paper series (2003).

Keohane, Robert, "International Institutions: Can Interdependence Work?" *Foreign Policy*, no. 110 (Spring 1998): 82–194.

"Multilateralism: An Agenda for Research," *International Journal* 45, no. 4 (1990): 731–64.

Keohane, Robert and Joseph S. Nye, *Power and Interdependence*, 3rd edition (New York: Longman, 2001).

Kittilson, Miki Caul and Leslie Schwindt-Bayer, "Engaging Citizens: The Role of Power-Sharing Institutions," *Journal of Politics* 72, no. 4 (October 2010): 990–1002.

Kjaer, Anne Mette, *Governance* (Cambridge: Polity Press, 2004).

Klasen, Stephan and Francesca Lamanna, "The Impact of Gender Inequality in Education and Employment on Economic Growth: New Evidence for a Panel of Countries," *Feminist Economics* 15, no. 3 (July 2009): 91–132.

Knack, Stephen and Philip Keefer, "Does Inequality Harm Growth Only in Democracies," *American Journal of Political Science* 41, no. 1 (1997): 323–332.

Knutsen, Carl Henrik, "Democracy and Economic Growth: A Summary of Arguments and Results," *International Area Studies Review* 15, no. 4 (2012): 393–415.

Koch, Michael and Sarah Fulton, "In the Defense of Women: Gender, Office Holding, and National Security Policy in Established Democracies," *Journal of Politics*, 73, no. 1 (2011): 1–16.

Kolbert, Elizabeth, "Peace in Our Time: Steven Pinker's History of Violence," *New Yorker*, October 3, 2011.

Kriesberg, Lewis, *Constructive Conflicts: From Escalation to Resolution*, 2nd ed. (Lanham: Rowman and Littlefield, 2003).

Krueger, Alan B. and Jitka Maleckova, "Education, Poverty and Terrorism: Is There a Causal Connection?" *Journal of Economic Perspectives* 17, no. 4 (2003): 119–144.

Lacina, Bethany, "Explaining the Severity of Civil Wars," *Journal of Conflict Resolution* 50, no. 2 (2006): 276–289.

Le Billon, Philippe, "Buying Peace or Fuelling War: The Role of Corruption in Armed Conflicts," *Journal of International Development* 15, no. 4 (2003): 413–426.

Lederach, John Paul, "Addressing Terrorism: A Theory of Change Approach," in John Paul Lederach, Douglas Ansel, Jessica Brandwein, Ashley Lyn Greene, Ryne Clos, Shinkyu Lee and Laura Weis, *Somalia: Creating Space for Fresh Approaches to Peacebuilding* (Uppsala: Life and Peace Institute, 2011).

Building Peace: Sustainable Reconciliation in Divided Societies (Washington, DC: U.S. Institute for Peace, 1997).

The Moral Imagination: The Art and Soul of Building Peace (Oxford University Press, 2005).

Leff, Nathaniel H., "Economic Development through Bureaucratic Corruption," *American Behavioral Scientist* 8 (1964): 8–14.

Levy, Yagil, "A Revised Model of Civilian Control of the Military: The Interaction between the Republican Exchange and the Control Exchange," *Armed Forces & Society* 38, no. 4 (2012): 529–556.

Lijphart, Arend, "Constitutional Design for Divided Societies," *Journal of Democracy* 15, no. 2 (2004): 96–109.

Patterns of Democracy: Government Forms and Participation in Thirty-six Countries (New Haven: Yale University Press, 1999).

Thinking about Democracy: Power Sharing and Majority Rule in Theory and Practice (New York: Routledge, 2008).

Linz, Juan J., "The Perils of Presidentialism," *Journal of Democracy* 1 (Winter 1990): 51–69.

Lipset, Seymour Martin, "Some Social Requisites of Democracy: Economic Development and Political Legitimacy," *American Political Science Review* 53, no. 1 (1959): 69–106.

Lord, Kristin M., *The Perils and Promise of Global Transparency: Why the Information Revolution May Not Lead to Security, Democracy, or Peace* (SUNY Press, 2012).

Luong, Pauline Jones and Erika Weinthal, "Rethinking the Resource Curse: Ownership Structure, Institutional Capacity, and Domestic Constraints," *Annual Review of Political Science* 9 (2006): 241–263.

Mack, Andrew, "A Signifier of Shared Values," *Security Dialogue* 35, no. 3 (2004): 366–367.

Mann, Michael, "The Autonomous Power of the State: Its Origins, Mechanisms, and Results," *European Journal of Sociology* 25, no. 2 (1984): 185–213.

Mauro, Paulo, "Corruption and Growth," *Quarterly Journal of Economics* 110, no. 3 (1995): 681–712.

McDonald, Patrick J., *The Invisible Hand of Peace: Capitalism, the War Machine, and International Relations Theory* (Cambridge University Press, 2009).

Melander, Erik, "Political Gender Equality and State Human Rights Abuse," *Journal of Peace Research* 42, no. 2 (2005): 149–166.

Miguel, Edward, "Economic Shocks, Weather and Civil War," *National Bureau of Economic Research, NBER Reporter 2011* Number 3: Research Summary.

Mitrany, David, *A Working Peace System* (Chicago: Quadrangle, 1966).

Moosa, Ebrahim, *What is a Madrasa?* (Chapel Hill: University of North Carolina Press, 2015).

Muller, Edward N. and Mitchell A. Seligson, "Inequality and Insurgency," *American Political Science Review* 81, no. 2 (1987): 425–452.

Müller, Lars, "The Force Intervention Brigade: United Nations Forces Beyond the Fine Line Between Peacekeeping and Peace Enforcement," *Journal of Conflict & Security Law* 20, no. 3 (2015): 359–380.

Naím, Moisés, *The End of Power: From Boardrooms to Battlefields and Churches to States, Why Being in Charge Isn't What It Used to Be* (New York: Basic Books, 2013).

Nathan, Laurie, "The Causes of Civil War: The False Logic of Collier and Hoeffler," *South African Review of Sociology* 39, no. 2 (2008): 262–275.

Nilsson, Desirée, "Anchoring the Peace: Civil Society Actors in Peace Accords and Durable Peace," *International Interactions: Empirical and Theoretical Research in International Relations*, 38 no. 2 (November 2012): 243–266.

Norris, Pippa, *Making Democratic Governance Work: How Regimes Shape Prosperity, Welfare, and Peace* (Cambridge University Press, 2012).

North, Douglas, *Institutions, Institutional Change and Economic Performance* (Cambridge University Press, 1990).

Nye, Joseph S., Jr., "Will the Liberal Order Survive?" *Foreign Affairs* 96, no. 1 (January/February 2017): 10–16.

The Future of Power (New York: Public Affairs, 2011).

Soft Power: The Means to Success in World Politics (New York: Public Affairs, 2004).

Østby, Gudrun, "Polarization, Horizontal Inequalities and Violent Civil Conflict," *Journal of Peace Research* 45, no. 2 (2008): 163–182.

Østby, Gudrun and Henrik Urdal, "Education and Civil Conflict: A Review of the Quantitative, Empirical Literature," background paper prepared for the Education for All Global Monitoring Report 2011, *The Hidden Crisis: Armed conflict and education*, 2011/ED/EFA/MRT/PI/29 (2010).

Ostrom, Elinor, "Crossing the Great Divide: Coproduction, Synergy, and Development," *World Development* 24, no. 6 (1996): 1073–1087.

Governing the Commons: The Evolution of Institutions for Collective Action (Cambridge University Press, 1990).

Ostrom, Elinor, James Walker and Roy Gardner, "Covenants With and Without a Sword: Self-governance is Possible," *American Political Science Review* 86 (1992): 404–417.

Paffenholz, Thania, *Civil Society and Peacebuilding: A Critical Assessment* (Boulder: Lynne Rienner, 2010)

Paris, Roland, *At War's End: Building Peace after Civil Conflict* (Cambridge University Press, 2004).

Pettersson, Thérése and Peter Wallensteen, "Armed Conflicts, 1947–2014," *Journal of Peace Research* 52, no. 4 (July 2015): 536–550.

Pevehouse, Jon and Bruce Russett, "Democratic International Governmental Organizations Promote Peace," *International Organization* 60 (Fall 2006): 969–1000.

Pickering, Jeffrey and Mark Penecy, "Forging Democracy at Gunpoint," *International Studies Quarterly* 50, no. 3 (2006): 539–560.

Piketty, Thomas, *Capital in the Twenty-First Century* (Cambridge, MA: Belknap/ Harvard University Press, 2014).

Pinker, Steven, *The Better Angels of Our Nature: Why Violence Has Declined* (New York: Viking, 2011).

Polachek, Solomon William, "Conflict and Trade," *Journal of Conflict Resolution* 24, no. 1 (1980): 55–78.

Pratto, Felicia, Lisa M. Stallworth, and Jim Sidanius, "The Gender Gap: Differences in Political Attitudes and Social Dominance Orientation," *British Journal of Social Psychology* 36 (1997): 49–68.

Przeworski, Adam and Fernando Limongi, "Modernization: Theories and Facts," *World Politics* 49 (1997): 155–183.

Putnam, Robert, *Bowling Alone: The Collapse and Revival of American Community* (New York: Simon & Schuster, 2000).

Making Democracy Work: Civic Traditions in Modern Italy (Princeton University Press, 1993).

Radelet, Steven, "Prosperity Rising: The Success of Global Development—and How to Keep It Going," *Foreign Affairs* 95, no. 1 (January/February 2016): 85–95.

Regan, Patrick and Daniel Norton, "Greed, Grievance, and Mobilization in Civil Wars," *Journal of Conflict Resolution* 49, no. 3 (2005): 319–336.

Regan, Patrick M. and Aida Paskeviciute, "Women's Access to Politics and Peaceful States," *Journal of Peace Research* 40 no. 3 (2003): 287–302.

Reinicke, Wolfgang H., *Global Public Policy: Governing without Government?* (Washington, DC: Brookings Institution, 1989)

Reynal-Querol, Marta, "Ethnicity, Political Systems, and Civil Wars," *Journal of Conflict Resolution* 46, no. 1 (2002): 29–54.

"Political Systems, Stability and Civil Wars," *Defence and Peace Economics* 13, no. 6 (2002): 465–483.

Reynolds, Andrew, *Designing Democracy in a Dangerous World* (Oxford University Press, 2011).

Rice, Susan E., Corinne Graff, and Janet Lewis, *Poverty and Civil War: What Policymakers Need to Know* (Washington, DC: Brookings Institution, December 2006).

Roberts, David, "Post-conflict Statebuilding and State Legitimacy: From Negative to Positive Peace?" *Development and Change* 39, no. 4 (2008): 537–555.

Roessler, Philip, "The Enemy Within: Personal Rule, Coups, and Civil War in Africa," *World Politics* 52 no. 2 (2011): 300–346.

Rosecrance, Richard, *The Rise of the Trading State: Commerce and Conquest in the Modern World* (New York: Basic Books, 1986).

Rosenau, James N., *Governance without Government* (Cambridge University Press, 1992).

"Governance in a New Global Order," in *Governing Globalization: Power, Authority and Global Governance*, edited by David Held and Anthony McGrew (Cambridge: Polity Press, 2002).

Ross, Michael, "A Closer Look at Oil, Diamonds and Civil War," *Annual Review of Political Science* 9 (2006): 265–300.

"What Do We Know About Resources and Civil War?" *Journal of Peace Research* 41, no. 3 (2004): 337–356.

Rotberg, Robert I., "The Challenge of Weak, Failing, and Collapsed States," in *Leashing the Dogs of War: Conflict Management in a Divided World*, edited by Chester A. Crocker, Fen Osler Hampson and Pamela Aall (Washington, DC: United States Institute of Peace Press, 2007).

ed. *On Governance: What It Is, What It Measures and Its Policy Uses* (Waterloo: Centre for International Governance Innovation, 2015).

"Governance Trumps Democracy," *Africa and Asia: The Key Issues* (2013), https://robertrotberg.wordpress.com/2013/02/01/governance-trumps-democracy/

Rothstein, Bo, "What is the Opposite of Corruption?" *Third World Quarterly* 35, no. 5 (2014): 737–752.

Rothstein, Bo and Eric Uslaner, "All for All: Equality, Corruption and Social Trust," *World Politics* 58, no. 1 (2005): 41–72.

Ruddick, Sara, *Maternal Thinking: Toward a Politics of Peace* (Boston, MA: Beacon Press, 1995, 1989).

Ruggie, John G., "Reconstituting the Global Public Domain: Issues, Actors, and Practices," *European Journal of International Relations* 10, no. 4 (2004): 499–531.

Rummel, Rudolph J., *Death by Government* (Piscataway: Transaction Books, 1994).

Russett, Bruce, *Grasping the Democratic Peace: Principles for a Post-Cold War World* (Princeton University Press, 1993).

Russett, Bruce and John R. Oneal, *Triangulating Peace: Democracy, Interdependence, and International Organizations* (New York: W.W. Norton & Company, 2001).

Sechser, Todd, "Are Soldiers Less War-Prone than Statesmen?" *Journal of Conflict Resolution* 48, no. 5 (2004): 746–774.

Sambanis, Nicholas and Håvard Hegre, "Sensitivity Analysis of the Empirical Literature on Civil War Onset," *Journal of Conflict Resolution* 50, no. 4 (2006): 508–535.

Sechser, Todd, "Are Soldiers Less War-Prone Than Statesmen?" *Journal of Conflict Resolution* 48, no. 5 (2004): 746–774.

Schirch, Lisa, *Conflict Assessment and Peacebuilding Planning: Toward a Participatory Approach to Human Security* (Boulder: Lynne Rienner, 2013).

Seligson, Mitchell A., "The Impact of Corruption on Regime Legitimacy: A Comparative Study of Four Latin American Countries," *Journal of Politics* 64 (2002): 408–433.

Sen, Amartya, *Development as Freedom* (New York: Anchor Books, 1999).

"Why India Trails China," *New York Times*, June 20, 2013.

Seyle, Conor and Matthew Newman, "A House Divided? The Psychology of Red and Blue America," *American Psychologist* 61, no. 6 (2006): 571–580.

Sharp, Gene, *The Politics of Nonviolent Action* (Boston: Porter Sargent, 1973).

Shattuck, John, "Resisting Trumpism in Europe and the United States," *American Prospect Longform* (December 2, 2016), http://prospect.org/article/resisting-trumpism-europe-and-united-states

Simpson, Matthew, "Terrorism and Corruption: Alternatives for Goal Attainment Within Political Opportunity Structures," *International Journal of Sociology* 44, no. 2 (2014): 87–104.

Singer, Peter, *Children at War* (New York: Pantheon Books, 2005).

Smith, Rupert, *The Utility of Force: The Art of War in the Modern World* (London: Penguin Books, 2006).

Spurk, Christopher, "Understanding Civil Society," in *Civil Society and Peacebuilding: A Critical Assessment*, edited by Thania Paffenholz (Boulder: Lynne Rienner, 2010).

Stewart, Frances, ed. *Horizontal Inequalities and Conflict: Understanding Group Violence in Multiethnic Societies* (Hampshire: Palgrave Macmillan, 2008).

Stiglitz, Joseph E., *Globalization and its Discontents* (New York: W.W. Norton & Company, 2002).

Taydas, Zeynep and Dursun Peksen, "Can States Buy Peace? Social Welfare Spending and Civil Conflicts," *Journal of Peace Research* 49, no. 2 (2012): 273–287.

Taub, Amanda, "How 'Islands of Honesty' Can Crush Corruption," *Interpreter, New York Times* (December 9, 2016), www.nytimes.com/2016/12/09/world/asia/south-korea-brazil-argentina-impeachment.html?ref=world

Tessler, Mark and Ina Warriner, "Gender Feminism, and Attitudes toward International Conflict," *World Politics* 49, no. 2 (1997): 250–281.

Thies, Cameron, "Of Rulers, Rebels, and Revenue: State Capacity, Civil War Onset, and Primary Commodities," *Journal of Peace Research* 47, no. 3 (2010): 321–332.

Thyne, Clayton, "ABC's, 123's, and the Golden Rule: The Pacifying Effect of Education on Civil War, 1980–1999," *International Studies Quarterly* 50, no. 4 (2006): 733–754.

Togeby, Lise, "The Gender Gap in Foreign Policy Attitudes," *Journal of Peace Research* 31, no. 4 (November 1994): 375–392.

Torres, Walter J. and Raymond M. Bergner, "Humiliation: Its Nature and Consequences," *Journal of the American Academy of Psychiatry and the Law* 38, no. 2 (2010): 195–204.

Treisman, Daniel, "The Causes of Corruption: A Cross-national Survey," *Journal of Public Economics* 76, no. 3 (2000): 399–457.

"What Have We Learned About the Causes of Corruption After Ten Years of Cross-National Empirical Research," *Annual Review of Political Science* 10 (2007): 211–244.

Tyler, Tom, "Psychological Models of the Justice Motive: Antecedents of Distributive and Procedural Justice," *Journal of Personality and Social Psychology* 62 (1994): 850–863.

U.S. Agency for International Development, *USAID Strategy on Democracy, Human Rights and Governance*, June 2013.

UNESCO, *EFA Global Monitoring Report 2009, Overcoming Inequality: Why Governance Matters* (Oxford University Press, 2008).

United Nations, *A New Global Partnership: Eradicate Poverty and Transform Economies through Sustainable Development*, The Report of the High-level Panel of Eminent Persons on the Post-2015 Development Agenda (United Nations, 2013).

The Millennium Development Goals Report 2015 (New York: United Nations, 2015).

United Nations Development Programme, *Governance for Peace: Securing the Social Contract* (New York: United Nations Development Programme and Bureau for Crisis Prevention and Recovery, 2012).

United Nations, General Assembly Security Council, *Report of the High-level Independent Panel on Peace Operations on Uniting Our Strengths for Peace: Politics, Partnership and People*, A/70/95 S/2015/446, June 17, 2015.

The Future of United Nations Peace Operations: Implementation of the Recommendations of the High-level Independent Panel on Peace Operations; Report of the Secretary-General, A/70/357–S/2015/682, September 2, 2015.

United States Dept of the Army, *The U.S. Army/U.S. Marine Corps Counterinsurgency Field Manual* (University of Chicago Press, 2007).

Urdal, Henrik, "A Clash of Generations? Youth Bulges and Political Violence," *International Studies Quarterly* 50, no. 3 (2006): 607–630.

Uslaner, Eric, *The Moral Foundations of Trust* (Cambridge University Press, 2002).

Varshney, Ashutosh, "Ethnic Conflict and Civil Society: India and Beyond," *World Politics* 53, no. 3 (April 2001): 362–398.

Wallensteen, Peter, *Quality Peace: Peacebuilding, Victory, and World Order* (Oxford University Press, 2015).

Walter, Barbara, *Committing to Peace: The Successful Settlement of Civil Wars* (Princeton University Press, 2002).

Walter, Barbara F., "Conflict Relapse and the Sustainability of Post-conflict Peace," World Development Report 2011 Background Paper (World Bank, September 2010).

Wanis-St. John, Anthony and Darren Kew, "Civil Society and Peace Negotiations: Confronting Exclusion," *International Negotiation* 13 (March 2008): 11–36.

Weiss, Thomas, Conor Seyle and Kelsey Coolidge, *Non-State Actors and Global Governance: A Look at the Numbers* (Broomfield: One Earth Future Foundation, 2013).

Weiss, Thomas G., Ramesh Thakur and John Gerard Ruggie, *Global Governance and the UN: An Unfinished Journey* (Bloomington: Indiana University Press, 2010).

Wenar, Leif, "Property Rights and the Resource Curse," *Philosophy and Public Affairs* 36, no. 1 (2008): 2–32.

Wilkinson, Richard and Kate Pickett, *The Spirit Level: Why Greater Equality Makes Societies Stronger* (New York: Bloomsbury Press, 2010).

World Bank, *The East Asian Miracle* (Oxford University Press, 1993).

Gender Equality and Development, World Development Report (Washington, DC, 2012).

World Development Report 2011: Conflict, Security, and Development (Washington, DC: World Bank, 2011).

Zenko, Micah, *Between Threats and War: Discrete Military Operations in the Post-Cold War World* (Stanford University Press, 2010).

Index